W9-BNX-637

BE ALERT
BE AWARE
HAVE A
PLAN

THE COMPLETE
GUIDE TO
PROTECTING
YOURSELF,
YOUR HOME,
YOUR FAMILY

Neal Rawls, with Sue Kovach

362.88
R261b

WITHDRAWN

Guilford, Connecticut
An Imprint of the Globe Pequot Press

Copyright © Neal Rawls and Sue Kovach

ALL RIGHTS RESERVED. No part of this book may be reproduced or transmitted in any form by any means, electronic or mechanical, including photocopying and recording, or by any information storage and retrieval system, except as may be expressly permitted by the 1976 Copyright Act or in writing from the publisher. Requests for permission should be addressed to The Globe Pequot Press, P.O. Box 480, Guilford, CT 06437.

10   9   8   7   6   5   4   3   2   1

Printed in The United States of America.

Library of Congress Cataloging-in-Publication Data is available on file.

To our parents,
Dallis L. and Katherine Neal Rawls;
and Charles and Judy Kovach.
They kept us safe.

Contents

Introduction:
A Sense of Security

On September 11, 2001, we lost our sense of security. It crumbled, along with New York's famed World Trade Center. The "bad guys" had just become the stuff of our worst nightmares.

Day-to-day life has changed in many ways since then. But it's important to remember that the world was far from perfect before that day. In the year 2000, of every one thousand people living in the United States, one was raped, two were assaulted, and three were robbed. Six of every hundred thousand people were murdered. In fact, a murder occurs every twenty-seven minutes; a robbery every fifty-nine seconds. Every year, nearly 25 percent of the households in the United States will be victimized by theft or violent crime. Now you can add to that the new personal security concerns:

- How secure is my workplace?
- Can I travel safely?
- How do I stay safe while out in public?
- What do I do if an emergency strikes and I'm separated from my loved ones?
- What can I do to be safe in a terrorist attack?
- Can anything be done to protect myself in a chemical or biological attack?

Be Alert, Be Aware, Have a Plan gives you the answers to these questions and more. This book is for all those who want to learn how to protect themselves and their families in almost any situation. In ten information-packed chapters, you'll learn practical ways to be secure and develop a sense of security in your day-to-day life, whether at home, at work, or traveling worldwide.

This book covers personal security in a wide range of situations, from street muggings, home burglaries, and auto theft to road rage, carjacking, home invasions, terrorism, chemical and biological attack, and hazardous material spills. The purpose is to give you concise, real-world advice that you can use, while teaching you to evaluate your own individual situation so you can make informed decisions regarding your personal security needs. Most importantly, I'll teach you how to protect yourself with minimal changes to your everyday life. Putting on a seatbelt when you're driving, for example, is an excellent way to protect yourself, and it's a small adjustment in your driving routine. Buckling your child in a car safety seat is a minimal change and can take less than a minute. But it's worth a lifetime — your child's lifetime. This book will show you how to protect yourself and your family against a range of security issues in the same way: Economically, with minimal change, in ways that can become as routine to you as buckling up.

I'll use examples of real-life incidents and security situations, but I won't bog you down in lengthy case studies of what others have done right or wrong in those instances. Quizzes, surveys, and checklists will help you learn the principles of personal security, evaluate your own life situations, and begin creating your personal security plan. Throughout the book, you'll find Top Ten Tips, which are short, concise pieces of advice regarding security and safety that will help guide you through the creation of your own personal security plan for you and your family.

You'll also find crime statistics for your information. They're not presented here to scare you, but rather to show you the reality of today's world, to reinforce the fact that you must take care of yourself. *You* are the one responsible for your own personal security, and this book will give you more confidence to accomplish that goal.

In my thirty years in the fields of law enforcement, education, and security, I've learned that a basic foundation of personal security begins with the three principles that are the title of this book: Be alert, be aware, have a plan. Combined with knowledge, they form the cornerstones of a foundation that can be expanded to serve you in even the worst circumstances. You'll learn that the ways in which you prepare and protect yourself in case of terrorism, natural disasters, and chemical/biological attack are rooted in the time-tested basics of security.

"Know the layout of your building, and its exit and escape routes" is a basic idea that likely saved thousands of lives in the World Trade Center attack. Survivors have told us how they trusted their instincts and used what they knew to get out alive. There can hardly be a better example of how it pays to be alert, be aware, and have a plan.

After the terrorist attacks, authorities often told citizens to be on "high alert" and to be more aware, but no one explained what that means or how to do it. In this book, I'll show you how to make security a part of your everyday life. Developing a good sense of security isn't about being paranoid or becoming a survivalist in a bunker. It's about learning to think differently, to be alert and aware to the dangers that are present every day, and to avoid becoming a victim by having a plan to deflect crime before it happens. The idea of security doesn't have to overwhelm you, and you certainly don't have to be obsessed with it. I believe personal security is a state of mind and a state of awareness that comes with practice. I call the basics Security 101, and this book shows you how to use them.

I've taught these techniques to both law enforcement officers and civilians, and they have worked for me on the streets as a police officer, in the corporate world as a bodyguard and security chief, and in my personal life. You and your loved ones are worth the effort of developing these same good habits in order to achieve a sense of security.

So much in our society is focused on fixing problems once they've happened, rather than preventing problems in the first place. Being in a security state of mind is all about prevention and being prepared. Anyone can do it, regardless of age, size, or strength, because it's a mental exercise as much as anything else. Remember, humans were never stronger than the saber-toothed tiger—only smarter. When you learn to be alert, be aware, and have a plan, you learn how to survive in today's troubled world.

Chapter 1

Security 101

In 2000 Americans over the age of 12 experienced 25.9 million crimes of which 24 percent were violent.

Having a sense of security means more than achieving a feeling of being secure. It also means cultivating an awareness of your environment, what security issues exist, and what you need to do in order to be secure. It's taking that extra second to look around when you walk out the door, to notice who's nearby and what they're doing, what cars are in your neighbors' driveways or parked on the street, and any other information you can pick up. Not to study it intensely, but to *notice* it, to be aware of that information, and to be alert to anything about it that causes your gut instinct to react.

Be Alert, Be Aware, Have a Plan

This simple but powerful mantra is the foundation for personal security. *Alert* is the state of being ready to receive and process information quickly about what's going on around you. *Aware* means that you *know* what's going on around you, that you have knowledge about your surroundings and are "tuned in" on many sensory levels. A *plan* is a predetermined course of action for responding to whatever situations you might encounter. Let's look at each of these individual components.

Alert

A soldier out on patrol or in combat is in a high state of alert. That state's exhausting and stressful. For your personal security purposes, I'm talking about being in tune to certain triggers that can put you instantly into that state of alert, without walking around constantly in that state. Living on the edge and being worried about things all the time can shorten your life—that's a fact. I know you can be alert to a certain degree and still have peace of mind. In fact, that's your goal.

Think of a scale of alertness from zero to five, and the soldier in the high state of alert is a five. Someone who walks down the street looking at his shoes all the time, either because he's lulled into a false security or he's scared to death by the world, is a zero. You never want to be a zero. Anyone could walk right up to a zero on the street and grab something or assault him, and he'd never see it coming. You've encountered people like this, always looking straight at the ground, avoiding eye contact with others. They're like a kid who burrows under the covers, thinking that if he can't see the monster under the bed, then it can't see him, either. Better yet, it can't touch him or hurt him. Denying the existence of criminals, who are the real-world monsters under the bed, won't make them go away and certainly won't keep you safe from them. Being a zero on the alertness scale makes you ripe for their picking.

The ideal state of alertness is between a zero and a five. It's when you've made it a habit to take mental snapshots of your surroundings anytime you're in transition from one place to another, much like checking all the car mirrors when you're driving. You've become so used to doing it, you're not always consciously aware that you're checking. In fact, the process of moving your head and checking your mirrors helps you remain in an alert state by preventing you from becoming lulled by the sound of your car engine and the monotony of the road. Likewise, you can be lulled into a false sense of security in your surroundings off the road. Quick glances at your surroundings keep you alert.

When you're home and your doors are locked, your alertness is down. You're a one or a two on the scale, barely in tune with those triggers in the outside world. Watching TV, cooking, or reading a book relaxes your mind, and we need to be in that kind of relaxed state in order to rest. But if there's a knock on the door, your body reacts and becomes alert, back up to a four or five. If you're busy or expecting someone to come and visit, you may just head to the door and fling it open. You need to be alert to the possibility that someone you're *not* expecting might be standing there.

Ideally, you want to be in the lower alert levels most of the time, not a zero, but always open to processing information so you can instantly go on high alert when needed. How do you achieve this? By practicing the skills and techniques I'll show you in this book until they become routine. Remember when you first began to wear a seat belt while driving—you consciously buckled up until it became so routine that you began doing it without thinking.

Aware

You're leaving home and walking out the door when you notice a car parked on the street in front of your house. In a second, you're aware that it's a familiar car—your neighbor's—and it's normal for it to be there. But suppose you're walking out of the grocery store and you see a car stopped in the no-parking zone with the engine running. A healthy young man is behind the wheel. Your brain can quickly and easily register the fact that the car is out of place. It also registers that he's waiting for someone. But take another second to look around and see if you can determine *who* he's waiting for—is it someone near you? Possibly his mother who was inside the store? Now you become aware of another young man not unlike the driver, standing next to a pay phone, holding the receiver but not talking. He's making eye contact with you and others, eyeing people coming out of the store, glancing occasionally at the man sitting patiently in the car. This changes things—now you need to make a split-second decision whether the car you first noticed might be the getaway car in a crime, or is harmless. Where is the driver's attention focused? On the people coming out of the store? On the man at the pay phone? On a newspaper he's reading? On *you?*

This is what it means to be aware. If you take those few seconds to look around, you can gather vital information about your surroundings, while being alert to triggers or changes in those surroundings. Your instincts process these clues and can signal you to action if necessary. If there's danger involved, the hair on the back of your neck might even stand up. If you sense this danger, your plan of action might be to retreat back inside the store and decide if you want to call the police to report a suspicious vehicle.

Awareness involves knowing what's going on around you. You can be quite alert, but if you aren't aware of the possibilities—that purse snatchers can operate this way, or that armed robbers may have a lookout and a getaway car—then being alert won't do much good. The situation could be harmless, and the young man may simply be waiting for his mother to come out of the store. But at the same time, it may not be harmless, and you need to be aware of that.

Interestingly, when you start to become aware, you then become more aware of how *little* you've been aware. Picture for a moment that you're walking to your car from the doctor's office. You might be thinking about what transpired during your appointment, mingled with thoughts about where you're going next. We all tend to walk around with a type of tunnel vision at times—we're looking straight ahead to where we're going, thinking about getting there, or thinking about where we just were. It's like having on blinders—you see only the path between the doctor's office and your car, and you've blocked out the rest of the world. When you become aware, it's like removing the blinders. Now you can see everything, and you begin to realize that there's a lot going on around you that you don't see a majority of the time. Two men sitting in a car parked next to yours; a woman and a child leaving another office a few doors down; a man on a bicycle coming toward you; a pickup truck leaving a parking space at the end of the row. Could any of these things hold potential danger? You need to be alert to the possibility now that you're aware of their presence. How long did it take to record these things in your mind? Perhaps two or three seconds. It wasn't a chore, and you didn't have to have your head on a swivel in a state of heightened alert. You took in the information just like you check the mirrors in your car when you're driving.

A Plan

Panic is often a sure way to become a victim. When people are caught by surprise, they can freeze and be unable to run or escape danger. They've made no plan, given no thought to what direction an assault might come from, or what might happen in case of a sudden emergency.

I was visiting a friend's home when a minor emergency occurred. She was in the kitchen cooking dinner when suddenly she screamed and ran out of the house. A skillet had burst into a flaming grease fire. I walked into the kitchen, picked up a pot lid, and placed it on the frying pan, smothering the fire. If she had thought even once about the possibilities of kitchen fires, how they occur and where, she likely would have done the same thing—or dumped flour on the grease fire—because it wouldn't have surprised her. Instead, she ran out the door in a panic, leaving the fire to possibly burn her house down. A well-thought-out plan in this case would include what to do if you didn't happen to find a pot lid lying nearby. Grabbing a fire extinguisher is another option, assuming you have one, it's charged up and works, and you've learned the basics of using one.

Let's say this same woman was cooking and someone suddenly burst through the back door. She might have panicked in the same manner as she did with the fire because she didn't have a plan. Had she thought about the possibility of home invasions and what to do, she would have immediately put her plan into action. That plan might be to set off a panic alarm located inside her house, or to immediately arm herself with a kitchen knife and escape from the closest exit to a neighbor's house. Whatever she might do, she at least had a plan to start with.

Formulating a plan can prevent you from panicking if that situation or something similar occurs. The odds are better that in an emergency, you'll act quickly, efficiently, and without panic. Thinking through different scenarios and planning what to do in any event isn't paranoia, pessimism, or expecting the worst. It's simply planning, and you only have to do it once. After that, it's filed away, but it can spring instantly to your mind should you ever find yourself in that situation. You don't need to sit down at work every day and wonder about how you might be trapped—your workplace doesn't usually change every day. Even if your workplace does change every day (you're a contractor and spend a day in a different location, or a salesperson who visits different clients all day by car), you'll still make your plan only once for *each* location.

Playing "What If . . . ?" is an important part of planning. In the chapters ahead, you'll learn how to use this technique to develop security risk scenarios and formulate plans to protect yourself and your loved ones. You want to play over the various scenarios in your mind, make your plans, and be prepared so you don't worry about the worst-case scenarios. I'm not going around telling people the world is coming to an end. More than one person has called me an optimist. But believe me, I've played out every type of worst-case scenario in my mind in order to be prepared for it so that I'll be able to act quickly if it happens. I have a burglar alarm, but I don't live in a bunker. Playing "What If . . . ?" doesn't make you a doomsayer.

Making It Work

When I was a police officer and stopped a suspicious vehicle, I had a plan when I approached the car. I was alert to what everyone in the car was doing, I was aware that the people were suspicious, and I had a plan for what to do in any of several scenarios.

Your personal security plan should always have the goal in mind of protecting yourself and your loved ones. It's not to go looking for trouble or putting yourself into a worse situation. When working security as a bodyguard, I carried a gun to protect myself and the people I was hired to protect. If I was aware of someone nearby acting suspiciously or in what I thought was a threatening manner, my plan wasn't to approach him to find out who he was or what he was doing—that wasn't my job. Instead, my plan was to call the police, who had the authority to approach him and discover those things. I was alert to the situation, was aware that the person was suspicious, and had a plan that covered what I would do to protect myself and the people I was hired to protect *if* the police didn't arrive in time, or the situation became a real threat. I didn't buy trouble. It had nothing to do with being afraid, but it had to do with what my job was and wasn't. As a cop, it *was* my job to approach suspicious people and determine the nature and extent of their threat. As a private citizen, your plan might be to call police if you see a suspicious car in your neighborhood, but it should never be to put yourself in a position of danger or confrontation.

How does all of this apply to the worst-case scenarios? We're simply not accustomed to the notion that we might get blown out of our cubicles while working "safe and sound" in our offices. And if a bomb explodes right under your desk, or a plane crashes right through your window, there's nothing you can do. Still, if the plane, bomb, or explosion *misses* you, and there's an escape route available, the same alertness, awareness, and planning that you've honed to protect yourself from a mugging or home invasion can help you escape a building that's burning and could possibly collapse. If you're aware of the dangers, are alert to the triggers (the sound of an explosion should get you moving fast), and have made a plan (you've learned the exits, have mapped out escape routes, and know the details of how to escape a fire), you stand a good chance of coming out a survivor. You can win if you play the mental game.

The Mind Is the Key

The term *personal security* is often used synonymously with *self-defense,* as in hand-to-hand combat and small weapons. That can be part of it, but I say it's a small part of it. To me, the mind is more powerful than weapons or fighting techniques. Personal security isn't just for the strong and well trained. I've seen muscular, well-trained people freeze in an emergency situation. All the strength and training in the world didn't matter. Why? Because their minds weren't prepared. They didn't have a plan. The key to personal security isn't strength, size, age, or gender—it's thinking. You're going to start to think about your own security and how to deflect crime to somebody else by being smarter, and by having a plan. The majority of criminals are lazy. If they weren't lazy, they'd get a job like the rest of us instead of living their lives in and out of the criminal justice system. You can out-think them. It's the same case when facing disasters—if you think about them and plan, you can be level-headed at a time when panic may run rampant.

Using your mind, you can do a lot to keep yourself from getting into situations in which you might otherwise have to resort to self-defense techniques. Good street cops always want to avoid having to use their firearms, and hundreds of arrests of armed felons are made every day where police officers never fire a shot. Indeed, many police officers go through their entire careers without discharging their weapons except on the practice range. It doesn't mean they never arrested anyone, or that they weren't good cops. It does mean they were able to out-think the crooks and put themselves in positions of having the upper hand. You can use those same techniques to protect yourself.

Transitions

In your home, you're in a static environment. You have a certain measure of control over that environment, which is why you feel comfortable there, and it's why your alertness level goes down. The more control you have over your static environment, the more comfortable you are. Your personal office is a static environment. A police officer considers his car to be a static environment and feels more comfortable there. Most people feel more comfortable in their cars, too, which is why they may ask someone to walk them to their car, but not to ride home with them.

Going to and from your car, however, is transitional. You have less control over that environment and are open to more security risk possibilities. This is why it's especially important to be alert and aware when in transitions. President Reagan was shot in a transition place between a building and a car. Transitions are where you most need to contemplate the security risk possibilities.

First, consider how many times you may be in transition during a typical day. It's more than you may think. Let's take a look at how many transitions might occur just going to work in the morning:

How many transitions?

1. Stepping out of your home.
2. Walking to your car.
3. Getting into your car.
4. Driving to work and stopping at traffic lights.
5. Parking your car.
6. Walking to the building where you work.
7. Stepping inside the building.
8. Walking through the lobby to the elevator.
9. Getting into the elevator.
10. Getting off the elevator into the lobby of the floor you work on.
11. Going into your work area.
12. Entering your office.

That's a dozen transitions, and your day has just begun! A dozen places where you're in a more vulnerable position than you are at home. Once inside your office, which is as familiar to you as your home, your alertness level is turned down a notch or so, just like at home. During this entire time, at least once you should make a plan for things that could possibly happen. Let your imagination run through scenarios and ask yourself, "What would I do?"

If you're on the way to the tenth floor, what would you do if the elevator lights went out and it stopped between floors? Can you work the emergency phone? Do you even know where it is, let alone how to use it? Remember, you're in the dark, so how do you find the phone? Before something like this occurs, it takes only a moment to look at the elevator control panel and learn where the phone is, or where the emergency alert button is in relation to all the others. Once you've done that, you'll have that knowledge and can draw on it when you need it.

Right now, where you're sitting reading this book, take a look around you. If someone were to threaten you in some way, is there an escape route? Can you call for help and be heard? Do you have any idea what you would do if the unexpected became reality right now? If you've not questioned yourself in this way before, you may be surprised at how unaware you've been. Later in the book, you'll examine your home and office, asking yourself questions like these. You may find it an eye-opening experience. You can uncover security weaknesses in your own home all by yourself, without consulting any experts. This is a good example of the enlightenment that you can gain from becoming aware.

Knowledge Is Another Key

Information is a powerful antidote to fear. It's important to educate yourself, your family, and especially your children on personal security and safety issues. Knowledge is what you use to formulate your plan, once you become alert and aware.

If you know that criminals like an easy target, you take steps to make yourself a difficult target. If you live in an earthquake-prone area, you learn as much as you can about quakes and how to prepare for them. The knowledge that anthrax is in the mail makes you alert to what's in your own mailbox. You must understand what to be alert for before you can become alert. This is why vague statements to be on alert only confuse people. If you're not told any specifics about a threat, how can you possibly know what to look out for?

Gathering knowledge involves being curious, but you must use common sense. Often we humans are too curious for our own good. Not that curiosity is always a bad thing; it's what leads us to leave our confines and explore new worlds and opportunities. But in dangerous circumstances, we need to learn to rein in our curiosity. How many times have you been caught in a traffic jam caused only by the curiosity of others rubber-necking at an accident? It may not be an accident at all, but simply someone changing a tire. The idea that it could be something worse, even something gory, can be overwhelming to some people, and that leads to slowdowns as everyone gawks. It can also lead to other traffic accidents and even fatalities. While your curiosity can kill you, it's important to remember that your curiosity can kill others, too. You can be aware that there's a traffic jam and alert to the dangers that a traffic jam can cause, but don't become part of the problem by being curious.

Likewise, if you're walking down the street and there's a loud, angry confrontation going on up ahead, your instinct should tell you to go the other direction and avoid the situation. If you're too curious, you may catch a stray bullet or become involved in an altercation. Your instinct tells you to protect yourself. It doesn't care exactly what's going on. But it may know enough to tell you that at this point, it's time to head in the opposite direction. And that's all you need to know. It's important to learn to trust your instincts.

Instincts

Police officers often work off a gut instinct, a "seat-of-the-pants" feeling that's not consciously developed. It comes from years of working on the streets and is a combination of knowledge and experience. It's not just cops who have it. Several times in my police career I've confronted armed felons and noticed an interesting phenomenon. They wouldn't drop their guns after several warnings. But as soon as I made the conscious decision to shoot them and my finger tightened down on the trigger, they gave up, just like that—milliseconds prior to my gun discharging. They sensed the fact that now I really was going to shoot them, perhaps kill them. I could see it, because their attitudes and demeanor changed in an instant. They sensed I wasn't just talking anymore—I was going to shoot. That sense protected them and kept them from getting shot, and probably saved their lives. That same sense is what can protect you from *them*.

People are usually taught to discount their gut-level feelings. It starts in childhood. Suppose a kid has an uneasy feeling about a new neighbor and expresses it to a parent. It's not uncommon for the response from the parent to go something like this: "You don't like the new neighbor? Now, don't be silly—he's such a nice man." *Silly*. An instinctual feeling is called silly, and now the child thinks he must keep his mouth shut the next time he gets a "silly" instinctual feeling. Yet instincts are what help us to survive, and the gut-level feeling this child got about the new neighbor may someday sadly prove itself out.

You use your instinct to pick up subtle clues. In a way, it's like extending your perception, the perception you—and all of us—already have. You incorporate this information with what you gather with all your other senses. If you think about it, you probably know that many of your own hunches prove themselves out. I've given serious thought to the idea of gut instincts and have come to the conclusion that they can be quite accurate. There can't be that many coincidences. I believe gut instinct played a part in helping many people survive such disasters as the World Trade Center event and Hurricane Andrew, one of the worst storms to ever hit south Florida. Too many people ignore their instinct and do the opposite of what it's telling them to do. I think it's important to give great consideration to what your feelings are in a given moment.

A woman I know ignored her instincts and became a crime victim. She was going to her mailbox at a private mailbox company in a shopping mall. As she parked her car, she noticed a young man sitting on the hood of a car not far away. Immediately she knew this kid was there to cause trouble. It was just a feeling. She didn't listen to her instincts entirely, but she did listen a little bit. Determined to get her mail, she decided to leave her purse in the car. Her instincts had told her that the kid might mug her for it. She left it on the car seat and went into the mailbox building. She was gone barely a minute, and when she came out, the driver's side window of her car was smashed and her purse was gone. She'd been half right. The kid wanted the purse. Had she listened fully to her instinct and decided she could have waited until the next day to pick up her mail, she would have been richer by three hundred dollars, the cost of replacing her window. That's not to mention the trouble of canceling all her credit cards and replacing documentation like her driver's license.

Putting It All Together

Statistics point to the fact that crime "prevention" techniques don't prevent crime. We still have crime, don't we? Technically, a person using proper crime prevention techniques won't prevent the crime from happening at all, but rather prevent it from happening to himself. He deflects the crime onto someone else who doesn't have a sense of security and is less prepared. I think crime *deflection* is a more accurate term.

In the coming chapters, you'll learn how to use your instincts, how to gain knowledge, and how to be alert and aware enough in your daily life to deflect crime, as well as plan for your survival in case of disaster. You'll learn how to think "out of the box" when formulating your plans, because you never know how things are going to go down. With this information, you can take charge of your own personal security, because in the end, you're the only one who can protect yourself.

Chapter 2

Streetwise

Seventy-three percent of violent crime occurs within five miles of the victim's home.

Rape occurs every six minutes.

Becoming streetwise as a way of life takes some practice, but after a while it will become second nature. It's not like practicing for a black belt in the martial arts, but it builds confidence in the same way. Instead of fighting and kicking your way to safety, however, you strive to avoid the threat in the first place. You're guarding yourself for a lot less than it would cost to hire a personal bodyguard—and after a while, it really won't take any effort. It will be a habit, one of the best habits you'll ever develop.

I didn't learn everything in school—sometimes the streets were the classroom, and "street people" were the teachers. They taught me how to be "streetwise," which is about surviving. Many people fall victim to crimes in the streets over and over; others in the same circumstances have never been victims.

Those who are streetwise have the skills and attitudes needed to take care of themselves. It's just another way of saying that they are alert, aware, and have a plan. It doesn't matter if you live in the city, the suburbs, or the country; there are certain dangers you may encounter as you go about your day-to-day business. You need to be streetwise wherever you go to avoid becoming a victim.

Quiz: Are You a (Street) Wise Guy? Test your street savvy.

How streetwise are you? The following quiz is designed to test your street savvy. Additionally, it will help you examine your habits when you're on the streets and get you thinking about being alert and aware. There aren't always right or wrong answers to these questions. In some circumstances, you need to size up what's going on at the moment and make an on-the-spot decision. But even in those cases, thinking about what could possibly happen, knowing your options, and formulating a plan ahead of time can ease the decision-making process if you find yourself in danger. When seconds count, it's much simpler to alter an existing plan than it is to try to create one.

Answer these questions honestly:

1. If your gut tells you to be alert, do you listen?
2. Even if you're in a rush, do you take a quick survey of your surroundings before leaving your car, or entering or leaving a building?
3. On the streets, do you walk confidently with your head up?
4. Do you often wear clothes that restrict your movement?

5. Do you wear obviously expensive jewelry at inappropriate times or places?

6. Ladies: Do you carry a larger handbag than you really need? Is your purse overstuffed?

7. Gentlemen: If you carry a money clip, do you keep the small bills on the outside?

8. How do you deal with strangers who talk to you on the street? If they ask for help? For directions? If they verbally harass you?

9. If you think someone is following you, what do you do?

10. Do you overload your arms with packages when shopping? Do you walk down the street with your hands buried deeply into your pockets?

11. If you run, bike, or roller skate regularly, do you vary your route from one day to the next?

12. Do you take shortcuts through parks, fields, and back roads?

13. When you enter a convenience store at night, do you look around before barging right in? Do you stay out if you don't see the clerk?

14. What would you do if you lost your keys? Where do you keep your spare keys?

15. When you are walking to your car, do you have your keys out? When walking to your apartment or home, do you have your keys out and ready?

16. Do you lock your car doors as soon as you enter the car? Do you lock them as soon as you get out? Do you keep them locked while driving?

17. Do you avoid parking your car next to buildings, Dumpsters, large vans, trucks, and other obstacles that limit visibility?

18. Do you avoid deserted or isolated parking areas?

19. Do you pick up hitchhikers? Do you hitchhike yourself?

20. Do you know the location of:
    - The closest police station to your home?
    - The nearest fire station?
    - The nearest hospital?
    - All-night stores with security?

So how did you do? Before this, had you ever thought about the possibility of being in any of the situations the quiz brings up? If any of the questions made you stop and think for a while, it probably means that you haven't considered that situation before and don't already have a plan for dealing with it. Let's discuss each individual question to learn more about what it means to be streetwise.

Answers:

1. Listen to your instincts.

As I've investigated crimes over the years, I've often heard people say, "I *knew* there was something wrong, but . . ." They finished the sentence with any number of things they went ahead and did anyway, despite warnings from their gut instincts. I've always been troubled by statements like these from crime victims: "I knew there was something wrong, but I didn't want to seem rude," or "I didn't want to upset him," or "I didn't want to be impolite"—or *prejudiced, scared, offensive, mean,* whatever. These victims explained their intuition away and ignored it in the name of being "nice." I find it fascinating that people care so much about what a total stranger thinks that they'll discount their own gut instincts and brush off potential danger. You need to ask yourself: Isn't it probably better to risk hurting someone's feelings in order to be safe and secure, even if it means suffering a little temporary embarrassment? Your hunch could be completely wrong, of course, but wouldn't that be a good thing, too? I think a lot of people would understand your position, and maybe even relate to it, if you exercised caution and listened to your instincts.

2. Be aware of your surroundings during transitions.

As I discussed in the introduction, going to and from your car and buildings are transition times when you need to be alert to both the environment you're leaving and the one you're about to enter. Learning to look around and quickly take in information at these times is one of the most valuable security habits you can develop.

3. Wearing an air of confidence comes naturally when you're alert, aware, and have a plan.

When you have a look of confidence, it tells everyone on the street: "I see you. I know you're there, and I know what's happening." Many street crimes are crimes of ambush committed on someone who appears to be distracted and not paying attention to what's going on around him. Appearing confident and aware can remove you from a criminal's target list: You no longer have the qualities he's looking for. When street cops go undercover, their confident looks have to go undercover, too. Criminals can pick up a cop's confidence from his walk and carriage. Citizens can often spot an off-duty police officer in a crowd because he walks with an air of confidence. Be aware of the difference between being confident and exhibiting behavior that challenges others. A swagger and attitude that says you think you own the streets can send the wrong message and possibly call others to take up your "challenge." Instead, be yourself, but with that confident air in which you're alert and aware of your surroundings at all times.

4. Your clothes can be hazardous to your personal security.

I don't like to suggest lifestyle changes, but what you wear can be detrimental to your security. Wearing certain types of clothing can hinder your escape from danger, whether it's going down fifty floors in a building to escape a fire or running to avoid being accosted on the street. Long flowing skirts, tight skirts, and high heels or thick, chunky soles are difficult to run in. Some types of jewelry can be grabbed, as can loose clothing such as vests, scarves, and neckties. Police officers prefer to wear clip-on ties for this reason.

What to wear that won't interfere with your ability to get yourself out of a dangerous situation is a judgment call you must make every time you dress to go somewhere. Stop and think about where you're going, who you'll be with, and the circumstances of your outing. Then you can make educated decisions about how your clothes might affect your security.

5. Don't tempt thieves with flashy, expensive jewelry.

So what's an inappropriate time or place to wear expensive jewelry? You need to remember that, unfortunately, we live at a time when people will kill a convenience store clerk for twenty bucks. This is one of those questions that begs you to use common sense and instinct. Go ahead and wear your favorite expensive jewelry to a formal party or when you're going out to dinner, but consider whether it's safe or even reasonable to wear expensive diamond necklaces or gold watches to the grocery store. I've heard enough cases of women joggers being attacked for their diamond tennis bracelets, or men joggers who were mugged and lost gold-and-diamond Rolex watches. Makes you think about why they were chosen as targets in the first place, right? A lot of thieves know what constitutes good jewelry; don't think for a minute that they can't recognize it from a distance, and don't think they aren't looking for it. Take a moment to consider your most expensive pieces of jewelry, even your most sentimental heirlooms, and ask yourself where and when you tend to wear them. You may need to reconsider some of your habits so you don't give thieves a reason to target you.

6. Keep it small, and other hints for handbag security.

Handbags, purses, pocketbooks—whatever you call them, they can cause you a lot of trouble due to their size, make, and contents (or, more correctly, *perceived* contents). Thieves are attracted to the biggest handbags. They seem convinced that the bigger the handbag, the more valuables it has in it,

Thieves are drawn to large handbags. A smaller purse can reduce your risk of being a target—and still hold all your essentials.

especially if it appears to be overstuffed. Purse snatchers and thieves want credit cards and cash first, but they certainly won't turn down a bonus. So if they see a fat purse, they think it may hold a cell phone, jewelry, even a firearm—all things they can easily fence or use. Of course, a large handbag could also contain used tissues, packets of artificial sweetener, and half-eaten chocolates. But the lure is so great that a thief might knock you over to find out what's really in the bag.

Overstuffed purses pose another security risk: It's harder for you to find things in one, so you must put a lot of attention into searching through it when you need your car or house keys, ATM card, or cell phone. This takes your attention away from your surroundings and focuses it on the purse, making you unaware of what's going on around you—and making you a target for thieves. Not only that, but if you're rummaging around while near others or in a crowd, people can see any goodies you might have in the bag, and the wrong person seeing this could target you on the spot.

Lastly, those designer handbags are a target in and of themselves. Forget about the contents; the bag itself is worth something on the street. Remember that such designer bags are made to be recognized, so they attract attention on their own.

Don't invite trouble. If your handbag is too big, see if you're carrying too many things unnecessarily, and consider switching to a smaller purse, or even a fanny pack. Just as thieves are drawn to larger purses, they tend to overlook smaller ones. It's amazing, but they almost don't see them at all. Here are some more quick security hints:

- If the purse is expensive, consider carefully where you'll be carrying it.
- Wear a shoulder-strap purse under coats or sweaters if you can, or hold it between your arm and body.
- Watch what your body language says to would-be thieves. Depending on the image you project, the above security measure can be taken two different ways. Do you casually hold your handbag securely between your arm and body, or do you clutch it madly as if it's full of gold? Remember, you want to project a confident feeling.
- Don't leave your purse hanging on the back of your chair when in a restaurant or at the theater. Hold it in your lap. If that's uncomfortable, place it on the floor in front of you, but put the strap around a chair leg, or your own leg.
- If your purse is snatched, let it go. Don't fight for it. Point at the thief and yell, "Police!" and "Stop him!" Don't simply say "Help!" Believe it or not, the word *police* can draw

more attention than the word *help,* and it usually gets others to look at where you're pointing rather than at you. If you say "help," you'll be lucky if they look at all. I've seen bystanders catch thieves when the victim pointed at the thief and yelled, "Help! Police! He's got my purse!"

7. Same advice, guys: Downsize.

It's tempting to tell the world how successful you are, but you don't want to tell *all* the world. Carrying a fat cash wad with the big bills on the outside of the roll can draw unwanted attention to you, including undeserved scrutiny.

As an undercover cop, I targeted men carrying big cash wads as possible smugglers or money launderers, and was right many times. If you tend to carry a much greater quantity of cash than you need, ask yourself why. You probably won't come up with a logical answer. Leave some cash at home, and consider switching from an open money clip to an enclosed wallet.

8. Use your intuition when dealing with strangers on the street.

I don't recommend being rude or impolite to strangers, but listen to your instincts if someone approaches you to ask for help, to offer you help, or to chat with you for any reason. If it doesn't feel right, excuse yourself and keep moving. Cross to the other side of the street if it makes you feel more comfortable. Whatever the reason, if someone you don't know approaches you, consider *why* the person has singled you out. Are you the only other person on the street? Are there stores or other businesses open nearby where they could seek help rather than ask your assistance? If things don't seem to add up, or if someone is harassing or verbally abusing you, move quickly to someplace where there are more people around, and don't hesitate to call the police if you feel threatened.

What if your intuition tells you that the stranger asking you for directions is legitimately in need of help? If you choose to help out, stay alert and aware. Keep your distance, at least farther away than the person's arms can reach. Don't approach a car so closely that you could be grabbed through a window.

9. Take the quickest route to the safest place you can find.

If you think someone is following you, it's important to move quickly to where there are a lot of people and you can summon help. What if you're not sure you're being followed? Test your theory by turning around and going in another direction. If your suspect does the same, then assume you're being followed. Don't panic; head quickly to the first safe place you can find—a store, a neighbor's house, a taxicab, directly to a police station, fire station, hospital, or any public place where you can call for help. Run if you have to. Take mental notes about who's following you: Are they in a car or on foot? What does the vehicle look like? Memorize the license tag numbers if possible. What does the person or people look like? When you get to safety, immediately call the police. Remember that you can make 911 calls from pay phones without change.

10. It's best to keep one arm free at all times.

It's much easier for you to be attacked if you overload your arms with packages, or bury your hands in your pockets. If you're struggling with packages, you're the perfect victim for an attacker called the "helpful stranger." His method of operation is to aggressively offer to help you while he grabs a package or bag you can barely hold on to. He walks along with you, and he won't take no for an answer. His goal is to get into your car or home to rob or otherwise harm you, and he hopes you'll simply continue on to one of those places. Now you're in a strange position: You need help, but he hasn't really done anything. What are you going to do? You can't yell out, "Help! I'm being helped!" But you might holler, "Police! He's harassing me!" Because you've overloaded yourself, you can't really make use of your hands unless you use the packages to move against the person.

It's the same with burying your hands deeply into your pockets—you can't get your hands out to defend yourself if someone grabs you in such a way that your arms are pinned against your body. For this reason, the police academy teaches officers not to keep more than three fingers in a pocket when walking or standing. Even if you're grabbed and pinned, you can still break your hands free.

11. Varying your route lessens your chances of being targeted.

If a would-be attacker sees you going along the same route day after day, he could learn the vulnerable points in that route. And when you're varying your route, don't vary it in the same manner. For example, if you can travel along either course A, course B, or course C, don't always do A, then B, then C. You'll end up just as predictable. When choosing your exercise routes, stay in populated places, avoiding isolated or thickly wooded areas. Consider carrying a cell phone with you when you exercise. Be sure you don't focus so strongly on your exercise that you get zoned out and don't pay attention to what's going on around you, or where you are. If you have to call for help on your cell phone, you'll need to tell the dispatcher where you're located.

12. Stick to well-traveled, populated routes, especially at night.

It may take you a little longer to get to where you're going, but at least you'll get there. Taking shortcuts through parks and other isolated areas after dark exposes you to danger. What if you can't avoid traveling through such areas? Remember to keep your head and confidence up, walk briskly, and stay alert and aware at all times. If you hear footsteps behind you or think you're being followed, run to a safer place. Don't be afraid to scream to get help or to scare your pursuer away.

13. Make sure you see the clerk before entering the store.

People have interrupted robberies in progress where the clerk was being held in the back—or worse. Wait at the door for a few minutes, and if you don't see someone soon, leave. Consider summoning police if you see anything suspicious. Use these same precautions before entering any small store or restaurant, especially at night.

14. Change your locks *immediately* if you lose your keys, and don't carry more keys than you need from day to day.

If you have no idea where you lost your keys, assume that they've been stolen. Your next assumption must be that whoever picked them up also knows where you live. Therefore, your first course of action is to change or rekey your locks.

Look at your keychain right now. How many keys are on it? How many of those do you use each day? Each week? Each month? People have been known to carry their spare car keys on the same ring as the primary keys (how useless can that be?), along with their sister's house key, the key to their neighbor's summer home, their bank safety deposit box—you get the picture. All of them are gone—and a big security risk—if your keys get swiped or you lose them. Carry only what you need regularly. Hide spare and little-used keys the same way you would hide valuables. I worked a case in which a woman's condo was burglarized while she was visiting a neighbor. This woman had a pretty key holder on the wall just inside her kitchen, in plain view from the front door. Adding insult to injury, the burglars took her spare car key, loaded her things into her car (which was parked in the space out front labeled with her unit number), and drove away with everything! Never label keys. Luckily she hadn't done that, or the thieves could have driven to her sister's or the neighbor's summer home and ransacked them, too.

15. Always have your keys out and ready in transition situations.

In transitions, you should always be alert and aware of your surroundings, not focusing your attention on *finding* your keys. Before leaving a building, put your car key discreetly into your hand. Before getting out of the car, put your house key between your fingers. If you have more than one lock on your door, it's helpful to put the two keys next to each other on your key ring.

Put your car key next to the house key so you can find it without fumbling in the dark—it can be one simple movement to go to the next key. If your car or home alarm system has a remote panic button, carry that during these times as well. You can set off either alarm to attract attention if you need to.

16. Keeping your car doors locked at all times gives you an edge.

Thieves can't get in as easily when you're not in the car, and muggers can't get in when you are. While driving, locked doors help protect from would-be assailants and carjackers at intersections, stop signs, and anywhere else you might stop. They also protect you in an accident by keeping your doors from flying open, and by strengthening the side of your car in case of a broadside hit.

17. Park where assailants don't have a hiding place.

Muggers often hide inside vans; they can slide the side door open and force you into the van at gunpoint. This is not limited to women—I've heard more than one chilling story of men being pulled into vans and forced to disclose their debit card PIN numbers. In some cases, the victims were driven to their homes, where the assailants stole their valuables.

18. Park in an area that won't *become* deserted at some time.

Few people consciously choose to park in an isolated or deserted lot. The lot's usually full when you get there, but depending on how long you stay, it can become deserted when it's time for you to leave. Often this can happen at work, especially if you end up staying later than you'd planned. You can't always avoid a deserted parking lot, but if you know you have to work late, you might go out before dark and see if you can move your car closer to the building. If you can't, then try to get someone to accompany you to the lot, particularly if your company has a security department.

19. Never pick up hitchhikers, male or female.

Nobody should have answered yes to this question. It's dangerous to hitchhike, and to pick up hitchhikers, period. There's a tendency to think it's probably okay to pick up a woman hitchhiker, but remember that female serial killer Aileen Wuornos found some of her victims while she hitchhiked. Don't pick up *anybody* you don't know, and don't get picked up by anybody you don't know.

20. Know the safe places in your neighborhood, and any area you frequent.

It's important to know the locations of the police station, the closest fire station and hospital, and businesses with security that are open late or all night. If you're ever being followed, you don't want to lead the person to your home. Any of the places mentioned are good safety zones to head for. Fire departments are usually close at hand and staffed by firefighters who are ready and willing to help people in any emergency situation. Hospitals, especially emergency room areas, have twenty-four-hour security. You don't have to park in the parking lot if you feel you're being threatened—drive right up to the ambulance emergency entrance, where there will be plenty of people and security. All-night stores with security on the premises are a good alternative to get assistance. Stop right up front and run inside to call the police. Just going to places like these will often scare away a pursuer.

Your Money or Your Life— ATM and Banking Security

In the course of normal banking, the most serious concern is for people who carry a lot of cash to or from the bank, such as retailers and small-business owners who may pick up cash at the bank for their businesses (for cash registers, or to make transactions). Other prime targets are people taking valuables to or from a safe deposit box. Robbers stake out banks waiting for people who look like they have cash, or who put something in the trunk as if it's valuable. If you do this, they'll follow you to determine if you're an easy mark. They may try a bump and rob, or follow you home and wait for you to open the trunk again. If you happen to be in an isolated area, or have pulled the car into your garage and left the door open, they have an opportunity to rob you.

Here's what to do to avoid becoming a victim:

- Be aware that someone may be watching you.
- Don't put items in the trunk right after coming out of the bank. Take them in the car with you.
- If you frequently carry cash or valuables to and from the bank, consider getting a lock box or small safe made especially for use in cars. They bolt to the floor under the front seat.
- Check to see if you're being followed by diverting from your regular route and seeing if any cars behind follow suit. Or

make a complete circle by making four right turns or four left turns—anyone still behind you after that is definitely following you. If so, don't go to your destination, but rather go to the police—or call them on your cell phone.

- Have someone meet you when you arrive at your destination.

ATM Security—Protecting Your PIN

When ATMs were new technology, you couldn't choose your own personal identification number (PIN). Banks assigned them to you; you had to accept your number and memorize it. Lots of people used to write their PIN numbers down somewhere, often right on the cards or the little envelope they came in, so they wouldn't forget, despite banks' warnings not to do so. I've come across too many cases in which thieves used stolen cards with PINs written on them to cash out victim's bank accounts, especially if the victim didn't know for a while that his card was missing.

Today, just about everyone chooses their own PIN, and that should be a good thing. If you thought it up in the first place, you should be able to remember it. Right? Not so—I'm always amazed at how many people still write their PINs down when they should know better, and they still write them somewhere they shouldn't, like directly on the card itself, or on a slip of paper kept in the wallet or purse, labeled ATM PIN NUMBER. The truth is, the PIN game today goes beyond the ATM, and the consequences can be far more devastating than losing a couple hundred dollars from your bank account. Don't write your PINs down. It's that simple. Here's why:

Take a moment to think about how many places you use a PIN or access code today.

Besides your ATM card, you might use a PIN:

- To gain access to *all* your bank accounts, including money markets and certificates of deposit, either by phone or on the Internet.
- To get cash advances from credit cards via ATMs.
- To refill prescription medication via a pharmacy's Web site or telephone automatic refill service.
- To access an online bill-paying service, including those that allow you to perform money wire transfers.
- To turn your home security system on and off.
- To log onto your Internet service provider.
- To log into various Internet services such as e-mail, subscription newsletters, shopping accounts, online securities trading, and more.
- To access job-hunting and résumé service accounts.
- To lock your cellular phone.
- To access long-distance telephone service.

See where this is going? Depending on how "wired" you are, there may be few areas of your life that aren't somehow accessed by security code. That said, here's the big problem: Humans are creatures of habit. If we choose a PIN, we often choose the easiest one to remember. And if we have to use lots of PINs, we probably choose the same one—or a slight variation of it—over and over.

I polled a few friends and was surprised to learn just how many of them use the *same* PIN or access code for nearly every need. Believe me, smart robbers and good identity thieves know this is probably the norm rather than the exception (more on identity theft in chapter 3). If your PIN is stolen, it's likely whoever gets it won't stop at trying to access your bank account. He could do far more damage.

PINs and access codes can be stolen in three ways: If you've written it down, someone can see it or steal whatever you've written it on; someone can see you using it; or someone can decipher it from an online or computer application. There are two steps to protecting your PIN.

The first is to select a code—or more than one—that's hard for others to guess.

Here are some PIN selection hints:

- Don't use the following for PIN or access codes: Your current phone number, street address, birth date, any consecutive digits in your Social Security number, any other number that can be found in the home.
- Consider using the first phone number you ever learned. This is one of the best pieces of advice I've ever found for picking a PIN number. In many cases, the first phone number you memorized when you were a kid has never been in any database. So if someone wanted to try to guess your PIN from old phone numbers, it would be extremely difficult to find it. This won't be true for everybody, particularly for people born in the 1970s or later whose families have had the same phone number since then.
- If possible, use more than four characters. Mix numbers and letters if you can. This won't always be possible. ATMs don't allow letters to be used, for example, and usually have a maximum of four digits. On the other hand, computers and Internet accounts often allow the use of symbols and case sensitivity in a code, such as puRELY?steeL.

- Choose a foreign word for your code, if you can. Are you multilingual? An obscure word in another language would be more difficult to figure out, especially if you mix numbers in with it. Just be sure it's something you can remember easily.
- Ideally, don't use the same PIN code for every application. You may need to remember a couple of codes, but it's really the best way to protect your accounts and other valuable information.

The second step in PIN security is to keep others from seeing you use the code. This, too, has moved beyond the ATM machine. With debit cards in wide use, everyone is merrily punching their PIN codes into debit terminals at the gas pump, in convenience stores, at the supermarket, the drive-through taco stand, and even some vending machines. Never have there been so many opportunities for others to peek over your shoulder and see your secret codes. It's been called "shoulder surfing," and there's more than one way for a crook to do it.

The old-fashioned way, of course, is to stand close to you and watch. But just because nobody's physically shoulder surfing you doesn't mean they aren't somehow reading over your shoulder from a distance. Criminals can use video cameras with telephoto lenses to tape as many ATM or debit customers as they want. Depending on where an ATM is located, a clever crook might sit in a van or even a tree with a pair of binoculars and write down codes. Some may relay the code to an accomplice on the ground, who would attack you to get the card and use it right away.

When keying in your PIN, you should always try to shield the keypad with your hand so others don't see. You may feel funny about doing this at first, especially at places like the grocery store. But you'll get over it. The truth is, if you don't make a big deal out of it, then probably few people will even notice. Using your cupped hand may not be enough to keep away prying eyes at the ATM, however. If someone is waiting in line too close to you for your comfort, turn sideways and watch when keying in your PIN, and divide your attention between the person and the machine. Doing this will usually cause the person to move back from you. Keep a pleasant manner when you do this—you don't want to start a confrontation, especially since you don't know what's going on in this person's head. If he doesn't back off, I advise you push the CANCEL button to end your transaction, take your card, and leave.

Robbery at the ATM

The most common ATM crime is robbery, PIN or no PIN. If you go to a bank ATM machine after the bank is closed, you're at greater risk of being robbed than during banking hours. Forty-nine percent of ATM-related crimes occur between 7:00 P.M. and midnight, the most dangerous hours for ATM crime. In many cases, robbers wait for you to withdraw cash, then mug you for it. Or they may attack you and force you to make a large withdrawal. In either case, they generally take your jewelry, credit cards, and other personal property, too.

Once again, crooks like people who are wrapped up in thoughts of where they've been and where they're going rather than where they are, which is at the ATM. Don't be distracted. Be alert to what's going on around you at the ATM, and follow these tips to avoid becoming a victim:

Top Ten Tips to Prevent ATM Robbery

1. Don't dawdle at the machine. Get your ATM card out and ready before you even get out of the car. If you're using a drive-up ATM, have your card ready to use as soon as you stop beside the machine.

2. Only use ATM machines that are well lit, or located in areas with lots of activity and people around.

3. Beware of machines that have "eaten" your ATM card. An ATM scam involves jamming the machine in such a way that the next user thinks the machine has malfunctioned and kept his card. If this happens to you, and someone who claims to be a bank representative quickly approaches you asking for your PIN, don't give it! The person gets you to give him your PIN, and when you leave, he pulls your card out of the machine with tweezers and uses it. Go inside the bank right away and ask to speak to the manager. If the bank is closed, leave. Note that this scam isn't as easy to pull off in this country as it once was, but if you travel to other countries, it's still done frequently.

4. When you get your cash, put it away quickly and leave. Don't stand around counting your money in the open. You can do a quick scan of the cash to make sure you got what you wanted by slightly fanning the bills out, like a hand of playing cards. You should be able to take a quick glance and know what you have while keeping the money, like cards, close to the vest.

5. When using drive-up ATMs, make sure all your doors are locked. Check mirrors and look around frequently.

6. At drive-up ATMs, pull your car as close to the machine as you can so you don't have to put your car in park and/or open your door to get to it.

7. Consider keeping your car in gear and your foot on the brake during the entire transaction. If someone is approaching you in a threatening manner, you can quickly drive away. As a plainclothes cop, I used this technique when informants came to the window to talk to me. I sometimes kept the car in reverse for the element of surprise.

8. Plan ahead to lessen the chances of needing to use an ATM at night. Try to have cash on hand. If you do have to use an ATM at night, go to one located inside a business, such as a gas station or grocery store.

9. Use your ATM card as a debit card in a grocery store to get cash after dark instead of going to an isolated ATM machine. There's always something you can buy—milk, bread, even a pack of gum. Pay with your ATM card and get cash back.

10. Don't use an ATM—walk-up or drive-up—if there are people around who make you suspicious, or you see or sense anything that causes you concern.

Muggings and Abductions

Muggers get you when your guard is down. They usually strike quickly, take your valuables, and run. To be mugged means to be struck or beaten by someone whose intent is robbery. But this doesn't mean that a mugger always ambushes you, jumping out from a dark alley or from behind a tree. Sometimes a mugger will approach you in the guise of the friendly stranger I discussed earlier, who looks for targets who appear to be lost, confused, or vulnerable in any way. As noted in the Streetwise quiz, you can become a target anytime your attention is drawn away from your surroundings—rummaging around in your purse for your keys or to put away money you just took from an ATM machine, for instance, as I just discussed.

Who is most likely to become a mugging victim? Interestingly, mugging is a popular criminal-on-criminal sport among dope dealers and their clients, and prostitutes and their johns. But the real victims are usually the elderly, women, and anyone who appears to be an easy target. The strong are seldom mugged—if they're victimized, they're usually robbed at gunpoint.

Advice in the case of a mugging is never as simple as to say "Fight back," or "Give up your property rather than risk your life." People will always do whatever they feel compelled to do at the moment. There's psychology involved that makes people want to stand up to this type of crime, even to act against most advice they may have been given on how to handle such a situation. The case of a star college football player from Florida who was robbed at gunpoint illustrates this. He was seriously injured when he was confronted by two attackers, one of whom pulled a gun and demanded the player hand over his championship ring. The player wasn't going to give it up—he turned to run, and the assailant shot him in the back. The player survived, but when questioned about the attack, he stated: "They didn't get my ring." To him, at that moment, it was extremely important to not let those thugs take something that didn't belong to them, something he had worked very hard to earn. The player put himself at great risk, something he might not normally do.

On the other hand, an elderly woman in south Florida fought back against a mugger who tried to steal her purse outside the office supply store where she worked. The woman was so brutally beaten that she was quite lucky to be alive. From her hospital bed, she wished she had handled the situation differently: "I wish I'd let him have the purse."

What would you do in the player's situation? In the elderly woman's situation? You must ask yourself questions like this as part of your personal security plan development. The answer is individual and situational. No one can say definitively what you should do. In my own experience, there are times when I've fought back, and times when I've thought better of it. It doesn't matter if you're a cop or a soldier—or a citizen—there are times to retreat, and times not to. There are times when your life or the lives of your loved ones are threatened, and no one can tell you to not fight back. The question of self-defense is one I'll cover in more detail in chapter 10. For now, I'll say that to fight back or not is an informed decision only you can make for yourself.

To avoid getting to the point of having to make that decision, the best prevention advice is to not make yourself a vulnerable target. As I've said before, those who are not alert or aware of what's going on around them are the best targets.

You generally don't have to worry about mugging and abduction in crowded areas. Being in the habit of taking a quick survey of your surroundings every time you're in a transition will let you know right away if you're in a place where you have to be more vigilant. You'll do well to walk close to the curb and avoid recessed doorways, bushes, and alleys where assailants could hide. It's a rare abduction that occurs in broad daylight on a crowded street—except on TV. I'm not saying it doesn't ever happen, but if it does, it sure makes the news.

Abduction usually occurs for the purpose of committing another crime, such as robbery or sexual crimes. Child abduction is every parent's nightmare, and I cover that in detail in chapter 5. Avoiding abduction in the case of adults is basically like avoiding mugging or being grabbed from ambush. Those who abduct get you to put your guard down, or use a weapon to intimidate and force you to do what they want. The defense against this is prevention by being streetwise, alert, and aware.

Public Transportation Security

When riding the bus or train, it's tempting to leave the driving to someone else and relax a bit. But check your surroundings before you do and note who's sitting next to you. Do this each time the bus or train stops. This quick mental snapshot tells you whether you need to be more vigilant, or if you can continue to relax and read your paper.

Staying safe when riding public transportation:

1. Stay awake and alert. Pickpockets and other crooks like to work on crowded public transportation. Tip for men: If you ride public transportation regularly, put a big rubber band around your wallet. This makes it more difficult to pick

your pocket without you feeling it, even for an experienced pickpocket. It's a good idea to do this when you're traveling, too.

2. If you're riding the bus or train with a friend, watch what you say and how loudly you say it. You never know who might be eavesdropping. It would be very easy to get into the following conversation with your friend: "It's sure been a hard week. But my husband and the kids are out of town for the weekend and I'm going home to put up my feet and relax all by myself." Isn't that just what a mugger or sexual predator nearby wants to hear? Remember, you can be followed when you disembark (see #7).

3. Be careful if you strike up a conversation with a stranger. Don't give out any personal information about where you live, your social life, vacation plans, or where you work.

4. Have the exact fare ready so you aren't exposing your wallet or purse in a crowd.

5. Know your bus schedule, and arrive at the bus stop only a few minutes before the bus gets there. Don't spend time standing around.

6. If someone's harassing you on the bus, tell the driver. Most drivers are in radio communication with dispatchers and can send for the police if you need it.

   I find it interesting that it's almost universally recommended to sit near the driver as a security precaution. Considering that bus driver is the tenth most likely profession to be attacked at work—right after convenience store clerk—I wouldn't want to sit too close.

7. If you believe someone is following you when you get off the bus or train, head quickly for a populated area, or go to a safe public place like a police station, fire station, or hospital.

Crowds and Other Problems in the Streets

I almost got caught in a riot in Paris in the mid-1980s. I saw a huge, noisy placard-carrying crowd coming toward me, and police were arriving in riot gear. I ducked into a side street to avoid the ruckus and found myself facing two gendarmes armed with submachine guns. They pointed the guns in my direction and yelled angrily in French—and I had no idea whether they were telling me to come forward, or saying, "Stop or I'll shoot!" I put my hands up, smiled, and backed off slowly, and they let me go. In retrospect, I'm still glad I avoided the crowd.

Why? Demonstrations can easily turn into riots. Tear gas usually follows, and after that you never know what might happen. While a demonstration may start out peaceful, there's always the chance of opposing demonstrators showing up and everyone getting into fights.

Not all crowds on the street are bad or hold the potential for being dangerous. I remember coming upon a crowd situation that turned out to be Muhammed Ali giving autographs to children. The point is that you should use all your senses, including your sixth sense, to decide your course of action when you see a crowd forming. Listen for police sirens. Analyze the voices—are they angry or upset? How large is the crowd? Even a happy crowd surging through the street can accidentally crush people to death, or suddenly erupt into violence. You've probably seen that on occasion when a pro sports team wins the championship title.

If you're ever swept up in a crowd, try to move toward the edge and away from anything you can be trapped against, like a fence or wall. If you're at a rowdy concert, for example, avoid being front and center stage. Sitting on the edge affords more escape options. If you're swept up and being crushed, as a last resort try to crouch into a fetal position and protect your head with your hands. Forming yourself into a ball creates a stronger position that can withstand more pressure and weight. You're protecting your lungs in this position, so it's not as easy to have the wind knocked out of you. And your rounded back helps repel other bodies. By being low to the ground, the pressure of the bodies won't be against you, only the legs. I'm not saying it won't be painful to be battered by a sea of legs, but the chances of getting crushed are diminished greatly.

Chapter 3

Security at Home

One-hundred-seventy-eight of every 1000 households will be a victim of some sort of property crime and 32 homes of every 1000 will be burglarized this year.

Your Home Is Your Castle

Personal security at home means more than just taking steps to keep your house safe from break-ins. It means planning for a full range of protection for you and your loved ones in a way that allows you to go about your normal lives, free from fear and anxiety.

Break-ins are just the start of your home security considerations. In this chapter, we'll discuss burglary and home invasion, the two most common intruder crimes. But also we'll look at domestic violence and fraud, two other common security considerations in the home. We'll look at electronic security alarm systems from a design point of view. I won't go into great detail about what hardware to buy or how to wire it up. Rather,

I'll help you determine how much, or how little, alarm system gadgetry you need to adequately secure your home within your budgetary concerns, and discuss the most popular options for security systems. The Home Security Assessment will take you step by step through your home to find its security strengths and weaknesses, information you need to make your home security plan.

You learned in the last chapter how to be alert and aware on the streets—now bring that increased awareness home.

Don't Be Intruder-Friendly

There is a tremendous feeling of personal violation and loss of security when someone breaks into your home. If you can't feel safe in your own home, where can you? The truth is, most burglars go into homes because they've been invited. Yes, you read that right: Homeowners regularly invite burglars to come right on in! How? By unconsciously giving them opportunity.

Some ways people regularly invite burglars into their homes:

- Leaving windows and doors unlocked when not home.
- Not arming security systems.
- Leaving garage and basement doors unlocked.
- Leaving windows open all night.
- Not making a home look occupied when they're on vacation.

In the Home Security Assessment to follow, you'll learn how to counteract these and other security risks.

What else makes a home inviting to intruders?

According to a study at Temple University in Philadelphia, three or more of the following things make a home a good target:

- It's located within three blocks of a major thoroughfare.
- It's on a cul-de-sac.
- It's situated adjacent to a wooded area, abandoned railroad tracks, or park.
- It's somewhat more expensive than others in the neighborhood.
- The home's occupants are newcomers to the neighborhood within the past year.

To have a plan for security at home, you first need to look carefully and honestly at how secure—or insecure—your home is currently. Many people think that having good strong locks on all the doors and windows is enough for security. Well, here's an interesting thing about locks: You do have to use them in order for them to work. This is no joke: In nearly half of burglaries in which the thief entered through a door or window, he got in through an unlocked door or window.

Many burglars I've arrested told me they usually spend less than a minute sizing up a potential target before deciding whether to break in or move on. Obvious deterrents such as an electronic security alarm system can cause them to go elsewhere (more on that later). Interestingly, some said certain visible, flamboyant security measures, such as huge padlocks, sometimes had the opposite effect of a deterrent. It raised the crooks' curiosity about what was so valuable that it required such extreme measures, and sometimes offered a challenge they couldn't pass up.

Even if you have good locks and use them, you need to know some important things I learned while investigating burglary cases:

- Most burglars enter a home through the front door. Whether they pick the lock, kick in the door, or simply turn the handle and push, the majority of thieves enter your home through exactly the same entry you do.

- The vast majority of windows can be easily broken. Break the lock or break the glass—it doesn't matter. The end result is that the thief gets in.

- Where there's a will, there's a way for a burglar to get in. Locks are only the first line of defense. A motivated, persistent criminal will quickly move to other means of gaining entrance, and homes with few security measures will open up to a clever crook rather quickly.

- Most stolen property is never recovered, and much of what is recovered can't be returned to its owner because proper steps weren't taken to identify the items.

The good news is that homes with well-thought-out security measures as part of an overall security plan can create enough obstacles for burglars that they'll take their business elsewhere, deflected to other, less prepared homeowners. This is where the Home Security Assessment comes in—whether you live in a single-family home, a condo, or an apartment. In the years I investigated burglaries, I saw everything from the simplest entries—through unlocked doors and windows—to some outlandish, highly creative ways of breaking into a home. This assessment will help you prepare for even the most obscure methods I've seen of gaining entry.

Read through the series of questions and think about how they apply to your own home. Each question is followed by information and advice on making a particular aspect of your home more secure.

Quiz: Home Security Assessment

1. How easy would it be to kick your doors in, pry them open, or smash them?

It's easiest to gain entry through a wooden door (with the exception of heavy hardwood doors like oak). Some hollow wooden doors can be chipped at and deformed to allow locks to be removed, or crowbars to be inserted between the door and frame to pry the door open. A little-used but highly effective way to get past a wooden door is to use a small battery-powered saw to literally slice the door in half horizontally below the lock. The end result is like a Dutch door, and the thief simply swings the bottom half of the door open. This technique defeats most alarm systems, too, since the magnetic contact is generally located on the top of the door.

The best doors are metal, or made of solid-core material that's difficult to smash through, even with a sledgehammer or an ax. While a burglar could theoretically use the "saw it in half" method on a metal door, the amount of noise and effort involved pretty much ensures he wouldn't bother trying.

2. How good are your locks, hinges, and other hardware?

If you don't have a deadbolt lock, get one. Handle-locks (key on the outside, push-button or turn-button on the inside) can be broken fairly easily with a good twist from a pipe wrench. Your lock's bolt should travel at least two inches into the door frame. A lock that's flush-mounted on the door is preferred to one that protrudes, which can be struck with a sledgehammer or pried off. When installing deadbolt locks, don't forget the door from your garage into the house. This is a common security weakness in many homes. Too many people rely on a handle-lock on this important door.

When you engage a deadbolt lock, you turn the handle and the bolt moves into the wall through a metal plate called a strike plate. The strike plate is mounted on the door frame, often on a piece of molding. The problem is that the screws used to mount the strike plate are often so short that they barely pass through the molding. Kicking the door will simply tear this molding away from the wall and defeat the lock. The most secure door uses an oversized strike plate mounted with three-inch screws that penetrate through the molding and deeply into the door frame.

You can secure sliding glass doors with special locks available at home improvement stores. A homemade method that works is to simply put a broomstick or a dowel cut to the proper length in the inside track to keep the door from being opened. A major sliding door security weakness is that they can be lifted off their tracks to gain entry. You can foil this by drilling a hole through the top or bottom track and into the door, then inserting a metal pin in the hole.

It's often recommended that you install double-cylinder deadbolt locks—the kind that require a key to open them from the inside as well as the outside. These locks are the subject of a lot of controversy because they may pose a hazard by creating a barrier to escape in case of fire or other emergency. I don't recommend using this type of lock, because to overcome the hazard, you need to leave a key in the inside lock at all times when you're home. This isn't always practical or easy to do if there are a number of people in your household. It's too easy for someone to take the key out and misplace it. If you live alone, it's easier to keep a key in the lock and not lose it.

Doors should be mounted so the hinges aren't exposed on the outside. Otherwise, someone can simply knock the bolts out of the hinge and take the door off. If your door is mounted in this way, either remount the door with the hinges on the inside, or try this fix to prevent your door from being removed from the hinges:

- Remove an opposing screw from each hinge leaf.

- Screw a long bolt into the door frame side of the hinge. Leave it protruding at least half an inch. Saw off the bolt head.

- Drill out the opposite hole so the bolt goes into it when the door is closed. Do this to the top and bottom hinge plates. Even if the hinge pins are removed, the door will stay firmly in place. It's really not a bad idea to do this to any door, no matter where the hinges are located.

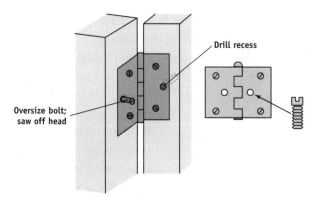

Drill recess

Oversize bolt;
saw off head

Inserting a larger bolt into a hinge and sawing off its head will prevent an intruder from removing the door. See page 53.

3. Do any of your doors contain glass panels?

If you have glass panels in doors, French doors, or sliding glass doors, they are nearly impossible to secure. Safety glass and some protective glass films can offer reinforcement by preventing shattering, but they can still be penetrated. When installing locks on doors with glass panels in them, the rule of thumb is to keep the locks at least two feet away from the glass, thus making it harder for someone to reach in through a broken pane and unlock the door.

4. Are windows secured by locks, security glass, stop pins, or other hardware?

While locks and other hardware won't prevent a determined burglar from breaking your window glass, they can erect enough of a roadblock to help deflect a criminal from your home to another. At the very least, sturdy locks can alert you to an attempted break-in while you're at home. There are downsides to some of these hardware items, however.

- Stop pins prevent your window from being opened more than a few inches, which may slow you down if you ever need to use your windows to escape your home during an emergency.
- Security glass and reinforcing films such as storm glazing will slow down a less persistent intruder, but are costly.
- Locks can be defeated either by breaking them or bypassing them and breaking the glass instead.

Of course, I still recommend installing strong locks. But the best overall security method for windows is an alarm system.

When assessing your windows, don't forget basement and attic openings. Pay attention to bathroom windows as well. Though they're small, they can still provide opportunity to thieves. I worked a case in which a father pulled off burglaries with his seven-year-old son. Dad boosted the kid into the house through a bathroom window. Little Junior was trained to grab jewelry, watches, cash, guns, cameras—anything he could easily pick up and pass through the small window to his waiting dad. The loot was stashed in a backpack, and after the heist, the two strolled away from the job hand in hand, the least likely pair of criminals you could ever conceive. They made several good hauls without ever going through a larger window or door.

5. Are your windows protected with metal grates or burglar bars?

These are the two best ways to physically protect windows. Both methods, however, are barriers to escape in an emergency, so consider their use carefully. Another effective method that doubles as storm protection is to install rolling aluminum shutters controlled from the inside of the home.

These three ways to protect windows aren't for everybody, though—they're considered extreme by most people, and they certainly don't do much for the looks of your home.

6. Where might a burglar or assailant hide outside your home?

Burglary is a crime of stealth—its perpetrators depend on not being seen to commit their crime. If you're not careful, criminals can find many places to lurk on your property. Consider trimming tall bushes and trees near your front door or windows to eliminate possible hiding spots and potential access to your upper floors. Light up dark areas and entryways, making sure to mount lights high enough to avoid tampering. I especially like motion sensors on lights, for two reasons: They alert you to any motion outside, and the prowler can't know if you've been alerted to his presence and turned on the light yourself.

Don't forget to lock any backyard storage sheds, cellar doors, and garage doors when not in use. Burglars can use such areas to place you under surveillance, learn your habits, and plan their crimes more thoroughly.

7. Can anything outside the home be used by an intruder to break in?

Burglars don't always carry their own tools of the trade with them. Often they rely on using the homeowner's personal items left lying around the house. Put away ladders that could be used to access upper stories, or any other tools that might help someone break into your home. Look carefully around your home and consider any other means a burglar might use to get into your home. Might he climb a sturdy trellis to an upper floor? Or perhaps shimmy up a downspout? Although I've never gone this far myself, I once met a homeowner who greased all his rainspouts with petroleum jelly so no one could climb them to get in the second story. But I have to give him credit for noticing the downspouts as a possible means of entry and creatively doing something about it.

8. Is your address plainly visible from the street?

Emergency services such as police, ambulance, or fire can respond more quickly and efficiently if your address is easily seen from the street. I've known people who took steps to make their address easily seen when they were having a big party, but never considered how important this small, inexpensive measure was to their safety and security each and every day. When minutes count, it can literally save your life in case of fire, medical emergency, or home invasion.

9. Have you taken simple security measures in your garage?

People tend to overlook the garage as a security weakness, whether it's attached to a house or freestanding. Make sure all doors lock, or you're offering criminals a good place to hide. If the garage is attached to your house and he can get in easily, he now has a safe place out of sight where he can work on getting into the house for hours. He could use tools stored there to pry off the connecting door, or even cut a hole through the wall between the garage and the house. He might also get into the garage ceiling and simply make his way across the crawl space to the house's ceiling, then knock a hole out and drop right in. If your garage is detached, the burglar can make it a comfortable hiding place to watch you over a period of time to learn your habits, preparing to strike in the future. He could also steal your car, or lie in wait to attack you.

Don't be caught in the dark in your garage. Keep it well lit, making sure all lights are in working order. It's best to provide for turning garage lights on from inside the house.

10. Have you engraved, photographed, or otherwise identified and inventoried your personal property?

It's easier to recover stolen property if you've identified it, but doing a thorough job of recording your items and marking them also makes it easier to deal with your insurance company should you need to. My favorite way of marking items is electric engraving. I like this method because it isn't easy to remove. Some burglars will actually leave engraved items behind because they're too difficult to fence. I recommend putting your state and your driver's license number on items in this way:

FL/DL#123-456-7890

Any police officer who finds stolen items marked in this way can immediately run a driver's license check—anywhere, any-time—and find out on the spot who owns the property. Anyone who's been stopped by the police knows how quickly they can run a driver's license. I don't recommend using your Social Security number as ID for two reasons: Police don't have ready access to those numbers to find out who you are, and your Social Security number is something you should be keeping as private as possible. Your SS number is tied to your finances, and a good cybercrook can use that to the fullest extent possible. Somehow mark your ID on all new purchases immediately so you don't put it off and forget to do it at all. You might also take photographs or video of your items. Keep a copy of any photos, videotapes, and a written list of serial numbers somewhere off the premises, like a bank safe deposit box or a friend's house. Always record serial numbers of items such as computers, TVs, firearms, and electronics. (Tip: Don't toss the user's manuals, even if you're an expert in the use of the equipment. For many insurance companies, possession of the user's manual is proof that you owned the item.)

When I graduated from college and was a (very) rookie cop, my house burned to the ground. Unfortunately, I hadn't done a complete inventory of my property. Months after settling with the insurance company, I discovered items I'd missed in my original claim. They were little-used antique items that I had truly forgotten about, such as old fishing reels and my grandfather's gold watch. Now I do regular yearly inventories just before hurricane season, in case I need to make storm insurance claims. I'm covered for anything that might happen.

11. How well do you know your neighbors?

Close-knit communities and neighborhoods have lower crime rates than areas where neighbors don't look out for each other. Residents are familiar with each other's work and recreational habits, as well as who's coming and going in the neighborhood. They're alert and aware of suspicious activity or unfamiliar people and vehicles in the area.

If you don't know your neighbors, it's time to get to know

them. That includes the nosy busybody down the street. Every neighborhood has one, and while you may not like it, this could be the person who is first alerted to criminal activity. Often during the course of investigating a burglary, victims told me about busybody neighbors and suggested I go talk with them immediately, since they might have seen something. Quite often, the busybodies not only saw someone, but could provide detailed descriptions. Yet many times, alert and aware neighbors who gave highly accurate descriptions of burglars and their movements didn't attempt to call police. Why? One woman told me that she didn't really know if the person she saw belonged in the house or not. She simply didn't know her neighbors, but if she had, the burglary may have been interrupted in progress by police.

Consider putting extra-vigilant neighbors in charge of a neighborhood crime watch program, or invite them to join a Citizens' Observer Patrol (COP) program through your local police department. They can actually make it their "job" to get to know everyone and be aware of what's happening in the neighborhood, and to call the police about suspicious activity or people.

Getting to know your neighbors can also clue you in to any potential threats in your midst. A friend told me that after her home was burglarized repeatedly, she talked to all of her neighbors to inform them of the thefts. While doing this, she learned that one of her neighbor's sons had been having a terrible time with a drug problem. This made my friend think that the teen could be a good suspect for the burglaries. She reported what she learned to the police, who were later able to match the kid's fingerprints to those lifted from inside my friend's house. An arrest was made as a result.

12. Apartment dwellers: Do you have a crawl space in your ceiling that's accessible from other apartments?

Attic spaces open across an entire building aren't uncommon. They're used to run air-conditioning ductwork, plumbing, and electrical wiring to units throughout the building. Such spaces are also a security risk—an intruder can enter the crawl space and have easy access to more than one apartment by simply kicking a hole in the ceiling and dropping into a unit. The burglar then leaves through the door.

There are two ways to secure this weakness. One is to block off access to the crawl space covering your unit. This is an expensive structural option that you may not be permitted to do, and even if you were, the cost may be your responsibility. The only other alternative is to use an alarm system. How to do this is explained in the next section on alarms.

13. Apartment dwellers: Do you have a balcony that's accessible from adjoining balconies?

Experienced cat burglars often use this method of entry. I investigated a case in which one prolific cat burglar gained access to nearly every unit in a small apartment building during one night. It amazed me how the burglar could move through nearly a dozen units without waking the occupants, nimbly climbing from one balcony to another. He was so stealthy, he even stepped over one family's sleeping dog—successfully—to get at a jewelry box.

When looking at your balcony for weaknesses, don't just look sideways—depending on how the building is designed, a burglar might be able to drop in from an upper balcony, or pull himself up from a lower one. It doesn't even take an expert. An acquaintance told me that she and her friends sneaked out of a college dormitory at night by dropping from the building's fifth floor to the ground level, one balcony at a time. It was surprisingly easy to do so because of how the building was designed. Professional cat burglars use a knotted half-inch line tied to a small grappling hook to move quietly up and down balconies. Learning how to do this is easy, too. Uncle Sam is more than willing to teach you if you enlist in the military. This method has been used to scale walls since the time of medieval castles.

There are few remedies for easy-to-breach balconies. The simplest one is to not leave balcony doors open all night, even if you live on an upper floor. Remember, cat burglars love to climb, so just because you live on the tenth floor doesn't mean you're secure. Some people may not want to "hunker down" and fortify themselves in such a way that they no longer feel they can enjoy living in their high-rise. I'm no different—I like to leave my balcony door open at night to enjoy nice weather. But I use an alarm to feel secure doing this, details of which are covered in the next section on alarms.

Another way to help secure a balcony is to erect some physical barricades between your balcony and the ones on either side. You might use heavy planters, a trellis, or some other decorative means to create a wall. It may not stop the most experienced or determined cat burglar, but it's a barrier that may serve to deflect him to a less prepared apartment dweller. A third security option is the use of an alarm system; again, see the discussion on page 63.

Most really good cat burglars seldom hit the middle class. Their skills are such that they tend to focus on the upper class, figuring if they're going to take such risks, they might as well have a big payoff. But nothing can really rule you out as a possible target in this way, so it's best to be alert and have a plan to cover the possibility.

More on the Fine Art of Deflecting Crime

I once arrested a successful cat burglar and was quite curious about how he'd gotten away with his crimes for so long. I asked him point blank to tell me his secret and was surprised when he gave up a lot of his personal "tricks of the trade." After finally getting caught, perhaps he had begun to think about retirement. I also asked him what deflected him from one target home to another and learned some interesting things I hadn't thought of.

"Leave a light on in the bathroom," he said. "That always sends me looking for another place to hit. I can never be certain if someone's really home or not if I see a bathroom light on."

People use the bathroom at all hours of the night, he explained. If he knocked on the door, as burglars often do to check if someone's home, no answer wouldn't automatically mean that the house was empty. Someone could indeed be in the bathroom and unable to jump up to answer the door.

"I never took a chance if I saw a bathroom light on. It just raised too many question marks," he said.

Different things deflect different burglars. I prefer the word deflect to deter, because when you take preventive measures, you really are deflecting the crime, not actually deterring or stopping it. You only stop it from occurring to you, and therefore deflect it to an easier target of opportunity. If we were truly deterring crime, we'd see the crime statistics go down every time a crime prevention program was initiated.

Everything discussed above is intended to deflect a home break-in. Here are some more ideas for crime deflection in and around your home:

Top Ten Tips for Added Security

1. When valet parking, give only your car's ignition key to the attendant. Never leave your house key—or other keys— with the valet. You probably have something in your car that has your address on it, such as an insurance card, car registration, even forgotten junk mail. An attendant or accomplice could quickly cut a copy of your house key and, armed with your address, head to your home to help himself to a few things while you're dining.

2. Replace or rekey all locks when you move into a new house or apartment. I'm always amazed at how many people don't do this, yet it seems like common sense.

3. If you live alone, don't advertise the fact. Put an extra name or two on your mailbox or apartment building directory. On your answering machine, say "we" instead of "I" when recording your greeting message, or simply say, "Please leave a message."

4. Completely secure your home anytime you leave it, even if—and especially if—it's only for a few minutes or you're just dropping by the neighbor's. Lock all doors and windows, and turn on your security system.

5. If you go away for a few days, set up some interior lights on timer control. Newer timers can be set to turn lights on and off in more random patterns. If possible, place a timer on your TV as well.

6. When leaving home, ask a friend or neighbor to collect your mail and newspaper, and to open and close your drapes or blinds enough to give the appearance that someone's home. See if a neighbor will park in your driveway.

7. Never leave a message on your answering machine that says you're out of town. If possible, don't leave such a message on your workplace voicemail, either. Many people routinely do this, thinking they must let work-related callers know they're out of town. But doing so is no different in terms of broadcasting the fact that your house may be completely unoccupied.

8. Anytime you have service people visit your home, consider removing valuables and firearms from view. I'm not telling you to distrust all home service personnel, but I've seen cases in which the service person casually talked about someone's nice home and possessions to a less trustworthy person, who then used the information to burglarize the home.

9. Make sure you can see someone at your front door. Security peepholes in the door are a must for every home, unless you can clearly see who's at your door from either a nearby window or a glass pane in the door.

10. Consider replacing louvered or jalousie windows, which are difficult to secure. It's too easy to remove the individual

glass panes in these types of windows. The only option for louvered windows is alarmed screens.

Sometimes, Burglary Happens

For any number of reasons—not having a security system, having one and not turning it on—burglary happens. Everyone needs to have a plan for what to do if you come home and discover a break-in.

If you don't currently have a home security system, you are at risk for break-ins. If you have a security system, it's important to use it. Again, this isn't a joke. Burglaries happen to homes with security systems, but when they do it's almost always because the system wasn't turned on. The odds of you coming home and finding a burglary if you've turned on your good, well-installed system are extremely low. You may find that someone tried to get in and was scared off by the alarm system, but rarely would you discover any of your property missing.

Think for a moment about what you would do if you came home and found your front door kicked in, or a window smashed out. Here's a situation in which having a plan can literally be a matter of life and death. Discovering that your home has been broken in to can be so shocking that you can make impulsive—and highly dangerous—moves.

In one burglary case I worked, a young single woman had left her home for only twenty minutes just before noon. When she returned, she saw that her front door was wide open. At first she though her landlady had gone inside for some reason, but as she walked closer to the house, she noticed the door frame was broken and splintered. Now she was struck with the realization that her home had been broken into. Here's where she made her first mistake: She hurried inside! She was concerned about her pets, and seeing one of her two cats through the screen door made her worried about the second one. Inside, she made her second mistake: She hurried throughout the house, opening closed closet doors and walking into all the rooms. She saw immediately that all her home office equipment was gone, as was her jewelry box. She also noticed, however, that her TV, VCR, and stereo were still there. (Take note—this is important.) After a few minutes, she grabbed the phone and called 911. The dispatcher asked where she was calling from, and she answered that she was inside her home. The dispatcher immediately told her to get out of the house and wait for the police outside. The woman did so. The police arrived, went inside, and began their investigation. In the process, they were able to determine that a pair of burglars had been scared off by a phone call to the woman's home only minutes before she returned! The message on her answering machine explained why the burglars fled: "Hey, I'm on my way over—see ya!" The burglars had no way of knowing that her friend lived more than an hour away and wouldn't be there for a while. But if that phone call hadn't happened, the burglars would probably have still been in her home when she walked brazenly inside. The ending to the story might have been quite different.

Often what starts out as a simple burglary can turn into assault, rape, or even murder if a burglar is surprised or trapped in the house. This is why it's so important to make these two items a part of your everyday security plan:

1. If you see a broken window, slit screen, open door, or anything else suspicious at your home, don't go inside. Call

911 from a cell phone or a neighbor's home, or if you have to, find a pay phone.

2. If you go inside your home and discover that a break-in has occurred from a door or window you couldn't see at first, go outside immediately and call 911.

You should also have a plan for what to do if you see a burglary or suspicious behavior at a neighbor's home or elsewhere in the neighborhood. Take these steps for your safety and security:

1. Call 911 to report the break-in or suspicious activity.

2. Stay inside. Don't go outside and put yourself in harm's way or do something to cause the criminal to flee. You may want to stop the crime in progress, but you also want the police to catch the crook, preferably in the act.

3. Don't challenge the crook. I investigated a case in which someone got shot confronting the criminal by yelling out the window at him, "Hey, you! You don't belong there!" Keep your mouth shut and don't let him know you've seen him.

4. Stay on the phone with the police. You may be able to act as their eyes and ears, providing valuable information on what's going on until they get to the scene. In one case, a woman called 911 to report two suspicious men in her condo complex and learned they were burglars in the process of being chased by police. From her vantage point, the woman provided police with a detailed play-by-play of the crooks' movements, leading to a successful capture and, eventually, two convictions.

Electronic Security Alarm Systems

People always ask me if I think they should get a security system, and I say yes. I have one, and I recommend them highly. I'm a firm believer in alarm systems and think they should be part of any personal security plan. They're the best way to deflect home burglary. I don't know of anybody with a well-installed system who isn't happy he got it.

Do alarms systems actually deter burglaries? Studies and experience say they do. A Temple University study says that a home without an alarm is nearly three times as likely to be broken into. In cases where a home with an alarm was burglarized, either the alarm wasn't activated, or the burglar grabbed a few things before being scared off by the alarm. In rare cases the burglar defeated the alarm system, either because he had inside knowledge of alarm systems, or because the system wasn't very well planned out.

Generally, burglars don't even get inside a home with an alarm system, because once it sounds, they flee. Yes, there are crooks who can bypass alarms, but I'm not overly concerned with them. I figure if they can do that, they're probably going to hit someplace really worth it to them—like Brink's, or a much bigger house than mine. Statistics say that's the case, too. So if you question whether or not it's worth it to install an alarm system in your home, I say: How much is a good night's sleep worth to you? People have reported to me that they really do sleep better at night after installing an alarm system. In fact, many said they didn't know how lightly they had been sleeping until they got the system. For many people, the security and peace of mind alone are worth the cost of a system.

What Kind of System?

The subject of alarms is broad and widely treated. Entire books have been written on the design and selection of home security systems. I think there are a few basics that are important for everyone to know; these basics can help you put together a system that will work well as part of your overall personal security plan.

When first contemplating the purchase of a home security system, many people have it in mind to protect their property when they're away from home. But a security system does far more than that: It protects your person first, and your property second. With that in mind, consider the goal of your home security system. Is it to scare off an intruder who would attempt to break in when you're away from home or, worse, when you're home? Or do you want to catch criminals in the act? To protect your person, you wouldn't want anyone to actually get inside your home. For this reason, a security system that makes a lot of noise to scare someone off would be the least you would want. There are silent alarms, which alert a monitoring station unbeknownst to the crook, but those are generally used on business properties. As a cop, I always enjoyed responding to a good silent alarm at a business after hours. I knew the suspect was still inside and I would have a chance to apprehend him without endangering the public. This is an alarm that's truly crime prevention, because police can take the crook off the streets, at least for a while. On the other hand, an audible alarm will scare the criminal off, and if he doesn't get caught, he may attempt to break in again some night.

In your home, however, you want to scare the intruder away

so you, your family, and your neighbors aren't injured. Basically, the goal is to keep the intruder out of your home, period.

As an aside, I know someone who actually got a basic alarm system not only to keep intruders out, but to keep a fun-loving teenager in at night. After discovering that the kid had been slipping out the bedroom window to party with friends, Mom installed the alarm so it wouldn't happen anymore. Talk about peace of mind!

When deciding how much—or how little—security you need, remember that your primary goal is to keep intruders from getting into your home. If they do happen to get in, you want them to be frightened away.

Buying suggestions:

Before you buy, or if you already have a security system and you want to update it, consider the following suggestions:

1. Contact several reputable alarm companies for quotes and design options. Get recommendations from friends, family, or business owners you know. Compare prices and advice.

2. Is the proposed system easy to use? The main point is to be able to turn it on and off easily. You don't want to get bogged down in technology so complex you can't understand or use it, or turn your home into a fortress. You want to be able to move around freely and enjoy your home, while still having an electronic "barrier" to criminals.

3. Don't overspend—select a system you can afford. Otherwise, you may create a monster that's so intimidating, you postpone the purchase or give it up entirely. Some security is better than none at all.

4. Choose a system that can be easily expanded and upgraded. You may build an addition on your home, or decide to add some options at a later time. With forethought, you won't have to install a completely new system.

5. Consider a system that includes smoke alarms. This way your alarm will go off in the presence of smoke and either someone will hear it or (if your system is monitored) the fire department will be called. The smoke detectors are in full operation at all times, whether the alarm system is armed or not.

6. Involve the whole family in the discussion and investigation of an alarm system. You can address and consider every family member's concerns. You also want to make sure you're buying something the kids can understand and use properly, too.

I want to mention that if you happen to have a dog, you've already got one of best security systems I know of, especially if you have a big, well-trained dog. I can recall investigating only one burglary case in which someone had a big dog in the house. It happens, but I'm equally sure that it can't be very often. Big dogs make a lot of noise, which burglars don't like any more than they like bright lights. Dogs bite, and the bigger they are, the harder they bite. Listen to a big dog crunching a thick bone between his teeth—no human, least of all a burglar, wants to know what that feels like firsthand. At the end of the day, a good dog is a far more enjoyable home alarm than a keypad and a loud horn. It's not necessarily the cheapest system, and in some ways may not be the best, but a dog can bring you your slippers, lick your hand, and keep you warm at night. This doesn't mean you can't have both dog and an alarm system, however.

The Basic System, Plus Options

The most basic home security system can offer you a great deal of protection. By using the preceding Home Security Assessment, you've located your home's weak spots. In most homes, those weak spots are doors, windows, basements, and attic crawl spaces, collectively known as the home's perimeter. For viable, basic security, all you need to do is protect your perimeter by covering your entrances. (Don't forget the door between your house and attached garage, as well as any other doors into the garage, including the big door.) Magnetic contacts set off the alarm if doors or windows are opened. With this measure alone, there's a high probability that a would-be intruder will set off the alarm, and it will have served its purpose. Many alarm companies offer this type of basic system for very little money to install, and a contract for monthly monitoring service. I've even seen some companies offer the system for free in exchange for signing a multiyear monitoring contract.

This is a very basic system, and it has weaknesses. But they can be covered with options.

Security system options:
Monitored or unmonitored.

A monitored system sends a signal directly to a twenty-four-hour monitoring station. Personnel there will do one of several things upon receiving a signal from your security system, from calling your home first to sending police immediately. You choose what you want the response to be. You can install a security system and choose not to use central monitoring, too. At this point, you have a major noisemaker, which is still good because it can alert neighbors and frighten away intruders. This does, however, require you to have neighbors, and for them to be home, which you can't always rely on.

If you want more protection, and a more immediate police or fire response, you need a monitored system. I prefer monitored systems and recommend them if you can afford them because they're highly effective—so effective that insurance companies often give a noticeable discount on homeowner's insurance if you have a monitored system. Monthly monitoring charges vary, but run from twenty dollars per month and up. They're usually less than the monthly charge for cable TV, however, and even a year's worth of monitoring charges can be cheaper than long-term sleep loss.

Cellular phone or radio backup.
This backup system is a safeguard that will allow your monitored system to still call into the station even if your phone lines have been cut. This is a good option to consider if your phone lines aren't underground and are vulnerable to being cut.

Wired or wireless.
The standard wired security system takes time to install, and skilled installers to do it in such a way that your home doesn't look like spaghetti is hanging from all the win-

dows. There used to be an advantage to wired systems in that they produced fewer, if any, false alarms. But wireless technology has improved greatly these days; false alarms are far less of a problem. Wireless systems may be less expensive to install, but they use more battery power, requiring more frequent replacement of expensive batteries.

Zones.

Designing a system with zones can allow you to turn off certain areas of your house if you wish. I used to spend a lot of time working in my backyard, but didn't want to lock up the whole house when I did. So I used zones with my security system and "zoned out," or turned off, only the back door. I could move freely in and out of the house all day, while the alarm system was on fully in the rest of the house.

Motion detectors.

The owner of an alarm company recently told me that he didn't like to install motion detectors in residences. "My job is to keep an intruder from getting inside," he explained. "If I put in motion detectors, then it implies that I'm not doing my job because I'm assuming someone is going to get inside." Interesting point. I agree, and am not a big fan of motion detectors in the general residence. Pets can set off improperly installed motion detectors, although there are some devices available that can be "tuned" to how much motion to sense according to how much the creature creating the motion weighs. There are places in the home where a motion detector can be quite useful, especially garages, basements, and crawl spaces.

But in general, I believe motion detectors are better used in business settings. The best kind sense not only motion, but heat as well, thus decreasing false alarms because they'll go off only when detecting a warm, moving body. A curtain waving around can set off a regular motion detector, but not one that also senses body heat.

Glass break detectors.

These devices used to be rather unsightly, with thick silver contact tape encircling the glass pane. But now their appearance has improved. If magnetic contacts alone are used on windows, they only detect when the windows are opened. A determined intruder can still break the glass and get inside without setting off an alarm. A major weakness in many homes for this reason is sliding glass doors. This is one place where glass break detectors can be useful.

Traps.

Crooks break into your home to find loot, and once they get in, they'll look everywhere for it. Usually they start in a master bedroom, opening doors and drawers in search of jewelry, cash, and firearms. They can't resist a closed door, especially a bedroom closet door, and that makes a perfect place to put a trap. An alarmed interior door that no one would expect to be alarmed is one way to make up for the inability to completely secure sliding glass doors or other weaknesses in your perimeter. Yes, someone still gets in, but he does eventually set off the alarm system. I know someone living in a second-floor apartment who has installed a minimum number of alarm contacts: the exit doors, and the bedroom walk-in closet. It's economical and viable. There's no way a burglar would break into that apartment and not open the closet door. An alarmed closet is also the perfect place to put your alarm system's transmitter, since an intruder can't get to it to disarm it without setting off the alarm. Traps aren't limited to closet doors—use your imagination when coming up with a good trap. You might think about a jewelry box, cabinet door, even a medicine cabinet. (You might even have fun with that one. Do you know many people who can resist a peek in a medicine cabinet?)

Remotes and panic buttons.

I think it's a good idea to have a remote panic alarm for every member of the household, if possible. It's a small push-button transmitter, not unlike your car remote, about the size of a standard pager. When activated, it sends a radio wave to a receiver connected to the alarm system so you can arm and disarm the system without using the keypad. For panic-button use, it should be designed to send a panic signal to the monitoring station and set off your audible alarm, whether you have armed the security system or not. If installed properly, your transmitter may work fifty yards or more away from your home. This allows you to use your remote as protection walking to and from your car late at night, walking to a neighbor's house, or to protect yourself while inside the house. You can also use it in case of a medical emergency if you can't get to the phone. I know of one instance where someone found a child unconscious in the swimming pool. Rather than leave the child, the person hit the panic alarm, then pulled the child out of the water and began CPR, knowing that police were on the way. This may have contributed to saving the child's life.

"Hostage codes."

If someone should force you to turn off your alarm system, you can do it and still summon help if your system is programmed with a hostage code. This is a code programmed into your system that turns your alarm off as usual, but sends a silent SOS signal to your monitoring company. Police are sent immediately, but to the home invaders, it appears that you've simply turned your system off. Generally, a hostage code is your regular access code plus one additional number. So if your regular code is 12345, the hostage code might be 123456. (Note: Don't ever make your security system code a series of consecutive numbers. The above example was only an example!)

Alarmed screens.

Alarmed screens are great—a regular window screen is refitted with new screen that has fine alarm wire woven through it and a magnetic contact on the frame. When installed, it allows you full access to opening and closing your windows while protecting your home from intrusion. If the screen is moved or sliced, the alarm goes off; an intruder thus triggers the alarm before even getting to the window. If you like to sleep with your window open at night, this is the perfect solution. It's also great for those high-rise dwellers who, like me, enjoy sleeping with balcony doors open. Use a sliding screen door and have the screen alarmed. This may not work for cat owners, however.

Infrared.

Like an electronic eye that sounds a bell when you enter a shop, an infrared beam will protect an entryway by setting off your alarm when someone passes through the beam. This is another good solution to the security problems of sliding glass doors and balcony doors. An additional advantage is that they can be installed taller than any pets in your home.

Fences.

In some settings, you may think about alarming a fence surrounding your home. One way to do this is with pressure-sensitive cables that are buried just beneath the ground surface. You can literally ring your home with this, and it can be adjusted to various sensitivities so that a raccoon or small animal prowling in your backyard won't set it off, but the weight of a human will. Unfortunately, the weight of human children may not set them off. These systems work fairly well, but tend to be pricey.

As you can see, you have plenty of options to choose from. Learn all you can about security systems before making a decision on what to buy. Keep in mind that you also want a system that eliminates false alarms. My current system has been operating for more than five years and has not had a single false alarm due to system malfunction. Guests in the house have accidentally set the alarm off on perhaps two or three occasions, but the system itself has never sent out a false signal. You don't want false alarms because it's like crying wolf. If it goes off all

NORTHEAST COMMUNITY COLLEGE LIBRARY

the time, your neighbors will no longer pay attention. My neighbors wouldn't even know I had an alarm if I hadn't told them and asked them to keep an extra eye on my apartment if they ever heard it go off. Some jurisdictions levy fines against homeowner and businesses for excessive false alarms, which can run from fifty to several hundred dollars per false alarm over a set number. I don't agree with this, because it discourages monitored alarm system use. I'd rather see the fines levied against the companies that installed a faulty system.

Do-It-Yourself Alarm Systems

There are many alarm systems that don't require professional installation. You can purchase them at home improvement stores, hardware stores, and even department stores. Individual security devices to do specific jobs are also available, some rather inexpensive. I've seen small vibration detectors that attach to a glass window pane—they sound an alarm if the window is opened or the glass is broken. They sell for less than twenty dollars each. While my alarm systems have always been professionally installed, I know people who have successfully installed viable systems they bought at such outlets for economical prices. If you consider this option, remember your goals: to make enough noise to dissuade an intruder, alert your neighbors, and alert you if you're at home. If an off-the-shelf system you install yourself can accomplish this to your satisfaction, then go for it. Any properly installed alarm system as part of your personal security plan is what's important, whether it's professionally designed and installed or not.

Living the Country Life

Crime doesn't occur only in big cities. Security is just as important for people who live in rural areas. Outlying and country areas are "statistically" safe, meaning that there is less crime per capita than in the city. Because of this, residents can be lulled into believing there is no danger at all. In fact, you often hear people who live in the country brag that they leave their doors unlocked in their homes because it's so safe. When I hear that, I say, "Yikes!" I don't believe anyone should leave their doors open, no matter where they live. I note that several high-profile crime cases have occurred in rural residential areas; one of the most famous was the subject of the Truman Capote book *In Cold Blood*.

Rural residents face essentially the same security threats as city dwellers. But those who reside on farms and ranches can also experience theft of crops, livestock, timber, outbuildings, expensive tools, and farm equipment. Most farmers don't hesitate to brand or tattoo their livestock, but they don't always think to engrave their driver's license number onto valuable tools and farm implements, or to take extra precautions with large, expensive machinery. I've seen such items left unsecured in the fields at night, and at great risk of theft. Crime rings dealing in farm machinery load the equipment into a tractor-trailer container, haul it to a seaport, and ship it to another country. Once there, the machine is put to work on a farm without any registration or licensing procedures; where the thing came from is never questioned. It's a big business, and it amounts to huge dollar losses for farmers. This problem could become bigger, because customs officials have shifted their emphasis even more to watching what's coming into our country rather than looking closely at things being shipped out.

My father was a farmer, and I grew up farming tomatoes, squash, and beans; for a while we had beef cattle and a few horses. Crime didn't pass us by. I remember having problems with the theft of gasoline from our bulk tanks, and that was when gas was about twenty-five cents a gallon. A neighbor's tractor was stolen, and we all experienced crop loss due to theft. People often stop by roadside fields to pick corn, strawberries, even dig up potatoes for their own use, never considering that a farmer's livelihood comes from those crops. My father and I once heard two men bragging about stealing watermelons from a field. He asked them if they would be openly bragging about shoplifting items from J. C. Penney. "It's no different. Those crops you took are money out of a hardworking person's pocket," he told them. "That's nothing to brag about." Needless to say, the men were embarrassed.

There are special steps rural residents can take for personal and property security. Besides following the home security tips offered above, rural residents should take these additional steps:

Top Ten Tips for Rural Security

1. Use vehicle locator and tracking devices on expensive farm machinery. Such a device recently helped intercept a container filled with farm equipment on a ship bound for South America. The device, placed on a tractor, was able to transmit even through the container walls.

2. Install plenty of outside lights. Consider using timers, photo-sensitive cells, or motion detectors to turn them on and off.

3. Trim trees and shrubs so that you can see your property from your house, and likewise see your house from the fields.

4. Make use of signs such as no trespassing, no hunting, and no fishing. You may not care if someone cuts across your property, or if your neighbors hunt and fish, but signs such as these tell people who don't know you (and who may be interested in stealing crops) that you're alert and aware of what's happening on your property. They also suggest that you're likely patrolling it.

5. Don't leave keys in farm machinery. This is done all the time. When I was growing up, a lot of farm machinery didn't have keys—you simply pushed the starter and off you went. Today, leaving keys in the tractor is just as much an invitation to theft as leaving keys in your car. Don't do either. If you plan to leave a machine unused for a period of time, I suggest taking the rotor out or turning the fuel supply off so it can't be driven away.

6. Use sturdy padlocks on farm buildings such as grain elevators, tool sheds, storage bins, and gasoline pumps. Secure heavy equipment together with heavy chain and large padlocks to thwart thieves.

7. Consider installing alarms on expensive farm machinery. Farmers often have alarms on their thirty-thousand-dollar automobiles, but it doesn't occur to them to install one on their two-hundred-thousand-dollar piece of farm machinery.

8. Use cellular phones or install regular phones in outbuildings. If you're in the fields and see someone breaking into your house, it can take you a long time to get to a phone

if you're riding a tractor or running. Or if you're injured in the fields, you could be there for a long time, unable to summon help.

9. Stay in touch with your neighbors. It's the best way to keep alert to crime in the community, suspicious people or activity, and general information. Often during growing season, farmers get so busy that they don't keep in contact. You might not know about security threats if you don't all help each other.

10. Carefully check references before hiring anyone to work on your farm. Criminals are often drifters—they'll travel from farm to farm and work the fields because farms historically don't ask for ID or references from temporary workers. I can count on both hands the number of victims of this I personally know, yet some of those victims still don't make an attempt to check references.

Home Invasion

The violent crime of home invasion robbery can be truly horrific. Consider these true accounts:

- A seventy-five-year-old retiree was working alone in his garage when someone sneaked up behind him and hit him with a tire iron. The man's wife, napping on the sofa, was beaten with a cell phone. The assailants ransacked the house.

- A fifty-nine-year-old man answered his door and found two armed men wearing masks. They forced their way in and demanded money. The offenders left the victim beaten and tied up.

- Four armed assailants crashed a party and forced partygoers to lie on the floor while they stole their money and jewelry. Some of the victims were pistol-whipped. The criminals got in through an unlocked door.
- Two suspects knocked on a resident's door, and when the victim answered it, they drew guns and demanded money. They forced the victim to the floor, and fled after ransacking the house.

Home invasion robbery has its roots in the "Cocaine Cowboy" drug culture of south Florida in the 1970s and 1980s. It was a "criminal's crime": Drug dealers viciously forced their way into each other's homes because of the vast amounts of cash and drugs they possessed. Most of the home invasions I investigated were this type, with criminals as the victims. In fact, it was so much a drug dealer's crime that non-drug-dealer victims were viewed suspiciously as possibly being drug dealers. That view is still sometimes held today.

This type of robbery isn't unknown to small businesses such as liquor stores, convenience stores, and gas stations. But as these targets began to beef up security with cameras, alarms, and armed guards, the crime once again evolved. Its perpetrators had to find other victims, so they moved on to residences that included not only drug dealers, but also the elderly, women, and anyone else who presented an easy opportunity. Like I said, crime isn't prevented—it gets deflected somewhere else.

I want to make a distinction here between robbery and burglary. Some police officers don't understand the difference, let alone the general public, and the terms are often interchanged.

Burglary is a crime of opportunity. Its perpetrators generally work alone, don't want to be seen, and rely on stealth to accomplish that. Robbery is an in-your-face crime—a robber uses threats and violence to make victims fearful. Therefore, you can't possibly rob a house. You would have to point a gun at it and say menacingly, "House! Give me your money!" Likewise, you can't burgle a person. You rob people, and burglarize buildings.

Home invasion robbery takes the term robbery to its most extreme. The intention from the start is violent confrontation with people in the residence in order to steal money and property. But the crime scenario doesn't always start violently. Home invaders often approach a house in a manner unlikely to get them noticed by residents or neighbors. Often they pretend to be delivery people, utility company workers, even police officers. They may enter through an open garage door, or follow a victim home from shopping. In this case, they may even pull the "helpful stranger" routine discussed in chapter 2. Home invaders rarely concern themselves with security systems, because most people don't have their systems turned on when they're at home. Once again, this makes a good case for the panic button, which will set off the alarm even if the system isn't armed. And a good case for the hostage code, should a home invader force you to turn off your alarm system.

After gaining entry and taking control, home invaders make their victims give them all their valuables. They're usually armed and frequently tie up their victims, so they have plenty of time to thoroughly ransack the house and escape the scene.

At the heart of preventing home invasion is being alert to people who come to your home. Remember, invaders often pose as people you're likely to not look at too closely. The following quiz poses some situations in which home invaders might try to trick you. Answers and discussion follow. All questions assume that you have some means of seeing someone standing at your front door. (If you don't, you need to go back to the beginning of this chapter, to #9 of the Top Ten Tips for Added Security.)

Quiz: What Would You Do Now?

1. Someone is pounding on your door and screaming that he's being chased and needs help. What would you do now?

2. Someone knocks at your door and says, "My car broke down and I need help," or "I ran out of gas and I need help." What would you do now?

3. There's a knock at your door and someone says, "I just hit your car." What would you do now?

4. Someone at your door says he has a flower delivery for you. What would you do now?

5. There's a knock at the door and the person says he's with the electric company (or other public utility); there's a problem that he needs to come inside the house to correct. In fact, your power may have gone out and the person at the door says he's come to fix it. What would you do now?

Answers

1. Even if you're in a position to physically help the person, dial 911 before opening the door. Then, before opening the door, tell the person that you've called 911 and police are on the way. If this is a ruse, the would-be home invader will probably run away fast.

2. Don't open the door or let the person in. Offer to call a tow truck or the AAA (American Auto Association) road service. Ask if there's someone else the person would like you to call for him. Don't hesitate to call police if you're suspicious and feel you—or he—may be in danger.

3. If your car's in the garage or there's no way someone could have hit it, call police immediately. If you believe it may be true, call police before you go outside. When you call, say that there are suspicious people at your front door. Don't say someone hit your parked car—police won't respond as quickly to a noninjury fender-bender as they will to a suspicious-persons call where the person is standing at your door. Ask the person to wait until police arrive.

   In an actual case, two men knocked on a woman's door and said they had hit her parked car. She opened the door and found herself facing guns. The assailants rushed inside, stole her cash and jewelry, and handcuffed the woman's wrists and ankles. Before leaving, they covered her head with a pillowcase, poured cooking oil over her, and threatened to set her on fire. Had she called police first, help would have been on the way.

4. If you're not expecting a flower delivery, use your instincts. Call a friend or neighbor to stay on the line while you accept the delivery. Ask for identification before opening the door if you feel threatened, or ask the person to leave the flowers outside, then pick them up when you're sure he has left. I've never known anyone who had to sign for a legitimate flower delivery.

Another true story: A man delivering flowers convinced a woman to open her door. He turned out to be an armed home invader, who handcuffed both the woman and her husband, then stole their cash and jewelry.

5. Ask immediately for identification. It's a rare occasion when a utility person shows up at your door if you haven't called for a specific reason. Even if your power has gone out, they have no way of knowing. Home invaders sometimes cut your power, then come to the door posing as utility workers. If you can't see their ID without opening your door, ask for the name of a supervisor you can call to check on the person. Don't call a phone number he gives you—call directory assistance and get the number if you don't have it handy. If you can't verify the person's identity, call police to report a suspicious person at your door.

There have been many true cases of home invaders falsely impersonating utility employees. Often they target elderly victims. Utility companies are aware of this and don't mind your calling to verify employee ID.

After reading these situations, you may wonder if you have to be suspicious of everyone who comes to your door. Frankly, yes, you do, but think of it more as being alert and aware without being fearful. If you have some suspicions but don't feel you need to call the police, you can always call a friend or neighbor and ask him to stay on the phone with you while you answer the door. You might even ask a neighbor to come to his front door and watch as you answer yours. You probably don't get that many deliveries, so don't worry about bothering your neighbors all the time. And you're only going to call if you think something's suspicious anyway. Whatever the case, don't discount intuitive feelings you may have. Don't let other feelings drive you to ignore your gut-level instincts.

A Plan in Case of Home Invasion

Now ask yourself: What would I do if someone burst into my home? Understand that you can become trapped in any room in your house. You must have a plan for what you would do in any circumstance. Go through the following process in every room in your house. I can't emphasize enough how much thinking things through and having a plan can keep you from panicking when a real emergency strikes. In each room, ask yourself:

1. What would I do if someone burst through my front door? The back door? Any window? A window in this room?

2. What direction could I run to avoid becoming trapped? What route might I take through my home to get out?

3. How would I summon help? Can neighbors hear me if I scream and make noise out the window of this room? Is there a phone easily available in this room?

4. What if someone breaks into my home in the middle of the night and I'm sleeping?

The idea here is to escape harm without escalating violence. Your first answer may be as simple as: "I don't have to do anything—my alarm is on and he's fled and police have been called." Or, "I hit the panic button, the alarm went off, he ran, and police have been called." Ideally, this is what you want to happen. Still, you should determine an escape route through the house. You might think about a route where you can throw obstacles in a pursuer's path, such as slamming doors behind you, or toppling chairs as you head out a door and to a neighbor's. As you think about it, you'll realize that you have many options. They may not all be good ones, but at least you have options you hadn't thought about before.

Here's another situation: If you're awakened at night by someone breaking into your home, having a plan can make it less likely that you'll panic. In this case, take the phone off the hook and dial 911 at first opportunity. Remember that you don't have to talk—while it's better to talk and give information, the system knows where you're calling from immediately. No response from you will send the police to your address.

I'll now introduce you to the concept of a safe room. If you have a safe room in your home, it can serve you in several circumstances.

Safe Room

The primary purpose of a safe room is to provide a place to escape from intruders and other dangers. A bathroom often makes a good safe room, but other options include interior closets, laundry rooms, or even a small den. The idea is to make this room a bit more fortified than anywhere else in the house, to help keep you safe while you summon help. Safe rooms are very common in some foreign countries and in many wealthy neighborhoods such as Beverly Hills.

How do you turn a room into a safe room? A basic safe room can be modified for other uses, which I'll discuss in later chapters.

To get started on a basic room:

1. Find a room that's easy to get to in a hurry from almost anyplace in the home.

2. Install a sturdy, solid-core door for this room if it doesn't already have one.

3. Install a heavy-duty lock, such as a deadbolt, that you can easily lock from the inside. Follow all advice regarding deadbolt locks earlier in this chapter. Note: If you have children, don't just install a sliding bolt. You must have a lock you can open using a key on the outside in case the kids lock themselves in.

4. Have some means of communicating that you're in danger. You might install a phone in this room, but realize that your phone lines might get cut, so another form of communication is necessary. I advise keeping a remote panic button for your alarm system in this room. It's a good idea to keep your cell phone's battery charger in this room so that you'll leave the phone here whenever you don't have it on you. If this room has a window, you might consider an air horn to get attention, or simply screaming out the window.

   If danger strikes, consider getting to your safe room as one of your escape routes. When planning escape routes, as outlined in the earlier quiz, remember that you always want to take the quickest and best route to safety. Going to your safe room may not always be the quickest or easiest route. Be sure you have alternate routes, just in case.

What else can you do to protect yourself from home invaders?

Here are some more security tips:

1. Install a wide-angle peephole to get a fuller view of the outside area. I recommend one that's much larger than a standard peephole. The viewer is larger than a half dollar, and you can practically see from the across the room who's at your door and what's behind them.

2. Don't open your door to unexpected visitors you don't know, and never let strangers into your home to use the phone. Always offer to make the call for them.

3. Don't give any personal information to telemarketers, door-to-door surveys, or phone surveys.

4. Keep a method of summoning help close at hand, such as a remote panic alarm, portable phone, cell phone, or something to make a lot of noise. My mother lived alone in a retirement community, and I gave her a handheld air horn

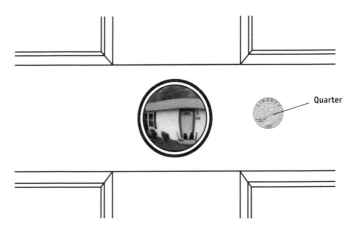

Quarter

Wide-angle peepholes afford a much better view than traditional models.

that was extremely loud. Someone suspicious came to her back door once and when she hit that horn, he fled. She wasn't afraid to use it.

5. Ladies: Beware of casual acquaintances who visit unannounced. Many rapists know their victims and plan the time of the attack.

6. Don't let your children open the door. Teach them to first yell, "I'll get my parents!" when someone knocks, then find you and let you know there's someone at the door.

7. If you lose your garage door opener, change the security code immediately and get a new opener. If you can't change the code right away, unplug the opener until you can. Often, circuit breakers for the home are located in the garage; just flip the appropriate breaker.

Violence in the Home

Twenty-five percent of violent crime occurs in or near the victim's home, and domestic violence destroys millions of families each year.

I want to say up front that both men and women are both victims and perpetrators of domestic abuse. For that reason, unless I'm talking about a specific case, I will always refer to those involved in domestic abuse as "victim" and "perpetrator." But I will note that in the vast majority of cases, women are victims and men are perpetrators. That's not my opinion—it's statistical fact.

As a police officer, I was often called to the scene of domestic violence. It's a call most cops dread because right, wrong, good, and bad aren't always well defined. It's not uncommon in some domestic disputes for a police officer to get into a scuffle with a male perpetrator, only to have the woman turn and attack the police officer for fighting with her man. Domestic violence laws have helped cops make decisions about when to make arrests. But often, they end up leaving a situation because no laws were broken. The people were in conflict—perhaps extreme conflict—but without violence. The anger may have been defused, but only temporarily.

There are people who fight. I know people who throw things at each other who've been married for twenty years, and it's not to be confused with domestic abuse. Yes, it's violent, but are they really trying to injure each other, or are they just truly making a lot of noise? It's often difficult to assess a situation, even from a police point of view. Still, these cases shouldn't be confused with systematic domestic abuse, in which the abuser methodically breaks down the mental and physical well-being of the victim. In such cases, police are usually called only when the victim is in the process of fighting back against the abuser. Rarely is the call made after the victim has been beaten. The systematic violence reduces victims to not calling for help at that point because they feel guilty, intimidated, and, most of all, hopeless. These are sometimes the worst cases. A victim who does call has taken the first step in defiance of the abuser.

As you can see, the cases aren't always black and white, and the shades of gray can be many. But one thing is certain: Different forms of violence in the home are not exclusive crimes. Their victims come from all walks of life, religions, cultures, income levels, all ages, and from both genders. The victims share certain things in common: feelings of guilt, shame, fear, helplessness, isolation, and a tendency to keep their experiences to themselves. The worst part is that many victims convince themselves—often for great periods of time—that they absolutely are not being abused. Likewise, many perpetrators don't admit that they are committing violence against loved ones.

Personal security in cases of domestic violence means protecting yourself and any children involved from the perpetrator of the violence. This also means being honest about whether or not you are a victim or a perpetrator.

Quiz: Are You a Victim of Abuse?

Does the person you love:

1. Monitor your comings and goings in great detail? ("Where did you go? How long could it have taken you to pick up a loaf of bread?")

2. Constantly accuse you of being unfaithful?

3. Isolate you from family, friends, and people in general?

4. Discourage you from working, joining organizations, attending school, or leaving the house?

5. Belittle or humiliate you routinely?

6. Become violent or angry using alcohol or drugs?

7. Control all finances and force you to account in detail for what you spend?

8. Destroy personal property or sentimental items?

9. Hit, punch, slap, kick, or bite you or the children, or threaten to harm you?

10. Use or threaten to use a weapon against you?

11. Control your behavior with threats, such as physical harm, or taking the children from you?
12. Force you to have sex against your will?

Quiz: Are You a Perpetrator of Abuse?

Do you mistreat someone you love by:

1. Monitoring their comings and goings in great detail?
2. Making constant accusations of unfaithfulness?
3. Isolating the person from family, friends, and people in general?
4. Discouraging the person from working, joining organizations, attending school, or leaving the house?
5. Routinely belittling or humiliating them?
6. Becoming violent or angry when using alcohol or drugs?
7. Controlling all finances and forcing them to account in detail for what is spent?
8. Destroying their personal property or sentimental items?
9. Hitting, punching, slapping, kicking, or biting them?
10. Using or threatening to use a weapon against them?
11. Controlling their behavior with threats, including physical harm, or taking the children from them?
12. Forcing the person to have sex against their will?

If you believe you are a victim of domestic violence, it's important for you to admit that fact. It's the first step toward escaping your situation. Those who feel trapped in domestic abuse often can't escape because they feel helpless. They need empowerment and encouragement to make a plan to escape.

Not everyone can take time to plan, however. If you believe you must escape a domestic violence situation immediately, you should do one or all of the following:

1. Call the police. Assault by anyone, even a family member, is a crime. Most police officers can refer you to agencies and personnel who can help you.

2. Call the National Domestic Violence Hotline: 800–799–7233.

3. Leave the home immediately and go to a trusted friend or relative, a local fire station, police station, or hospital emergency room.

If you have time make a plan for escaping a violent or abusive situation, I suggest you try these:

Top Ten Tips for Escaping an Abusive Situation

1. Confide in someone. Remember that abusers isolate victims from others to keep domestic violence a hidden crime. Breaking the isolation is empowering, and the support of others will help you carry out your escape plan. Confide in a friend, neighbor, or family member, either living nearby or in another location.

2. Plan how you'll leave. If by car, make sure you have a key when you need it by hiding a spare somewhere safe. Or hide enough money for other transportation, and prepare phone numbers to call when you're ready—for instance, cab fare and phone numbers of cab companies.

3. Plan where you'll go. This is your safe place. Can you stay with friends or relatives you trust and who support your

decision? (Anybody who tells you to stay in a dangerous situation is not supporting you.) If not, discreetly find local abuse shelters. Call the National Domestic Abuse Hotline or a local hot line for information. When making calls to plan where you'll go, remember that your phone bill may show long-distance calls or local charged calls, thus giving your abuser clues to locate you later.

4. Get some money. If you have access to checking accounts, take everything you can the day you leave. Don't use ATM cards or credit cards after that, because you'll leave clues for your abuser to find you. If the abuser controls the finances completely, you can still get cash, but it will be difficult and you may get only small amounts at a time. Some suggestions:

   • Siphon off some of the grocery money.
   • Get change from clothing pockets; check the floor and seats in the car—check everywhere.
   • Swap products for refund cash. For example, buy boxed cereal and keep the expensive box. When you run out, buy the same cereal, but after the abuser checks your receipts, return it and buy much cheaper cereal in a bag to refill the first box. Save the cash difference. Other items you can do this with include shampoo and toiletries, peanut butter, toilet tissue and other paper products, even aspirin and other over-the-counter medicines. Use your imagination.

5. The day you go, take jewelry and other valuables you can pawn for cash, including wedding rings, silver service, and wedding dresses. (It might even make you feel better!)

6. If you don't have your own checking account but have a joint account, take a few checks from the back of the book. They're less likely to be found missing.

7. Collect important papers such as birth certificates for you and your children, passports, and anything else you need, and keep them in an envelope in a safe place. Your driver's license and Social Security card should be carried in your wallet at all times.

8. Plan the escape day. For example, you might have a trip to the Laundromat or a shopping day. Leave and go to your planned safe place instead.

9. Shortly before you leave, either don't pay bills or don't mail the envelopes. Keep that money for yourself for your escape.

10. Don't leave clues behind for your abuser to use. Take your address book containing all your friends' addresses and phone numbers. Take or destroy notes, letters, envelopes, phone bills, or anything that might have addresses and phone numbers.

The best solution to this problem is to prevent violence and abuse in the first place. That means managing conflict in a reasonable way that can lead to solutions to problems, not leaving things to simmer and boil up again and again. When under duress, you have trouble seeing yourself as others see you. As a police officer, I've intervened in enough situations to know that when things have escalated to the point of abuse, it's time for those involved to seek professional help. Here are some suggestions:

1. Consider professional counseling. Individual or couples therapy with a psychologist or other licensed mental health counselor is the place to start.
2. Call your local domestic abuse hot line, which is generally listed in the government pages of your phone book. Other agencies to contact might include your state or local family services agency.
3. Join a support group. Professionals and agencies often sponsor such groups. You might also check your church or a local domestic abuse shelter for advice.

If you find yourself trapped and unable to make plans because you're frozen in fear, don't forget that you can call the National Domestic Abuse Hotline at 800-799-7233. You don't have to go through this situation alone.

Violence Against the Elderly

Unfortunately, this has become such a problem that many states have implemented laws. Often older people are targets for the same reasons women and children are: They're not as physically able to defend themselves, and they're often financially dependent on others. So the strategies for women and children will work for the elderly as well.

If elderly people are being abused through domestic violence, they have the same opportunities to call domestic abuse hot lines and seek shelter from an abusive situation. As frequent targets of crime, it's especially important for them to have a plan to protect themselves.

Alzheimer's Disease and Dementia

If you have a relative suffering from Alzheimer's disease or another form of dementia, you may wish to care for your loved one at home for as long as possible before considering nursing home options. Home security takes a different turn in this case, because not only do you want to keep intruders out, but you also want to keep loved ones in. The statistics tell us why: 90 percent of dementia patients wander at some point.

If you've taken steps to secure your home using tips and advice from earlier in this chapter, there are some additional things you can do for more security in your special situation.

Top Ten Tips for the Security of Alzheimer's and Dementia Patients

1. Install sliding bolts and hook-and-eye locks in unusual places such as the top of doors or windows, above the line of sight, to prevent wandering.

2. Install an additional lock on exit doors to make unlocking the door too complicated. In fact, you could install numerous locks, but leave half of them unlocked. If the patient gets systematic about going down the line and turning the lock knobs, he'll always be locking some as he unlocks others.

3. An ID or Medic-Alert bracelet or necklace (including at least a name, phone number, and medical condition) is a good idea.

4. Tell neighbors about your loved one's condition. Though you may wish to keep your privacy, your neighbors can be a big help by being alert to possible wandering.

5. Camouflage windows with decorations to help distract the patient's attention from them. Tapestries, blinds, even hanging glass decorations can grab the patient's attention enough that he forgets about the window—and possibly escaping through it.

6. Leave squeaky doors squeaky to alert you if the patient wanders. Or simply set your alarm system.

7. Put decals on sliding glass doors, both to prevent the patient from walking through them, and to camouflage them.

8. Secure doors leading to garages, basements, balconies, attics, and other obscure ways of exiting the home.

9. Use a simple doorknob alarm on the patient's bedroom door to alert you to nighttime wanderings.

10. Consider a locator device to help find your loved one if he does get out and wander. Some devices use the same technology as the ankle bracelets used for house arrest. These proximity alarms sound when the person moves beyond a set perimeter.

Preventing Fraud

Crime doesn't always sneak into your home through a broken window or an unlocked door. It doesn't always need cover of darkness. Sometimes it enters your home by telephone or the mail, or strolls up to your front door in broad daylight. Perpetrators of fraud are simply a different form of robber or burglar, but the results of their handiwork are the same: You're a victim of crime. Con artists are as varied as their victims—they are men, women, even children who work alone, in pairs, or in groups.

As a detective, fraud was one of the most difficult crimes I worked. There was little satisfaction from investigating these cases, because the perpetrator was usually long gone by the time the victims realized they had been conned. The crimes are detailed and complex, often difficult for even astute attorneys to understand fully, let alone juries. Perpetrators move quickly from one jurisdiction to another. Convictions are few and far between, and victims rarely recover what they've lost.

Nobody wants to think they could fall victim to a con artist, but most of us have been scammed about something at least once in our lives. The first time I was scammed was by a carnie at the local county fair. He claimed he could accurately guess my weight, and I took the challenge. What I didn't know was that I was standing on a scale hidden in the ground beneath my feet.

It's difficult to resist an offer that sounds too good to be true, but you must remember the old adage: "If it sounds too good to be true, it probably is." The people who perpetrate these crimes are smart, pushy, flamboyant, and usually quite charming. They're smooth operators, conning people with college degrees as easily as those without. Anyone can fall victim to their thieving charms, from the elderly to teenagers, from the poor to the very rich, from individuals to institutions. Their line is so good, the same con games keep working over and over, year after year.

Classic Cons and Why They Still Work

Clever cons are coming up with new schemes and scams all the time. Some classic con games, however, never seem to go out of style. As long as people fall for them, they'll always be around.

The most well-known and successful cons are:

The home improvement swindle.

A "contractor" comes to your door and offers a free service, anything from checking your air-conditioning system to inspecting your roof, plumbing, or heating system. During the inspection, he discovers that something is broken, worn, torn, or otherwise in need of repair or replacement, sometimes actually breaking something when you're not looking. Through various means, he offers visible "proof" to you. You hire him to make the repair, and are charged a large sum of money for nothing. Either a repair isn't done, or none was needed in the first place. The bogus contractor is long gone when you discover the scam.

The zip code scam.

You get a phone call from someone who says he's with the post office. He'll ask you to confirm your zip code. When you tell him, you're then told that you're eligible to receive gift vouchers or some other premium. You'll be asked to verify your home address and zip code so your gifts can be sent to you special delivery. He'll also ask when someone will be home to accept delivery. Now he knows where you live, and when will be a good time to break into your home.

I've seen this scam done with a general "survey" designed to elicit enough information from the victim to stage a burglary, or even steal credit card numbers. Victims are sometimes told the survey is anonymous, but be assured that they know exactly who you are. Believing it to be anonymous, gullible victims answer all types of questions they might not normally answer, such as: Do you have a home security system? What is you annual household income? Do you have a VCR? (Or home computer, thirty-one-inch television, DVD player, professional camera equipment—a complete inventory of potential loot.) Always be leery of surveys.

The bank examiner.

The con artist poses as a banking official or government agent and tries to enlist your help in catching a crooked bank teller. Either in person or on the phone, you're asked to take money out of your account and give it to the "official" so the money can be marked and the serial numbers recorded. Anyone who does this will not see his money—or the bogus official—again.

"Take over payment" scams.

The advertisement says something along the lines of: "Having problems making your car payments? We can help!" You're told that your lease or purchase problems are over: The company will take over your payments, sell your car for you, and settle your account, sometimes for a small fee. You might get a call like this if you're advertising your vehicle for sale in the paper. If you agree to use the service, you'll receive an agreement to sign in which you give the con artist permission to take your vehicle, either to sell it or to arrange a takeover of payments. Once you hand over the vehicle, that's it—you've been had. The con artist sells the car or ships it out of the country. You may get a call telling you the vehicle has been stolen and you should file an insurance claim. This could actually cost you a bundle if you owe a large sum and the vehicle's value is less than what's owed.

The pigeon drop.

You "fortuitously" stumble upon a lot of "lost" money, jewelry, and other valuables in the street at the same time as two other strangers, who supposedly don't know each other. They offer to share the stash with you and rely on greed to get you to give in to their way of doing it. This involves you giving them some "good faith" money while they go off to sell jewelry and other noncash items. They allow you to hold the cash portion of the found loot as "insurance." But what you've really got is a bag of newspaper cut to resemble money. The strangers—and your money—are long gone when you discover the switch.

The pyramid scheme.

You're offered what sounds too good to be true: a once-in-a-lifetime chance at an investment that's allegedly risk-free and guaranteed to pay a gigantic return. All you have to do is invest and get others to do so, too. Each time you bring a person into the fold, you get a cut of his investment. He, in turn, brings more people into the investment. Of course, the money from investors at the bottom of this pyramid is being used to pay the "investors" at the top. Once the money runs out, the pyramid collapses, and only those crooks at the top make out like the bandits they are.

Auto repair swindles.

Usually these scams occur in out-of-the-way locations or small towns near interstate highways. There are two commonly "needed" repairs. The first is new hoses. (The con artist has a small razor concealed in his hand. As he examines the hoses, he's actually cutting them.) The second is a new battery. (Yours suddenly doesn't work. As the mechanic checks the water, he slips an antacid tablet like a Tums into the battery, which neutralizes the acid and ruins the battery.) An old southern "tourist trap" con was to tell northern drivers that they needed to have the winter air in their tires replaced with summer air!

"Work at home" scams.

You're offered a chance to be free of bosses and commuting and have your own business. All you have to do is send money for a course, instruction book, materials, or supplies to do a certain type of work from home that will supposedly bring you plenty of money. After you've sent the money, what you receive in return doesn't live up to expectations—or you discover that there's little or no market for what you're learning to do. Chances of getting your money refunded are slim or none.

Not all work-at-home offers are scams—there are some legitimate ones. Generally these won't ask for any money up front. As with any other offers, be aware and beware.

900-number credit fix.

The ad says that if you have bad credit, you can fix it or obtain a new credit card by calling a 900 number. If you call, you'll be charged for each minute you're connected. (The charges go straight to your phone bill.) After listening to a telemarketer's pitch or a recorded message designed to keep you on the phone for a long time, you usually end up getting a booklet or pamphlet in the mail that gives general advice to fix bad credit, or a list of institutions offering low-rate credit cards. The cost of the call can be outrageous, often fifty dollars or more, and it's not easy to get the charges dropped.

Don't lose a dime to a con artist! To avoid becoming a victim, make sure you follow a few basic rules:

1. Like the old adage says, if it sounds too good to be true, it probably is. So be suspicious!

2. If strangers tell you they've found a large sum of money and want to share it with you, leave immediately. If they persist in following you, go somewhere for help. Tell them you're calling the police now.

3. If someone claiming to be a bank official contacts you either in person or on the phone and wants you to withdraw money from your account, call police immediately. Banks don't do business in this way. Never take money out of your account and give it to the person.

4. If someone calls and wants to verify your credit card number because you've won a prize, hang up. Often the con artist tells you that you've won if your Visa card number begins with 4 or your MasterCard number begins with 5. The problem is that all Visa cards start with 4, and all MasterCards start with 5.

Some of the newer con games are being played on the Internet and through the credit system. Let's look at some of these very modern crimes of fraud.

Identity Theft

This fast-growing crime claimed seven hundred thousand victims in the year 2000 and cost businesses billions of dollars. It has attracted added scrutiny after the terrorist attacks in New York and Washington, because some of the suspected hijackers used false identities. Purloined passports, falsely obtained driver's licenses, and other official documents weren't difficult for them to get. Officials said the terrorists actually became the people whose identities they stole.

Are you at risk for identity theft?

Test Your IQ (Identity Quotient)

1. I receive several offers of preapproved credit every week. (5 points) Add 5 more points if you do not shred them before putting them in the trash.
2. I carry my Social Security card in my wallet. (10 points)
3. I do not have a P.O. box or a locked, secured mailbox. (5 points)
4. I use an unlocked, open box at work or at my home to drop off my outgoing mail. (10 points)
5. I carry my military ID in my wallet at all times. (10 points)
6. I do not shred or tear banking and credit information when I throw it in the trash. (10 points)
7. I provide my Social Security number (SSN) whenever asked, without asking questions as to how that information will be safeguarded. (10 points) Add 5 points if you provide it orally without checking to see who might be listening.
8. I am required to use my SSN at work as an employee or student ID number. (5 points)

9. I have my SSN printed on the employee badge that I wear at work or in public. (10 points)

10. I have my SSN or driver's license number printed on my personal checks. (20 points)

11. I am listed in a "Who's Who" guide. (5 points)

12. I carry my insurance card in my wallet and either my SSN or my spouse's is the ID number. (20 points)

13. I have not ordered a copy of my credit reports for at least two years. (10 points)

14. I do not believe that people would root around in my trash looking for credit or financial information. (10 points)

15. My driver's license has my Social Security number on it, and I have not contacted the motor vehicle department to request a different ID number. (10 points)

Each one of these questions represents a possible avenue for an ID theft.

100+ points:	More than half a million people will become victims of ID theft this year. You are at high risk. I recommend you purchase a paper shredder, become more security aware in document handling, and start to question why people need your personal data.
50–100 points:	Your odds of being victimized are about average. Higher if you have good credit.
0–50 points:	Congratulations: You have a high "IQ." Keep up the good work and don't let your guard down now.

(ID Theft test courtesy of Privacy Rights Clearinghouse; www.privacyrights.org)

How did you do? If you had a high score, you'll definitely want to read on to learn more about preventing identity theft, especially credit card theft.

Credit card theft has essentially become a class of identity theft. It's really the most basic form. Thieves use your Social Security number, birth date, or driver's license to get credit cards, loans, and merchandise. They can ruin your credit, or worse. In some cases, identity thieves stole rental cars and took out second mortgages on homes.

While merchants and credit card companies usually pick up the tab, that cost is passed on to consumers. So is the hassle. Cleaning up the mess identity thieves leave behind can take many agonizing years. We use our IDs in so many places that it's often hard to backtrack and find them all. In a recent case in Florida, a couple whose identity was stolen finally cleaned up their credit reports after six years of fighting off creditors for more than thirty-four thousand dollars in charges. It was astounding what they had to go through when they were completely innocent. Who stole their identity? An employee at their bank, who saw the couple's pristine credit rating.

Those who steal credit card numbers get them by rummaging through trash for credit card receipts, or by paying restaurant employees to poach numbers. Anyone who works anywhere that processes credit card transactions can steal your numbers. It's that simple.

What can you do? Decrease your risk of identity theft with the following:

Top Ten Tips to Prevent Identity Theft

1. Use a cross-cut paper shredder to destroy papers you no longer need that contain sensitive or identifying information.

2. Don't carry your Social Security card with you, or anything else that has your SSN on it. Never write your SSN on checks or give it out unless absolutely necessary.

3. Check your credit reports once a year. Contact all three major credit bureaus. This is one of the best ways to find out if someone is using your information without your knowledge. Reports cost a small fee, less than ten dollars, unless you're a victim of financial crime or have been turned down for a job or credit due to information in your report. The three credit reporting bureaus are:

    TransUnion: 800-888-4213; fraud victim assistance: 800-680-7289

    Experian: 888-EXPERIAN (397-3742); www.experian.com; fraud division: 888-397-3742

    Equifax: 800-685-1111; fraud assistance line: 800-525-6285

4. Reduce the number of preapproved credit card offers you receive. They're security risks. Call 888-5-OPTOUT to permanently get off the credit bureaus' lists for unsolicited credit and insurance offers, which is where the credit card companies get your name.

5. Guard your personal information. Carry as little as possible in your wallet. Get credit cards with your picture on them. Be alert to shoulder surfers listening for information.

6. Keep confidential information in a locked place.

7. Keep an eye on your credit card when you give it to a clerk. Make sure your card information isn't being copied somewhere, or onto a computer to make copies of the card later.

8. Cancel any credit cards you no longer use. Don't just cut up the card—call the company to cancel the account, and ask them to send you a letter confirming that at your request, the account was closed with a zero balance.

9. If your credit card is lost or stolen, immediately notify the company, even if someone calls and says he's found your card and is returning it. Thieves often make such calls. If you don't cancel your cards, the thief goes on a charging spree.

10. Put passwords on your credit card, bank, and phone accounts. Follow the PIN code tips from chapter 2 to avoid choosing codes based on easily available information.

Telemarketers—"If their stock tip is so good, why are they working a cheap telephone job?"

A telemarketer called me with a "hot" stock tip. I listened for a moment, only because I wanted to wait for the guy to stop talking so I could ask him why he was working in a telemarketing job if his investment advice was so good.

I get telemarketing calls all the time, and I have a standard way of dealing with them. Here's what I say:

> "I do not accept telephone solicitations. If you'd like to contact me by mail, feel free to. Thank you very much. Good-bye."

As you can see, I don't give out any information—not my full name, address, nothing. I'm polite, but firm. I use this standard response whether the call is asking me to support my local Police Benevolent Association, or if it's someone telling me I've won a prize. If they won't put it in writing and sign their name to it, I'm not interested.

I don't believe there's really any other way to handle unwanted telephone solicitations, and my way does protect you and your private information. You could just hang up, but if you think that's rude, try a standard response like I have.

At this point, you might ask: Is there ever a wanted tele-marketer? Is there any time you should listen to a telemarketer? For myself, the answer is no. You might completely disagree with me on this, and everyone has to make their own decisions in the end, but I can't think of one instance in which I need to listen to a telemarketer. If I need something, I'll go to the store and get it. If someone's telling me I need something, I probably don't, or I would have thought of it myself. And that's why I don't listen to telemarketers.

Don't confuse telemarketing calls with legitimate business calls, however. If my phone company calls me with new plans that save me money over what I'm currently using, that's a business call, in my opinion. I'm already doing business with that company and it's a legitimate business call. My insurance company, cable TV—anyone I'm currently doing business with isn't a telemarketing call.

Some telemarketers try to pretend they know you when they call. A lot of older people who have memory problems can be taken by this, then easily swayed into buying things. The telemarketers can be really good at this. Be on alert for this tactic. I have a friend whose phone book listing contains her cat's name first (Jake) and her name second. If someone calls and asks for Jake, she knows he got her number from the phone book and has no idea who he's calling.

What to Do If You've Been Conned

If you suspect fraud, contact your local authorities, your local or state consumer protection agency, your state or district attorney's office, or a consumer advocacy group. One such organization is the National Fraud Information Center (800-876-7060, or on the Internet at http://www.fraud.org/).

Many people who've been taken by telemarketers or other con artists don't report what happened because they feel foolish. It's important to report frauds to the authorities, so try to get over your feelings. If you don't report it, how can the criminals be caught? Do your part and report the con.

Chapter 4 Vehicle Security and Safety

Every **13 minutes** someone dies in an automobile, aggressive driving occurred in two-thirds of these deaths.

One out of every 100 households will have an automobile stolen and 2 percent of them will be by **carjacking.**

I used to be able to discuss vehicle security by covering auto theft and how to prevent someone from breaking into your car to rip off your radio. Not anymore—now we have road rage, carjacking, bump-and-rob crimes, and other serious situations that you encounter when you're behind the wheel.

Safety First

Security begins with safety. If you pay attention to safety issues, you're less likely to find yourself in a position—like broken down on the side of the road—where you're more prone to becoming a victim. You probably check the tire pressure, make sure there's gas in the tank, and get the car a good oil and lube job regularly, but do you put off checking a noise under the hood? Is it because you're too "busy?" Be aware that when you put off investigating such problems, you could very well be compromising your security.

Consider these potential situations:

- You run low on gas in a "bad" part of town at night.
- The bad tire you didn't replace goes flat on the interstate.
- The noise you ignored under the hood causes your car to break down on a deserted road.

In each scenario, a simple safety issue, left unaddressed, has put you in a position of security risk that probably could have been avoided. It's true that finances can sometimes keep you from dealing with a car problem immediately. If that's the case, and you feel sure that the problem isn't a safety risk, try to travel on well-lit streets and avoid isolated or dangerous neighborhoods until you can take care of things.

You know that proper vehicle maintenance is essential to preventing breakdowns. That's what keeps you from becoming stranded on the side of the road, with your car sitting up on jacks. A well-maintained car keeps you up and running, and not a sitting duck. I believe in carrying a few useful items in the car at all times, not a full tool kit. Consider the following simple items that serve safety and security purposes:

- Flashlight—A police officer wouldn't be without one. It's probably second only to his radio when it comes to usefulness for safety and security, from providing light to acting as a weapon.

- Flat tire fixer in a can—A great invention that can at least get you out of an isolated or potentially dangerous situation and to a repair shop.
- Tire gauges—You should always have proper pressure in your tires, because underinflated tires will hydroplane on wet roads. You want to stay on the road and driving.

Jumper cables and tools, on the other hand, aren't a big deal to me. They're more of a convenience than a security and safety concern, maybe at best eliminating the need to call road service or a tow truck. I think if your car doesn't start and it's not the battery, it's probably something you can't deal with on your own anyway in this age of highly computerized vehicles.

Taking care of some basic auto safety issues can be your best security measure on the road.

Simple Safety Issues

- Keep the gas tank at least half full at all times. This prevents having to buy gas in unknown or bad neighborhoods or late at night.
- Plan your route and check a map before starting on a trip. People who get lost can be targets for robbers. Don't think it can't happen to you at home—if you're not familiar with every single nook and cranny of your city, you can get lost.
- Park at an unusual angle to the road if your car breaks down or you need to pull over for any emergency. Police look for out-of-the-ordinary things, but parking parallel to the road looks normal.
- If you don't already have one, consider buying a cellular phone for ready access to emergency communication.

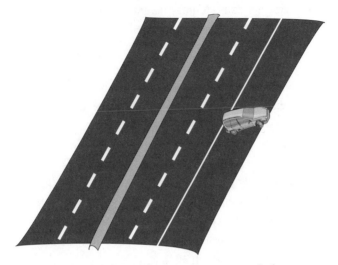

If you need to attract the attention of police or passers-by in an emergency, pull off the road at an unusual angle.

Defensive Driving

I don't like saying that you should obey the "Rules of the Road"—it can sound too much like a lecture. Everyone talks about these rules when discussing defensive driving, but I don't believe that simply obeying the rules is what makes you a good defensive driver anyway. You may know every rule there is about who has the right-of-way and who doesn't, but the graveyards are full of people who had the right-of-way and took it. What's more important is to look out for what the *other* guy is doing, because he may have forgotten what the rules are, or perhaps never knew them in the first place.

Defensive driving is best described as being alert and aware, and having a plan on the road. Practicing and perfecting your observation skills are a big part of it. A good defensive driver has several qualities:

- A state of being alert to what others on the road are doing, expecting the unexpected at all times.
- An awareness of road conditions, climate, and other factors in the environment.
- A plan in mind for any potential emergency.
- An attitude of wanting to be safe behind the wheel.

With these qualities, a defensive driver can look at other drivers with a different perspective. There's less of a "me versus them" feeling, which unfortunately seems to be the attitude of many drivers in recent years. You can see this in how some drivers describe what others are doing. For example, on the subject of speed, the competitive driver tends to believe that anyone going slower than him is blocking the road, and anyone going faster than him is an idiot. Isn't it amazing how he's always going the perfect speed, but nobody else on the road is? Everyone has probably felt this way at one time or another. I know someone who often gets distracted sitting at a red light. When the light turns green, she's still sitting there, until drivers behind her toot their horns to remind her to pay attention. But if she ever gets stuck behind such a driver, her inclination is to shout out the window, "What's the matter? Don't you see any colors you like?!"

Playing "What If . . . ?" on the Road

You never know what you'll find on the road from day to day. Traffic conditions differ, the weather changes, sometimes the highway is clear and other times it's mired down in construction work. Planning for what might happen is a constant thing, and it's necessary to always ask yourself, "What If . . . ?" When you do this and answer your own questions, you'll naturally begin to avoid such common situations as tailgating, riding in other drivers' blind spots, not signaling intention to turn or change lanes—or not moving when the red light turns green. If you continually ask yourself, "What If . . . ?" you become aware of how many things your senses may have been missing in the past. You come to realize that every intersection hides potential dangers, that not every driver is as attentive as you are, or that the soccer ball bouncing into the street in front of you may have a small child chasing it.

Try playing "What If . . . ?" with the three highway situations discussed next.

What would you do if you found yourself in these positions?

1. The "bump and rob."

This is literally highway robbery. A driver bumps your car from behind when you're stopped at a light or stop sign in an isolated area. When you get out to check the damage and exchange information, the perpetrators rob you, steal your car, or possibly kill you.

Avoiding this crime is a matter of stopping to think before acting. In the vast majority of cases, you've been in an legitimate accident and no one is out to rob you. But how can you know if that's the case or if someone is threatening you? Don't get out of the car right away—take a moment to look around, and listen to your intuition. Look carefully at the people involved. What kind of feeling do you get from them? You can usually trust your gut instinct.

Here's what else to do:

- If you have any doubts at all, don't get out of the car. Here's where it's good to have a cell phone. Call the police, and take note of the other car's license plate number if you can.
- If you're at all suspicious of the other people, don't simply tell police you've been in a fender-bender accident— tell them you've been hit and you're concerned that you might be in danger of being robbed or attacked. Stay on the phone with the police dispatcher and follow his instructions.
- Consider leaving your car in gear with your foot on the brake—if someone from the other car approaches you in a threatening manner, you can easily drive away.

If this is truly a bump and rob, it's likely the perpetrators will leave once they see you talking on the cell phone. They'll assume you've called the police. In most actual bump-and-rob cases, there's really little or no damage to the car—the perpetrators' intention is to rob you, and they don't want to leave any damage that could be used to identify them, such as paint on your fender.

If you believe the accident is legitimate and you don't feel threatened by the other people involved:

- Make sure there are others around before getting out of your car.

- Trade insurance cards only—not driver's licenses—and write each other's information down.
- Stay alert. This is essentially how you can avoid becoming a victim of this crime in the first place. Perpetrators I've arrested have told me they often choose their victims by looking for distracted drivers who are traveling alone. It always pays to stay alert.

2. Being followed.

A woman I know had the scary experience of being followed in her car by a stranger. The man had apparently become angry when she tooted the horn at him in traffic. He followed her from downtown Los Angeles all the way to the beach town of Santa Monica, where the woman lived. She had no idea what his intentions were, and she didn't really want to find out. The look of determination on his face and how closely he tailgated her was all the information she needed. The man didn't yell at her, honk his horn, or even look particularly angry or disturbed. He drove stone-faced, serious, and determined, period. This happened at a time B.C. (before cellulars), so the woman had few options. But she did think quickly. Not wanting her pursuer to know where she lived, she didn't go home; instead she led him right to the Santa Monica police station. It became obvious to her that the man was unfamiliar with the town and had no idea where he was being taken. When they turned a blind corner to find a massive parking lot full of police cars, the man's eyes widened and nearly popped out of his face. He did a quick U-turn and sped away. End of incident.

This is an example of exactly what you should do if you're followed and don't have a cell phone. Take your pursuer to the police. With that in mind, it helps to know where the police stations are, so find out. If going to a police station is impractical, go to any fire station—there are usually plenty of them—or a hospital emergency entrance. You want to look for anyplace where you'll feel safe to summon help. If you have a cell phone, call the police and follow the dispatcher's instructions.

It's often advised that you shouldn't go home in this situation. I don't always agree with that advice. It's one of those "rules" that I think may have to be broken from time to time, depending on circumstances. It's true that you don't want a stranger who's following you to know where you live, but it may be that your safest place is home. For example, if you're a young person in a rural area, then going home to your parents may be best.

3. Insurance traps.

Distracted drivers traveling alone are once again the targets, especially those who are driving expensive cars. An added twist the crooks look for is any driver talking on a cell phone, eating, or drinking. Insurance traps are a type of insurance fraud, and it usually takes two cars to pull you into it. The first car gets in front of you, and almost simultaneously a second car moves into position beside you. The first car slams on the brakes so quickly that you can't avoid hitting him. The other car blocks you from swerving out of the way. You rear-end the car in front of you, and everyone in it claims to be injured. Usually the first car is filled with people to take advantage of insurance liability limits. Amazingly, this accident is sometimes set up at higher speeds and can be quite serious. The perpetrators' goal is to collect lots of insurance money, and they're willing to take great risks to do it. This is why they look for distracted drivers, and they especially like it if you're talking on the cell phone. Why? Because your cellular phone bill provides evidence that you were distracted at exactly the time the accident happened. A half-eaten sandwich lying on your front seat or a spilled soda or coffee is also evidence of your distraction.

The advice to avoid being targeted for this crime is simple:

- Don't be distracted.
- If you use a cell phone while driving, get a hands-free device, rapidly becoming the law in many cities and states.
- Don't eat, drink, put on makeup, shave, or do anything else while driving except *drive*.

Ask yourself "What If . . . ?" any of these situations happened to you. The more alert and aware you become while driving, the easier it can be to avoid the more serious crimes I'm about to discuss.

Carjacking

In some ways, technology advances have spawned the crime of carjacking. I once arrested a carjacker who told me that the reason he moved from nonviolent auto theft to carjacking was that he couldn't "hot-wire" cars anymore. The new ignition systems forced him to find another way to accomplish his goal—stealing cars. It just goes to show you that with criminals, where there's a will, there's a way. Common street thugs who used to be able to pop an ignition with a dent puller or vise grips can't do that anymore, so they've turned to even lower-tech methods. And you can't get more low-tech than this: Use deadly force or intimidation to steal a vehicle. The crooks aren't deterred—only deflected from one crime method to another.

Carjackings can be horrifying. News stories tell of brutal beatings, murders, and cars speeding off with a child secured in a safety seat in the back. I can't comprehend why such violence occurs just because someone wants to steal a car. Though the odds are slight that you or your loved ones will be a victim, you can make these odds even more favorable by following some prevention tips and learning more about this deadly crime.

What Is Carjacking?

Carjacking is robbery, auto theft, mugging, and assault—and sometimes murder—all wrapped into one. Because it's so encompassing, carjacking usually gets lumped into the robbery statistics, which makes it difficult to know statistically just how prevalent the crime really is.

We know how the crime originated, but sometimes carjackings are pulled off for a thrill. Gangs often use it as an initiation or a rite of passage. Most carjackers who do it "professionally" are looking for flashier, expensive cars, figuring if they're going to put that much effort into it, the result should at least be worth it. Sometimes carjacking is the first step in a crime spree—the crooks jack the car, then commit a robbery or a series of robberies, and usually ditch the car in the end, perhaps stripping it for parts or selling it to a "chop shop." If anyone sees them during the crime spree and gets the license number, it turns out to belong to an innocent person.

Carjacking can also be part of a bump and rob, discussed earlier. Instead of theft of money or possessions being the goal, the target is the car itself. Most carjackings take place late at night, and they don't just happen in big cities—many occur in the suburbs, small towns, even rural areas.

Reducing the Risk of Being Carjacked

Carjacking is a crime of opportunity, so the way to reduce your risk is to eliminate or avoid the carjacker's opportunities.

Carjackers usually don't take their own vehicles when they're going to commit their crime, so they don't do things like run potential victims off the road. You're safest from this crime while you're driving down the road. It's when you have to stop that you become vulnerable, and especially when you're in the transition of getting out of or into your car. Thus, carjackings occur most often at intersections, parking garages, parking lots, self-service gas stations and car washes, ATM machines, shopping malls, grocery stores—anywhere you would be in that transition to and from your car, particularly in an isolated area. The isolation gives carjackers some advantages: They can get your car without interference from anyone nearby, it takes you more time to report the theft, and it's easier for them to hang around without being noticed or looking too suspicious. Also, places like convenience stores or out-of-the-way bars or restaurants have enough activity that a variety of victims and autos can be available to them.

If you're walking toward your car and a carjacker approaches you, you might try throwing your keys a short distance away. I know someone who did this, making the carjacker choose between taking the car and chasing her. (This guy had a gun, too.) He decided to take the car, and she got away. I think most carjackers would do the same thing and go after the car, since that's their goal in the first place.

How else can you avoid carjacking?

Top Ten Tips to Reduce Your Risk of Being Carjacked

1. Lock your doors after entering or leaving your vehicle. Keep your windows rolled up until you're moving.

2. Check your mirrors when you're sitting still at intersections. If you see anyone approaching you who makes you feel uncomfortable, take action (see #10).

3. Be aware that some carjackers actually impersonate police officers. A rash of such crimes occurred in the South several years ago, with well-publicized incidents of motorists, particularly women, being pulled over by someone they thought was a police officer. It's easy to get a blue light for a vehicle, believe it or not.

4. If a suspicious person or group of people approaches you while you're stopped at a traffic signal or at a deserted intersection, look for an escape route. Consider running the light if your intuition tells you that the situation could get dangerous. It could be your best escape—just be careful! Pay special attention when stopped at railroad crossings, too (see #10)—trains run on schedules, and carjackers who know the late-night timetable might decide to head down to the tracks to pick up a nice car.

5. Hold your key discreetly in your hand when heading to your car, and be alert to what's going on around you in this transition period. If something doesn't look right, trust your instincts—turn around and go back to where you were coming from. Likewise, if you're ready to get out of your car and feel threatened, don't get out. Drive on. (This is a good reason to always have enough gas in your tank, too!)

6. At night, particularly in desolate areas, try to drive in the center lanes of the road to make it harder for would-be carjackers to approach the car.

7. If you see someone whose car is broken down, don't stop to help unless you know the person. You can still be of assistance without stopping—drive to the nearest phone and call police to help the person, or call on your cell phone.

8. Be careful how you respond to anyone who pulls up beside you and tells you there's something wrong with your car. Don't stop unless you're in a well-lit place with plenty of people around. Here's a situation where you really need to use your instincts—does it feel like there's something wrong with your car? You probably know the feel of your own car pretty well. If not, you can probably afford to get to a good place to stop. If you feel anxious about the possibility of a car problem, drive to a service station.

9. Be careful of people who approach you asking for directions or handing out flyers. Again, trust your instincts—if something doesn't feel right, hurry up and get into the car, then drive away.

10. Leave enough room to maneuver anytime you stop your car at an intersection. A good rule of thumb: Be sure you can see where the rear tires of the car in front of you contact the road. This should leave you enough room to drive away from the spot if you need to.

Is He Really a Police Officer?

Carjackers sometimes pose as cops. It doesn't happen very often, but it has happened. How can you spot a phony? If he's in uniform and driving a marked police car, I'd say he's probably a real cop. If he's accompanied by someone like that, he's probably a cop. But be suspicious if:

1. He's wearing civilian clothing—plainclothes police officers don't work traffic. One might show up at a traffic stop only as a backup to a uniformed officer.

2. There's only one blue light on the car's dashboard. Marked police cars have lights on top of the car. Unmarked cars usually have lights in the grill or on the dash to be seen in the front, but they generally have another light flashing out the back so cars behind can see them.

3. He doesn't have a radio. Nearly all police officers carry radios.

4. He asks you to get out of the car and there's no uniformed backup there. This would be highly unusual. Police generally don't want you to get out of the car, and would ask you to do so only after a backup officer has arrived. This is for everyone's safety.

If he's simply writing you a ticket, there's no cause for suspicion. Only if he asks you to do something unusual should your suspicions be raised. At that point, tell him you're not sure he's really a police officer and ask him to prove who he is by calling his dispatcher. Don't be afraid to do this. I was working plainclothes once and had to stop a suspicious person who made no bones about saying that he didn't think I was really a cop. I didn't take it personally. I asked him to remain in his car with his hands on the steering wheel until a marked unit arrived. I had a radio and my badge in my hand.

You might also ask if the officer would follow you to a place where there are more people around before writing you a ticket. If he refuses to do either of those things, don't speed away, but drive away—and keep going until either another police officer arrives or you're in a place where you feel safe to pull over and report the incident.

If Carjacking Happens to You

If you're alert and aware, looking around and paying attention, carjackers are probably going to pick another target. But if it should happen to you, there are no hard-and-fast rules about what to do. Can you escape a carjacking in progress? Yes. If I were being carjacked, I would have to decide right then what to do. People who have complied with everything carjackers demanded of them have been shot anyway; others who've resisted were shot as well. This is one of the more violent crimes being perpetrated today. It doesn't happen often, but when it does, it can be extremely dangerous. Therefore, you have to think about it and make your own plan. I know that even if I had a pistol in my pocket, surrendering might be the only logical alternative: It could give me a chance where I might have no chance at all if I were to resist.

Here's a scenario to think about:

You're sitting at an isolated intersection with your doors locked and your windows rolled up, when suddenly your driver's side window shatters, done deliberately by a person who came up beside you without being noticed. What would you do now?

There's a tool that can quickly and easily shatter a window called a spring-loaded center punch. In Florida, drivers are often encouraged to carry one of these tools in their cars, just in case they ever find themselves flipped over in the water of one of the state's many canals. A trapped driver can quickly and efficiently shatter a window and escape drowning. I've seen it work. Unfortunately, carjackers can use this device, too, as in the situation described.

Depending on which window the carjacker shattered, he could reach in and turn the ignition off to give him time to continue the robbery, or point a weapon in the car, or unlock the passenger door and get in. (Most carjackers target auto models they're familiar with—they know where the locks are.)

When the above scenario happens, people without a plan often freeze, allowing a carjacker to have the upper hand. You must be ready to move on the approach of any threatening situation prior to being attacked, and hopefully not let anyone with bad intentions get close enough to shatter the window in the first place. Still, if carjackers have already shattered your window, there are options:

- If you're parked properly, use the accelerator to escape. This is where you need to leave enough room between you and the vehicle in front of you anywhere you stop. It's not a bad habit to get into. Anytime I stop at a railroad track at night and I'm the first car closest to the track, I stop about fifty feet back, then move closer after the car behind me begins to stop and I feel everything is safe. I've seen drunk drivers knock the front car into the train.

- If you can, you may just want to get out of the car and run. Don't argue—let them have the car.

- Lay on the horn, or hit the panic button on your car alarm. Enough noise may scare the carjackers away.

- Put your car in reverse and back out of the situation, if there's no one behind you.

Anticarjacking Devices

Carjacking is taken quite seriously in South Africa. Someone there developed a powerful anticarjacking device that's the hottest thing going, literally. For $655, motorists can protect themselves with a car-mounted flamethrower. As of this writing, it's still fully legal to own and operate in that country. The "Blaster" shoots gas through nozzles mounted under each front door. A spark ignites the gas, which comes from a tank stored in the trunk. The resulting flame won't kill anyone, claims the device's inventor, but a would-be carjacker sure isn't going to stand around and get a hot foot. Apparently police in South Africa are all for the device, since the flamethrower's first buyer was the police superintendent of Johannesburg's crime intelligence unit.

If the Blaster sounds like a bit much for you—and it's probably illegal here anyway—there are a few other choices:

- Immobilizers, which disable a car or reduce its speed to a safe level shortly after a pager signal is sent to the vehicle. The system blows the horn and flashes headlights while further reducing the car's speed to a crawl. Another type of immobilizer provides the vehicle owner with a toll-free number to call, which activates a kill-switch mechanism that stops the car.

- Locator systems that pinpoint the car to within a quarter mile. Most have regular service fees.

There's not too much that technology can do to help you

against carjackers, even though it was likely technology that helped create the crime.

Road Rage

A man whom I'll call Don told me this story: He was on his way to a softball game and had all the equipment in the car with him. He was cut off in traffic by two men riding in a pickup truck. For some reason, something in Don just snapped.

"It absolutely enraged me when these guys cut me off. I'm basically a calm person, and this has never happened to me before, but on that day, it just happened, out of the blue. I got really angry, for no good reason."

Truly out of character for Don, he then sped up and pulled next to the pickup truck, grabbed a softball bat from the front seat, and shook it menacingly at the truck's occupants. If his own actions surprised him, he sure didn't expected what happened next. At a traffic light, both men got out of the truck and strode quickly toward him, each brandishing a baseball bat of his own.

"These guys were huge—and mad! Now I knew I was in trouble," Don recalled. "I looked at these guys heading at me, realized I'd made a major mistake, and wondered how in the world I was going to defuse this situation. Then I got this weird idea that at least we all had one thing in common—softball. I don't know where the idea came from, but I quickly grabbed my softball and glove, put the glove on, and casually tossed the ball into the mitt, all the while wearing an expression on my face that I hoped would convey my message: 'Sorry, guys! Wanna play ball?'"

The two men stopped dead in their tracks and stared, then their expressions changed and they began to laugh. They shook their heads, turned around, and got back into their truck. Don managed to save the situation.

"I was very scared and would never, *ever* do anything like that again," he vowed. "I'm almost certain those guys would have smashed my windows, and possibly my face, if I hadn't had the ball and glove in the car to create a funny situation."

It's been called "Highway Madness," and that may not be far from the truth. Road rage is a growing problem that has potential for great violence. No one is immune from it, and anyone is capable of it. Unfortunately, not all road rage incidents end defused, as in the story above.

Often, the endings are quite different:

- A thirty-year-old Detroit man driving on a freeway fired two shots into a sport utility vehicle, missing the driver's head by inches. The man became angry because the SUV merged into traffic between him and the car behind him, which was being driven by his sister.

- Two teenage girls—ages seventeen and nineteen—beat a young mother to death in a Virginia road rage incident. The teens slammed the woman's head against the pavement, kicked her, then stomped on her head after the woman exchanged harsh words with them for blocking the road out of a residential cul-de-sac.

- A former financial analyst riding a motorcycle on a Texas highway shot and killed two truck drivers and wounded a third in a fit of road rage. The man claimed one of the truck drivers nearly ran him over. Two months after his arrest, he wrote in a letter to a former girlfriend: "I will tell you this: I found it quite pleasurable to kill those two men! If you are an angry person and someone provokes you to violence . . . it feels wonderful to cause their death and to watch their pain."

- A seventy-year-old Minneapolis woman was forced off the road and hit in the face by an enraged driver who sped away from the scene when other motorists intervened. He was later caught. The forty-four-year-old anesthesiologist had become angry when the elderly woman pulled in front of him on a highway ramp, nearly causing an accident.

Why are incidents like this on the rise? In fact, why are they happening at all? This may have something to do with it: Since 1990, traffic has increased by 35 percent, but new roads by only 1 percent, according to the American Automobile Association (AAA). That means more congestion on the roads and more problems, creating more frayed nerves—and more aggressive drivers. Frustration from day-to-day living may also contribute to road rage—if you get behind the wheel after a bad day, you might vent your frustrations and anger at other drivers. But most often, road rage can be directly traced to one incident between drivers, whether it's real or perceived—an incident that can be anything from an oversight, mistake, or poor judgment to actual "bad driving." Behavior and incidents that commonly set off road rage can include tailgating, not using a signal for a lane change or turn, honking your horn, cutting too quickly into a lane, or going slower than the traffic around you, especially in any lane other than the right lane on a freeway or highway.

What else contributes to road rage? The size and isolation of cars can give aggressive drivers a license to take out their aggression on others. Cars can make people feel invincible, as if they can retaliate for perceived wrongs done against them and not worry about consequences. This can be especially true for some people who feel they have little or no control over other aspects of their life. A car gives them not only a chance to thumb their noses at society, but also an aggressive way to win—by getting the best parking space, being first to stop at the light, or standing up to others in a way they normally wouldn't. Additionally, there's a quality of anonymity in a car. Some people act as though they're invisible—how many times have you seen someone behind the wheel talking out loud to himself, singing wildly, or picking his nose as if no one was watching?

Some psychology experts believe that road rage has its roots in childhood; that kids learn certain behaviors from watching how their parents behave in traffic. If parents get angry, swear, call other drivers names, and act aggressively behind the wheel, kids may think it's okay and normal to act that way when driving. Others say bad driving and road rage depictions on TV and in the movies have an effect on young people, validating this as "okay" behavior.

Road rage can turn into a power struggle, at least on the part of the road rager. This is where it can really get dangerous, as the driver who wants total control engages in potentially inciteful or deadly behaviors.

Bad tactics:

- Blocking passing lanes and refusing to move over.

- Obscene gesturing.
- Insulting, threatening, and yelling.
- Blowing the horn repeatedly, or "laying" on it.
- Tailgating to intimidate, coerce, or punish.
- Engaging in a highway "duel," cutting off the other vehicle and cutting in and out of traffic.
- Suddenly slamming on the brakes in retaliation.

Wherever it comes from, road rage is emotion out of control, and any such situation should be handled with great care. Prevention and avoidance are the keys in the case of road rage. Remember that most aggressive drivers believe they've done nothing wrong, but rather believe that they are being "wronged."

There are two goals: to avoid becoming a victim of a road rager, and to avoid becoming a road rager yourself.

Top Ten Tips to Avoid Road Rage Incidents

1. Don't use obscene gestures or shout foul language. That's a surefire way to get someone angry.

2. Don't blow the horn unless you absolutely need to. Horn blowing is often misinterpreted.

3. Signal your intentions! That cute little lever on your steering column has a purpose—it makes really neat red and orange lights on the outside of your car flash and blink.

4. Don't tie up traffic waiting for the closest parking space. Get some exercise! I got caught behind a lady once who waited for an eternity to get the first space in line. I parked, walked into my gym, and there she was on the treadmill. Go figure.

5. Watch your high-beam headlights. Don't blind other drivers, either oncoming or from behind, with your brights.

6. Observe parking lot courtesy. If you're going to leave a parking space, do it as quickly as you can after getting into the car. Someone might be waiting for you to leave, and he won't necessarily take it well if you suddenly start putting on makeup or looking for a good radio station while he sits there. Also, if someone's already waiting for a space that's about to be vacated, don't steal the space. Both of these situations can lead to confrontations between mature adults, especially during holiday shopping season, when stress is high and it doesn't take much to set some people off.

7. Move up close enough to the intersection (not into the pedestrian crosswalk!) to trip the traffic light. Many traffic lights are changed by pressure sensors buried in the asphalt. When you stop on the sensor, the light changes. If you don't hit the sensor, you may sit a long time. Many people know this, and many people don't. Often, the ones who do get stuck behind the ones who don't, and an angry confrontation is usually the result if the one who doesn't know won't move forward when prompted by the one who does.

8. Don't take traffic personally. No one's out to "get" you. When other drivers make mistakes, they aren't directed at you. Suppose you're impatient for the driver in front of you to make a right turn on red, but he won't do it. Check all signs in the intersection carefully and you might see one that says, no right turn on red. The other driver may simply be obeying the law, so calm down.

9. Allow plenty of time for your commutes so you don't end up rushing—and thus be tempted to do things that provoke road rage in others, like cut in and out of traffic, tailgate, or worse.

10. See the world from a different perspective once in a while by taking a break from driving. Ride the bus every now and then if it's available, carpool, or take the train. Let someone else worry about traffic.

If Road Rage Happens to You

1. Use the same escape techniques as if you're being followed. Don't let yourself be forced off the road and into a confrontation. If someone tries, turn and go down another street. If he's driving beside you, slow down abruptly or stop if it's safe to do so, and let traffic force him past you.

2. Don't do anything that might escalate the situation. Some aggressive drivers carry guns. People are getting killed or going to jail for a momentary flare-up of anger.

3. Don't get out of your car under any circumstances!

Consider an Apology

I don't think many people really *want* to anger other drivers. Usually an incident that causes road rage was simply a mistake on the part of the offending driver. An apology might defuse the situation, but the danger of being misread exists. Mouthing the words "I'm sorry" could look like something a whole lot different as seen through angry road rage eyes. There are experts who advocate the use of an I'M SORRY sign to help control anger on the road. One is Dr. R. Jerry Adams, an educator and executive director of the Evaluation and Development Institute in Portland, Oregon. Dr. Adams has shown through several studies that a SORRY sign can be quite effective in warding off anger. In fact, more than 85 percent of road ragers studied said they would drop the matter if the other "careless" driver simply apologized. Otherwise, they felt the "careless" driver needed to be taught a lesson.

Dr. Adams suggests keeping the apology sign where it's easy to retrieve; if you goof, just hold it up. I think it's a great idea. Dr. Adams suggests making the sign at least nine inches wide and three and a half inches high, finished dimensions. The print should be thick, black on a white background, and at least two inches high, so the other driver can read it easily. Dr. Adams advocates laminating the sign.

Give it a try. Anytime you can inject some humor into a situation, as my friend "Don" did, may help, too. I know two people who actually carry a red clown nose in the car with them. If a driver gets angry at them, they put on the clown nose. They swear it never fails to make the other person crack up laughing and leave them alone. I say, whatever works!

Auto Theft

A vehicle is stolen every twenty-three seconds.

Just like home burglaries, auto theft is a crime of opportunity. Auto theft often happens when people are distracted or don't pay attention. I know a lady who dropped her child off at day care, but was in such a hurry that she left the car running and the door open as she walked less than fifty feet away to hand the child over to the teacher. She turned just in time to see her car being driven away. The worst part is that the woman is a probation and parole officer with a degree in criminology. She had the knowledge and knew better, but she wasn't alert or aware. If she hadn't provided the opportunity, she wouldn't have lost her car to criminals.

Sometimes, however, the crooks get so sharp, you don't know you've given them the opportunity. I know of several instances where people pulled up in front of a restaurant or nightclub and were approached by a "valet parking attendant" who was a clever, well-dressed thief. They handed over the key, even got a valet ticket, and went inside, oblivious to the fact that their car had already left the premises. They discovered the theft when they came out later and learned there never was a valet parking service. Always make sure a business has a legitimate valet parking service before handing your key over.

Professional Car Thieves

When I was a cop, I heard about a car theft that happened over the phone, so to speak. I got hold of the police phone tape and listened to the incident, timing the whole thing. Here's how it went:

Victim:	I see someone next to my car, they're trying to get in.
Dispatcher:	Where are you?
	[Victim gives address]
Dispatcher:	What kind of car is it?
Victim:	A white Lincoln Town Car. Wait . . . they just opened the door . . .
	[Dispatcher sends police units to address]

Victim: . . . and they've started the car. Now
               they're driving north.

The car thieves walked up to the car, broke in, and drove
away in less than thirty seconds. Police did find the car and
catch the thieves shortly afterward, but I'm sure it was only
because the woman happened to see the crime as it was taking
place. A few more seconds and those guys would have been
gone, and the car not likely recovered. One of the men who did
it had three previous arrests for auto theft and was a true professional. When police arrested him, the only thing he said was,
"I want an attorney."

Those were high-tech, professional car thieves who made
their livings by stealing cars. They either sent them out of the
country, or sold them to a wrecker yard/chop shop. There the
car would be cut up for parts, or the serial numbers would be
switched with a wrecked car. The stolen car would then be sold
as a rebuilt auto. Depending on serial number location, it might
require only changing a door or a dashboard. To thwart this,
automobiles have hidden serial numbers, the locations of which
are known only to the FBI and to insurance investigative agencies. They're so secret that local law enforcement doesn't even
know where they are, and must contact these agencies to send
someone to look if they believe they've come across a "rebuilt"
stolen vehicle.

There are auto thieves out there—and I've caught them—
who travel around with beepers and cell phones. They're beeped
for a certain type of car, sort of like "theft on request." They're
pros, and they're not carjackers. They usually deal in one of several popular car models, and they're experts on every aspect of

that one type of car. They involve themselves in continuing education on these vehicles. They patrol, looking for these cars to steal, and they can do it quickly, usually in less than half a minute.

What can you do about such professional car thieves? Not much, actually, but what you can do might surprise you. Let's look at some ways to protect your vehicle.

Go Low-Tech

The way to thwart the high-tech car thieves is to go low-tech. The Club steering wheel lock would probably stop them cold. Why? High-tech guys have all the fancy tools to break into the computerized locks and bypass ignitions, but they rarely carry the brute-force type of tools needed to deal with the low-tech devices. Removing The Club usually requires using a saw to cut through the steering wheel, or huge bolt cutters. Popping an ignition takes a dent puller or vise grips. You can see already that this would be a lot of hardware for a thief or two to haul around, making it more difficult for them to blend into their surroundings. They won't waste time trying to remove The Club when they can find a car that doesn't have it.

Low-tech auto security solutions such as The Club can deflect car thieves to an easier target.

Alarm Devices/Security Systems

Do vehicle alarms and security systems really work? If you use them properly, yes, and that means being sure to actually *use* it. You'd be surprised how many people have a car security system but don't turn it on. These are active systems, requiring you to enable and disable them. On the other hand are passive systems, which arm and disarm automatically. Improper use of this type can lead to the alarm going off all the time, thus acclimating your neighbors—and indeed much of humanity—to the sound of car alarms. Many people no longer look when they hear an alarm thanks to this type of misuse.

Properly used, security and alarm systems do discourage car theft. They throw a technical roadblock in front of thieves that requires them to keep up their skills. Remember that criminals are lazy, especially amateurs. The more sophisticated the alarm, the more likely it is to thwart auto theft. There really aren't many thieves out there who can bypass your alarm. Still, nearly anyone who's had experience installing alarms and working on car ignitions can usually disable any alarm he's learned to install. A combination of a low-tech device like The Club and a high-tech alarm system is thus your best chance to reduce the likelihood of your vehicle being stolen. Hint: When using The Club, turn your wheels completely away from the curb before putting it on. This makes it more difficult for the vehicle to be towed.

What type of security system should you get? Newer cars often come with factory-installed systems that, at the very least, set off an alarm if someone opens the doors, the hood, or trunk. Like home security systems, some car systems are silent, sending a signal to a pager rather than blaring an alarm siren.

Law enforcement generally recommends audible alarms to draw attention to the car and scare off the intruder, rather than setting up a situation in which the vehicle's owner arrives to confront a possibly armed and dangerous criminal.

Consider these components and options:

Ignition kill systems.

These devices protect against hot-wiring, and can even prevent you from starting the car with the key. This is how many smart keys work (see below). Install-it-yourself kill-switch kits can be found for less than twenty dollars, if you're mechanically inclined.

Proximity alarms.

These alarms can be triggered by someone getting near the vehicle, let alone touching it. Systems range from under a hundred dollars to a few hundred. Some "talk" and announce to anyone who crosses the set perimeter that he's too close to the vehicle. These can be an asset or a pain in the neck, depending on where you live and how many people walk by your vehicle in the course of living their daily lives. Frankly, I find them annoying most of the time.

Motion sensors.

These devices are generally part of a complete security system. They set off the car alarm if the vehicle is lifted to be towed. The sensitivity can be set to go off if the car is moved or shaken in any way, or if the glass is broken. Highly sensitive settings can cause many false alarms— even a strong wind will set them off.

Vehicle locators.

Some of these really work well. People have found their cars in containers on cargo ships ready to be shipped out of the country, or actually found them in another country, tracked by satellite. The cost of such devices ranges from a few hundred dollars to more than a thousand.

Steering wheel locks.

This is usually a metal bar designed to keep the steering wheel from turning. The Club is an example. Since it's visible through the car window, it's an excellent deterrent against a thief who wants to move quickly, especially if the car doors are also locked. Most steering wheel locks can be cut off, but thieves rarely take the time and effort. That would be the exception rather than the rule.

Steering column collars.

These devices protect your car from being hot-wired through the steering column. They have to be physically put on or removed each time you drive or park the car. They cost a couple of hundred dollars and, like steering wheel locks, are a visible deterrent that can deflect many thieves.

Decals and flashing lights.

You've seen stickers on car windows announcing the presence of a security system. A flashing red light on the dash shows an armed system in use. These, too, can be deterrents—and you can therefore bluff potential thieves by simply putting decals on your window, or installing a simple flashing red light on your dash, saving the cost of an actual security system. Once again, only amateurs or thieves with a lot of time will find out it's a bluff. Inexpensive compared to a working alarm.

Smart keys.

Using computer chips or electronic transmitters, these keys are the sole means of starting a car's engine. They are incorporated into an ignition kill system. So far, they only come standard in some car models; you can't purchase them independently.

Kill switches.

Also called "hidden switches," these are designed to work with either the electrical or the fuel system. Flip the toggle when you leave the car and it prevents the flow of fuel or electricity, rendering the car inoperable until you flip the switch again. Experienced thieves may search for this switch, however. The cost depends on the complexity of the system.

Locks—A Simple Solution?

Do locks really do anything to help prevent car theft? Yes, they do help. About half of car thieves who successfully broke into a car did so by simply opening an unlocked door. A lot of thieves are amateurs who make a little money from car thieving, or joyriders who look for unlocked cars, those with a spare key kept in the visor, or older cars that are easy to steal. Neither will waste a lot of time trying to get into a car, because they're not as picky about what type of car to steal as professionals are.

Almost any regular door lock can be jimmied by an expert. Luckily, there are few experts out there. So use your door locks—they're the first line of defense. But at the same time, make sure you don't leave anything in the car that might tempt those amateurs into trying to break in.

The Traffic Stop

When I was a police officer, I rarely wrote traffic tickets. I don't believe that policemen should work traffic. Most traffic violations aren't considered crimes. They're civil violations for which you simply pay a fine, sort of like a tax on speeding or rolling through a stop sign. Traffic enforcement is the most common contact most people have with police officers, and the main conflict between cops and honest citizens. It's one that citizens really resent. Whenever I'm in social situations, everyone wants to tell me about the time he got pulled over for a traffic violation.

Emotions and anxiety during traffic stops have led to tragic consequences on both sides. We've heard of innocent drivers being shot by police because they made the wrong moves, and we've certainly heard of police officers being shot because the "average driver" they pulled over turned out to be a wanted criminal on the run. I can tell you that if you're stopped, there are things you should do and say, and things you absolutely *shouldn't* do and say. Following some simple suggestions can help prevent such tragedies by keeping emotions and the situation under control.

Top Ten Tips for Traffic Stops

1. If you see the police blue lights behind you, pull off the road as quickly as possible in the safest manner possible. Officers are trained to initiate a traffic stop in a safe place and may have followed you for some distance before actually pulling you over.

2. Don't tell the officer, "I know the chief." He'll probably say, "That's nice, tell him I said hi." He may or may not believe you, but even if you do know the chief, it probably won't help in the least. Almost everywhere in the country, tickets are issued by the state to the police departments, and those tickets can't be fixed by anyone once they get into the system. So once it's written, it's a done deal.

3. Don't give the officer bad attitude. Saying something like, "Why aren't you out catching criminals instead of picking on honest citizens?" is clichéd; every cop has heard it. Whether the officer likes it or not, writing tickets can be part of the job. In fact, job performance can often be tied to the number of tickets written. I wrote so few of them that a supervisor once asked me how I could possibly patrol all day and not see one single ticket to write. It won't hurt you to take your medicine with a good attitude, and can make the whole stop go more smoothly.

4. Keep your registration and insurance card readily available. Take your driver's license out of your wallet and hand it to the officer. If you don't, the cop will ask you to take it out—he doesn't want to handle your wallet or anything else that may have money or valuables in it.

5. Don't make any sudden or suspicious movements. Most people stopped by police are decent, law-abiding citizens who simply committed a traffic infraction, but the police officer can't possibly know beforehand who's sitting in the car he just pulled over. It could be you or me, or a guy who just robbed a bank—or worse. Remember, it was a traffic cop who caught Timothy McVeigh speeding away from the Oklahoma City bombing. McVeigh had just killed hundreds of people and had a pistol tucked into his waistband.

6. If you have to reach into your console or glove compartment for your registration and insurance card, tell the officer and ask permission. If you don't, he may assume you're going for a gun. It's happened—too often.

7. Don't get out of the car unless the officer asks you to. If you get out, a good police officer will immediately be suspicious and will probably ask you to get right back into the car. Do it. Cops keep a wary eye on the passenger compartment until they can check the car—remember that an assailant can hide in the backseat, and police officers have been ambushed in this way.

8. Don't be offended if a police officer "blinds" you with a flashlight or spotlight. When a cop shines a spotlight in your rearview mirror, it's to light up the inside of your car, once again to see what's inside for his own protection. In fact, consider turning on your dome light to assist the officer, especially at night.

9. Don't jump to conclusions if you're stopped. If you're thinking, I didn't do anything!—you may be right. Your

car may simply match the description of a stolen vehicle, or a burglar may be in the neighborhood and the officer is checking out the situation.

10. Don't resist signing the citation. Signing the ticket doesn't mean you're admitting guilt. You're just acknowledging that you've read the instructions on the ticket. The whole idea of signing the citation came about for the public's convenience. It used to be that accused violators had to post bond; now you simply sign the citation. Not signing, however, can lead to arrest and the need to post bond.

There may be nothing you can do or say that will keep you from getting a ticket, especially if you really did commit a violation. But having the best attitude you can during a traffic stop can make the experience a little less painful for all concerned.

Chapter 5

Protecting Our Children

More than thirty-five thousand children are **forcibly abducted** each year.

In 1999, Child Protective Service (CPS) agencies investigated **three million** reports that involved the maltreatment of approximately four million children.

In the year 2000, one out of every seven victims of **sexual assault** reported to the police were **under** the **age of six.**

From the time my son was born, I carried great concerns and awareness for his safety. As a cop, I answered far too many calls involving death and injury to children. I saw it all, and then some: Abduction, accidents, abuse, and drowning are only part of the list. All parents understand—and dread—that feeling you get inside when you think your child might be in danger. We all want to protect our children from the people and things in the world that would do them harm. The best we can do is to learn about these dangers, be alert to them, and educate our children to protect themselves.

Child Abduction—Every Parent's Nightmare

In the blink of an eye, a child can go missing. Grabbed off the street, thrown into a car, plucked from a bicycle or scooter—all it takes is a second or two. A naive child can be ripe for a predator's picking, but even a savvy child can be in the wrong place at the wrong time. What can you do to protect children against those who would prey on them?

Education is the first line of defense. Teach children how to recognize those who mean them harm and how to get away when they sense danger. But first, find out what your children already know and what you need to teach them.

Survey: How Streetwise Is Your Child?

Children can become streetwise by learning personal security skills, and they're never too young. Well, maybe a little—those under age three can't really grasp the concepts of personal security. But starting at age three, children can begin to learn skills vital to protecting themselves if you're patient and teach them slowly, over a period of time, with repetition and rein-forcement. By the time children are in school, they should have mastered the skills listed in the following survey under "Safety Assets." In general, preschoolers have few safety skills and require constant supervision, so they'll score high in the "Safety Liabilities" category.

This test can help you determine what safety skills and savvy your child has now, and what you need to teach. Complete this inventory for each of your children. Ask preteens to fill out their own inventory. Then compare theirs with yours and discuss what skills need to be improved. Armed with this information, you can read on to learn the next steps in teaching personal security to your kids.

Teach Your Children—How Abductors Lure Them Away

I served briefly as the public information officer for my police department, and in that capacity I often spoke with schoolchildren about safety and security. I've found that kids are ready, willing, and eager to learn if you're patient in explaining things, don't use scare tactics, and let them know that you're always there to talk with them about anything that concerns them.

Abduction is a topic you must discuss with your children. It's every parent's nightmare, and it happens far too often. Children are lured away by predators who know how to play to what makes kids compliant. They know how to gain children's confidence, how to make them think they're helping an adult or a small animal in need. They play on a child's desire for things, or use ruses to make the child think the predator is a "special" person. They can even use a child's sense of self, even vanity, to lure him with lavish praise. It's easy to understand how some of the most common lures used by child predators can work—some of the same lures will even work with adults. The keys are to teach children to ask your permission before accepting any

Safety Assets

1. Can say no to adults.
2. Can name all parts of his or her body, including private parts (genitals).
3. Can turn down a dare.
4. Can recognize and trust his feelings.
5. Can recognize and say no to uncomfortable touches.
6. Can follow rules well.
7. Can talk about problems or feelings.
8. Will risk making a scene if necessary.
9. Can call 911 or Operator in an emergency.
10. Knows name, address, and phone number.
11. Knows how to safely interact with strangers.
12. Would refuse a bribe from an adult.

Safety Liabilities

1. Is compliant with all adults.
2. Is embarrassed by or cannot talk about his or her genitals.
3. Will accept dares.
4. Ignores or cancels out feelings.
5. Seeks or accepts affection from most or all adults.
6. Has trouble following rules.
7. Has difficulty talking about feelings.
8. Doesn't draw attention to himself or ask people for help.
9. Doesn't know how to call 911 or Operator in an emergency.
10. Does not know all identifying information.
11. Is terrified by or very friendly toward strangers.
12. Would accept a bribe from an adult.

13. Tells callers too much information.

14. Opens the door to anyone.

15. Would freeze and not be able to think or act in an emergency.

16. Is easily persuaded by adults.

17. Doesn't know what to do if lost or separated from you.

18. Would obey anyone who was wearing a uniform or flashed a badge.

19. Would keep a secret if scared or threatened.

20. Could be tricked by someone who gained his trust and confidence.

TOTAL LIABILITIES _____

13. Knows how to answer the phone with out disclosing too much information.

14. Will only open the door with your permission.

15. Would "Yell, Run, and Tell" if in trouble.

16. Questions adults' motives and doesn't immediately trust them.

17. Knows what to do if he gets lost or separated from you.

18. Can distinguish between uniformed officers and imposters.

19. Would share a secret with you if scared or threatened.

20. Would be able to recognize and avoid common lures.

TOTAL ASSETS _____

[Test courtesy of Paula Statman, from her book, *Raising Careful, Confident Kids in a Crazy World*. Copyright © 1999 Piccolo Press, Oakland, CA. A psychotherapist and educator with twenty years' experience, Statman is the founder of the KidWISE Institute.]

gifts or doing anything to assist a stranger. You also want to teach children, as you have learned, that not everyone in the world is out to get you. But you need to be alert and trust your instincts to help you recognize when something just isn't right.

Here are the most common lures used by child abductors, and what your kids should do if they encounter these lures:

Common lures:

- **The lure:** "My pet is missing!"

  This is a difficult one for many kids to resist. An adult approaches the child and tells him how sad he is because he's lost his puppy or kitten. He asks the child, even begs the child, to please help him find his lost pet. Children are taught to help adults when they ask, and they have a great desire to please adults. This lure also plays to a child's love of animals, so it's that much more difficult to resist.

  Teach your child: No matter how sad he might feel or how much he wants to help, tell your child to come and get you *immediately,* and you'll all look for the lost pet. By saying this, you're not telling the child to never believe what anyone tells him, but you instill the idea that the child must tell you about any such contact first. Teach the child to shout, "I have to go get my parents first!" and to immediately run to you. You never know—someone may have indeed lost a pet. If that's the case, then you really can all help. Otherwise, a would-be predator will be scared off.

- **The lure:** "I got my little boy a new video game and his grandma got him the exact same one. You can have the other one if you like."

Gifts are an age-old bribe. Kids want things, and if they're offered the latest trendy toy, or candy, money, a puppy, even a burger and fries, they may readily accept. Not only that, but kids learn that someone who gives them gifts tends to be a "special" person—like Grandma and Grandpa, Aunt Mary Jo, or your next-door neighbor—special people who think the child is pretty special, too. The gifts make the child happy, and the child sees that the adult is happy from giving the gift. That all adds up to a dangerous combination when a predator is playing the game and offering the gifts.
Teach your child: Gifts are nice, but the child must come and get you *immediately* and is never to accept anything from strangers. Once again, teach the child to shout, "I have to go get my parents first!" and to immediately run to you.

- **The lure:** "I'm a friend of your mommy's [or daddy's] and s/he sent me to bring you home right away."

    This lure definitely plays on the compliance of a well-behaved child. "Your daddy said . . ." and "Mommy wants you to . . ." are things a child hears all the time from babysitters, neighbors, siblings, and other relatives. It's an automatic reaction for the child to do what he's told at this point. He's conditioned, and used to it.
Teach your child: If anyone says he knows Mommy, Daddy, Grandma, Grandpa, Sis, or Brother, find out for sure by coming to get you *immediately*. Never accept a ride from a stranger, and never get close to a stranger's car. Run away as fast as possible.

- **The lure:** "Aren't you just the prettiest little girl [cutest little boy]? Can I take your picture?"

Children can be vain, and an adult who praises or flatters a child may well get that child's undivided attention.

Teach your child: *Never* let anyone take his photograph. If someone does, run home and get you *immediately*. This is a common method of luring not only children, but also adults. Notorious serial killer Christopher Wilder used photography to lure women and gain their trust.

You see that in all the lure scenarios, the answer is always for the child to go and get the parents right away. They must trust and believe that they won't "get in trouble" for telling Mommy and Daddy anything. It's important for children to feel secure in telling parents anything and know they'll be loved, without fear of judgment or punishment. You know you'll love your kids, but you have to make sure they know it, too. Here's why:

Children who become victims can fall into a cycle of guilt and victimization. They keep secrets and feel guilty for not having done what they were told—for instance, for not getting into a car with a stranger. If they do fall victim, though, they think it's their fault because they fell for a lure they were warned about. Sometimes this combination of guilt and fear of punishment and rejection allows the child to be victimized repeatedly. In cases of child victimization by figures of authority to children, such as teachers, scout leaders, even clergy, this guilt is what they use to keep their crimes secret. This is one of the reasons these crimes can go undiscovered for so long.

Do You Know a Predator?

We don't want to consider that someone we know might victimize children. But the fact is, children are often victimized by someone they know. That's why it's very important for you to know who the adults are that your child comes into contact with on a day-to-day basis. Teachers, coaches, the friendly neighbor down the street—you should meet all these people face to face, and tune in to your instincts. If something doesn't feel right, don't allow your child to be with the person, period.

Neighbors and friends who want to take your child somewhere or give gifts should ask your permission first. Perhaps in the case of gifts, they should bring it to your home and hand it to you first, then let you give it to the child. Especially in young children, this helps reinforce the idea of not taking anything from strangers. Enlist your family to help reinforce this message. If your child's uncle and aunt want to bring a gift when they come to visit, they can remind the child not to take anything from anyone unless Mommy or Daddy is present.

You make the rules regarding your children, so make sure you let everyone knows what those rules are. Most people want to help and are willing to try. Sometimes you'll come across a friend or relative who may take the situation lightly and say their piece: "Oh, don't be ridiculous! If I want to give little Bobby a gift, I'm going to do just that!" If that's the case, show them this book and what the statistics are. Let them know that you aren't rejecting them, but trying to protect your child.

When the child is older, there will be plenty of opportunities to give gifts without you present. Many adults didn't grow up with the same dangers our children face today. When given an opportunity to think about it, they'll usually understand and probably be one of your biggest supporters.

How to Escape an Attacker

It's possible for a child, even a small one, to get away from an adult attacker. You might not believe so, but it can be done. Even a big adult trying to grab a small child can be foiled if the child knows what to do, and isn't afraid to do it. The child usually can't fight off an adult, but he can make enough of a commotion to draw attention to his plight.

Here are two escape techniques I recommend. They're easy to teach to kids, and you can all have fun learning.

Escape techniques:

Drop, kick, and scream.

The child drops to the ground on his back and protects himself by raising his legs in the air and kicking in the direction of the attacker, screaming loudly for help at the same time. I believe it's always good to yell, "Help! Police!" Using the word *police* has a psychological effect on the would-be abductor, but also passersby won't think that it's just a kid playing around. "Police!" is one of those things that makes people come to their windows and look out. If you saw a kid kicking an adult who was trying to grab him, all the while calling for the police, I think you'd go to help or call 911 right away.

The leg latch.

I've often heard it advised that a child latch on to the abductor's leg, then twist around to tangle himself in the would-be abductor's legs while screaming for help. I don't always agree with this method. I think it looks like what kids do to their own parents when they aren't getting their way. I'm not so sure onlookers would know the difference between this and a real emergency. I prefer teaching a child to use the leg latch on *another adult* nearby (if there are any)—or a bush or lamppost—while yelling, "Help! Someone's trying to take me!" It's visually confusing if a child is holding on to the person he's trying to get away from. Picture it yourself for a moment, and I think you'll see how confusing it can be. Now, if a kid puts a leg latch on *me* and screams that someone's trying to kidnap him, he's definitely got *my* attention! I think this is much better to do than latching on to the attacker. This is a case where the child must be unafraid to raise a ruckus and cause a scene. And that's really the point of both these escape tactics—to draw attention so the predator will let the child go and run off.

If there's nobody else around, however, and "drop, kick, and scream" doesn't seem to do much good, then I think the child should try the leg latch on the attacker. This should be only as a last resort, if there's nothing else to do, because it will slow the attacker down.

I want to emphasize that it's important to teach a child to yell, "Police!" Kids yell and scream while playing, and often they'll yell for help when they're being chased or playing tag. But they don't always call out for the police, so anyone who hears "Help! Police!" can be pretty sure the kid's not playing around.

Practicing Safety and Security

I advise parents to work with the assets and liabilities survey presented earlier and practice role-playing with their children. Kids enjoy the game part of it, and at the same time you've got their attention and can teach them valuable security information and techniques.

For example, you can play "What If . . . ?" to teach your child to turn down a dare. Where I grew up in Florida, a big dare for kids was to jump off a bridge that spanned an inlet of fast-moving water leading to the ocean. "I dare you to jump off the bridge" was part of growing up in my town. I got dared a lot—all kids do. It can be major peer pressure. Just the word implies danger, but kids still take dares, from shoplifting to vandalism, running across the interstate, and painting their name on an overpass. Then there's "I double-dare you."

Kids should be taught to never take a dare. In the "What If . . . ?" exercise, you pretend to be another child daring your own child to do a number of things. First, discuss dares and how dangerous they are, impressing on your child that dares aren't to be taken. Tell him that it's okay to refuse a dare, that you can say no to friends. Give him some examples of what to say in response to a dare. For example, "I don't take dares!" or "Friends don't dare friends." Better yet, have the child respond with a question: "That's dangerous, why do you want me to do that if you're my friend?" "I could get in trouble, why do you want to see me get in trouble?" This can empower a child and give him an understandable reason to walk away from the situation, which is often what he must do anyway.

Now play "What If . . . ?" You say to the child, "I dare you to . . ." and present different scenarios. Work with the responses, and include the idea that the child can come home and tell you about it, especially if something really risky is involved. Praise the child for his strength in saying no, and give plenty of reinforcement.

Don't forget to include typical drug and alcohol scenarios in your dares. "I dare you to drink that beer" and "I dare you to take that pill" are commonly heard by kids. All the while, your goal is to let them know you care and help them understand the dangers in taking dares.

Keep Them Safe

You can't enclose your kids in a protective bubble, but you can take steps to help them stay safe. Here are some tips:

Top Ten Tips for General Child Safety

1. Talk with kids about following and trusting their instincts. Even small children can be very in tune with their sixth sense. Teach kids to leave any situation that doesn't seem right to them.

2. Know your child's friends and who he's with at all times. Landmark studies in criminology have proven what Grandma always said: If you lie down with dogs, you get up with fleas. People tend to behave and act in the same manner as the people they associate with.

3. Check the references of day cares, preschools, and baby-sitters before leaving your child with them. Call the local juvenile authorities and Better Business Bureau to find out

if they have had any complaints lodged against them. Make sure they're licensed and inspected by the local government.

4. Talk to your child regularly about his day at school and what he did. Let him know that you care, and that if he has any problems he can tell you about them.

5. Make sure your child knows where the safe places to go are if he feels threatened while walking or riding his bicycle. Walk the route with your child and point out safe places, such as people you know and trust, hospitals, a fire station.

6. Never leave your child unattended in a public place. The bustle and confusion of crowds can make it easy for a predator to take a child unnoticed.

7. Review the security policy of your school or day care, especially in regard to picking up children. Do they maintain a list of approved people who are allowed to pick up your child? Would they release the child to just anyone? Many schools require a list of approved people, and anyone who shows up to pick up the child—even a teenager—must be on the list and show appropriate ID.

8. Don't "over-ID" your child by putting names on book bags, books, or clothing. This tells everyone your child's name, and a stranger can immediately remove the stranger barrier by calling your child by name.

9. When possible, encourage your children to walk and play with friends and avoid going anywhere alone. There's safety in numbers. Encourage friendships in general—lonely children can fall prey more easily because they're lonely.

10. Teach your children to avoid potentially dangerous places such as junkyards, alleys, empty buildings and houses, bridges, and railroad tracks. Children have a natural tendency to explore, so you must explain the dangers to them, especially since such settings are perfect for the start of "I dare you" games.

Child Abuse

Child abuse is everybody's business. Anytime you suspect child abuse, you should report it to your local police or child welfare agencies. If you wish to remain anonymous or are unsure about getting involved, call the child abuse hot line in your state, or the national hot line at 800-4-ACHILD.

If you're not sure how local police might handle your complaint, don't be afraid to ask questions. You can set up an appointment with a juvenile detective in your local police department and discuss your worries. These officers are very committed and are usually experienced in handling such complaints. They can sympathize with your concerns for the child involved, while understanding the apprehension you have about becoming involved in someone else's family business.

Children depend on us to protect them because they can't protect themselves.

Home Alone

What do you do if your twelve-year-old gets home from school at three-thirty, but you don't get home from work until six? You may not be able to change this situation, but you can protect your kids when they're home alone.

More kids are spending time home alone than ever because both parents work, or a single parent works. Some kids do well alone, but others may be uncomfortable, anxious, or frightened. Kids who are home alone run a greater risk of becoming crime or accident victims, of being victimized by adults (strangers or people they know), and of becoming involved in minor crimes. I strongly advise not leaving a child under age ten alone for any extended period of time. You know your child's strengths and weaknesses—judge his maturity level before deciding if he can be home alone for any period of time. What can you do? If you can't eliminate the time a child spends alone between school and when you get home, you may be able to at least reduce it.

Reducing time alone at home:

- Find after-school day care.
- Arrange for your child to stay with a friend or relative.
- Involve the child in after-school activities he's interested in.
- Arrange for a trusted neighbor to look in on your child.
- Hire a sitter to spend this time with your child at your home.

Spend lots of quality time with your child discussing his day and how he feels about being home alone. The more you can do to boost his self-confidence, the safer and more secure the situation can be.

Here are some more quick tips to make home-alone time more secure:

Top Ten Tips—Home Alone

1. Review basic home security procedures with your child,

teaching him to lock doors and windows, and how to operate the alarm system.

2. Teach your child to keep his keys in a secure location, and develop a plan for lost, stolen, or forgotten keys. Consider leaving an extra key with a trusted neighbor.

3. Show your child how to look for possible break-ins when he's coming home, and teach him to never go into your house or apartment if the door is ajar or if a window is broken. Make plans with a neighbor for the child to go to their home to call police.

4. Write emergency phone numbers where your child can easily find them. When my son was young, I wrote the emergency phone numbers on the wall near the phone and hung a calendar over them. Some people will think it tacky to write on the wall, but we all knew where the list was and that it couldn't be misplaced.

5. Set up regular check-in times when your child calls you at work. Perhaps ask a neighbor to check in on the child at a regular time.

6. Teach kids how to answer the door when they're home alone (see the next section for more detail).

7. Teach kids how to answer the phone when they're home alone. They should never let callers know they're alone—always say that his parents are busy and take a message. I prefer that kids say Dad's busy or taking a nap, rather than Mom.

8. Periodically quiz your child on procedures, and to make sure he's memorized your home and work phone numbers,

the complete name of your place of employment, and how to dial emergency numbers for police and the fire department.

9. Talk to kids about fire hazards and make sure they understand your family plan for escaping fire.

10. Lock up items you don't want kids to get into. Talk with them about the dangers of drugs, alcohol, firearms, tools, or other items of concern. Time alone can lead to curious exploration. I've heard many cases in which a small child started a fire by playing with matches, then became so scared and felt so guilty for doing something he shouldn't have that he hid in a closet or under the bed instead of running outside. The outcome was fatal because firefighters couldn't even find the child.

Answering the Door

It's often advised that children home alone shouldn't answer the door at all, but I strongly disagree. As I discussed in chapter 3, burglars often knock on the door to determine if anyone's home before they go ahead and break the door in. If a child is home alone and pretends there's no one there when he hears a knock—well, you can see what might happen. I think it's better for the child to say: "My dad's asleep and I don't know how to turn the burglar alarm off! You're going to have to come back later." It's a pretty good chance no burglar would kick the door in at that point.

If kids feel unsure about what to do, instruct them to call you at work, or a neighbor. They should never open the door for anyone they aren't expecting. No one should be just "dropping in" on a child home alone.

Baby-Sitters

Leaving your children with baby-sitters isn't an easy decision, particularly in light of news stories about abusive or careless sitters. Still, most of us do have to leave our kids with sitters at some point. For their security and your peace of mind, you must screen prospective baby-sitters thoroughly. Use the checklist below for questioning every potential baby-sitter.

Questions to Ask a Prospective Baby-Sitter

QUESTION: Why have you chosen the job of baby-sitting?
REASON TO ASK: By asking this question, you may get a good or bad feeling—does the applicant want to baby-sit because he loves children? Does he need the money?

QUESTION: How long have you been baby-sitting?
REASON TO ASK: This is one way to find out how much experience the applicant has.

QUESTION: Are you currently baby-sitting for other families? Will you continue to baby-sit for them if we hire you?
REASON TO ASK: You may be able to estimate how available the applicant will be for your family.

QUESTION: Have you ever had an emergency situation arise while baby-sitting? If so, how did you handle the situation?
REASON TO ASK: You can find out how the applicant responds to emergencies, which may occur while caring for your children.

QUESTION: Do you know CPR or have any other training?
REASON TO ASK: It's good to know if your baby-sitter will be able to handle emergency situations, should they occur.

QUESTION: Do you swim? Would you ever want to take our children into our pool?

REASON TO ASK: If yes, your baby-sitter should be skilled in CPR. If not, have them pass up the pool when you're not at home.

QUESTION: What would you do if my child refuses to listen to you?

REASON TO ASK: You want to be sure that your baby-sitter continues the manner of discipline that you have set up for your family. Be sure to discuss how you would handle the situation if your response differs from his, and mention whether you approve or disapprove of physical discipline.

QUESTION: Do you have any children of your own? Do you have any younger brothers or sisters?

REASON TO ASK: Knowing the answers to these questions may help you learn how the applicant feels about children, and if he ever did any baby-sitting for siblings.

QUESTION: Can you tell me about the best child you ever baby-sat for? How about the worst?

REASON TO ASK: Learning the answers to these questions can tell you how the applicant feels about children in general. How did he describe the "best child" and the "worst child"? What happened to make a child the "best" or the "worst"? How did the applicant handle that situation? Could he have handled it any differently?

QUESTION: What type of activities would you do with my children? How would you pass the time with them?

REASON TO ASK: Wouldn't you want to know what a prospective baby-sitter has planned to entertain your children?

QUESTION: During your experiences as a baby-sitter, have you ever suspected any child to be abused?

REASON TO ASK: After you've asked and discussed the easy questions, it's time to get down to business. You want to be sure that your children's baby-sitter will actually care for your children—not cause them any harm. Keep close attention to the applicant's response to this question. If he brushes off this topic or becomes evasive, there may be a reason for it. If he discusses abuse and how to spot it openly and honestly, he gains a point here.

Once you've found the right sitter, go through this checklist of things to do before leaving your child with the sitter. Add any other items you can think of that pertain to your individual situation.

Baby-sitting checklist:

1. Write down the rules regarding: bedtime, what your child can and can't eat, what's okay on TV and what's off limits, and so on. This gives the baby-sitter guidelines to follow and leaves no question as to what's permitted and what isn't.

2. Make a list of names and phone numbers to call in case of emergency. Go over it with the sitter so it's all understood. Include police, fire, trusted friends or relatives, pediatrician, and other important contacts.

3. Discuss what to do in an emergency. Make sure the sitter knows your home fire escape plan.

[Questions to Ask a Prospective Baby-Sitter courtesy of Joi M. Lasnick of StopSex Offenders.com, a Web site dedicated to child and family safety. Copyright © 2000 Joi M. Lasnick.]

4. Instruct the sitter how to respond to telephone calls or if someone's at the door.

5. Teach the sitter how to use your home security system. Most systems allow for "guest" codes to be programmed in—these are easily enabled and disabled as needed, so you can turn it on when the sitter is at your home and off after he leaves. Instruct the sitter to keep the alarm on while you're away.

6. Instruct the sitter to ask your permission to have any guests. It's often advised to never allow a sitter to have guests. I don't think this should be a hard-and-fast rule. When I was in high school, I used to visit my girlfriend while she was baby-sitting. I knew the people she worked for, and they gave me permission to visit her at their home. If you grant permission to have guests, make sure you know the person and that he knows your rules.

7. Make sure the sitter knows where you'll be and what time you'll be home. Make sure he knows who to call in an emergency if you can't be reached. If you're going to be late, call and let the sitter know.

8. With sitters who are young people or teenagers, tend to their security needs. Walk them to the car or drive them home. Make sure they call home and tell their parents when they've arrived at your home and when they're leaving. If you drive them home, you make the call right before you leave, for both your protection.

Our children are our most valuable asset, and sometime we have as much to learn from them as they do from us. Enjoy them, watch them, and protect them.

Chapter 6 **The Prudent Traveler**

Twenty-five to 35 percent of
hotel crimes take place
in parking areas.

Theft accounts for more than
90 percent of crimes reported
at airports worldwide.

A gentleman I know (I'll call him Jack) asked me for advice after he had been mugged in Atlantic City. He was lost and trying to find his hotel when a man approached him and offered to help. The friendly stranger pointed down the street to show Jack where the hotel was; when Jack turned to look, the man blindsided him with several blows to the head and face. He stole Jack's money and credit cards, then vanished into the night. Jack asked me how he could avoid being mugged again.

I told Jack the truth: He had targeted himself as a tourist. How? Jack is British, and like many men from Europe and the UK, he carried all his money, credit cards, and ID in a small handbag, which he called his "purse." That right there made him ripe for a mugger's picking, as it was obvious he was from out of town. Jack also wore trousers with no back pockets, underscoring the fact that his purse had to contain his valuables. He was wandering around at night looking lost, and he openly admitted to a perfect stranger that he was lost. The mugger probably hadn't come across such an easy target in a long time.

Jack wasn't aware that he stood out as a target. He wasn't alert to the man who meant him harm. He obviously hadn't planned his trip very well, and didn't have a plan for what to do if he became lost.

Whether you're traveling for business or leisure, abroad or in your home state—even across town—it pays to be alert, be aware, and have a plan for any circumstance that may arise, from accident to theft to terrorist activity.

I don't want to scare you into staying home and not taking that dream trip to Europe you've looked forward to. Nor do I want you to become overly vigilant to the point that you don't have a good time when you travel. Rather, I want you to sit down and think your trip through before you leave, giving consideration to what obstacles may present themselves and how you might get around them. Prudence doesn't mean being afraid. I take plenty of precautions when I travel; they're second nature to me. Putting together a few checklists and making plans before leaving home can really help make your trips more safe and secure.

Don't worry—this isn't an elaborate ritual you must undertake every time you walk out the door. Sometimes the only plan you'll need is to check your car, grab a map, and hit the road. If you're planning a longer stay in a more out-of-the-way place, put more thought into the trip. Part of the fun of visiting new places and foreign lands is the unknown factor, the sense of adventure that comes from learning new things and daring to move outside your familiar territory. But the unknown doesn't have to be scary, and a little study ahead of time can make you more confident and secure.

You can integrate security planning into your regular travel planning sessions. When I was a kid, the time we spent planning our vacation trips was almost as much fun as the vacation itself. Shopping was always a big part of planning, and we bought new clothes, and camping and picnicking supplies. We mapped out routes, and everyone had input on where to go and what to see. We also discussed what to do if we got separated from one another, or how to act if there was a fire in the hotel. We were reminded to always carry something with the hotel's address on it, like a piece of hotel stationery or a matchbook, so we could simply show a cab driver where we wanted to go. This was personal security information made part of the planning, and it wasn't a chore. It may not have been as much fun as shopping, but it did have an element of fun as we came up with creative ideas to deal with problems and pitfalls.

As an adult, personal travel is still fun, but business travel is another matter. My business travel sometimes sends me to foreign countries and trouble spots, and not knowing where I'm going until the last minute produces more security challenges. I often travel on short notice, and I mean *short* notice—the time from when a decision is made to send me somewhere until I arrive at the airport is often less than an hour. Planning is the key to making a spur-of-the-moment trip go smoothly, and believe me, it will make *any* trip a lot more hassle-free.

Before Leaving Home

Travel security starts with security at home. Why? If you aren't worried about someone breaking into your home while you're gone, you'll enjoy your trip more and, most importantly, you won't be distracted. You'll be able to keep your mind on what you're doing in the place you are, and you know how important that is to personal security. The last thing you want to do is clue potential burglars in to the fact that you're away for any period of time. Taking care of everything at home before you leave gives you confidence that you'll find things intact when you return.

Your goal is to make your home appear as though you never left, while making your travel preparations easier. Toward that end, I've created my "Before Leaving Home Checklist." It covers things I do to secure my home while I'm away, and still make it look as if somebody's there. It also covers other important items of concern before going on a trip. When I have to leave town, I often have a lot on my mind. I know that if I go through my checklist, I won't overlook anything and I'll be confident that my home is locked and secure.

Create a similar list of your own. To get you started, here are some tips for securing your home before you leave on a trip. No two households are exactly alike, so I'm sure you'll have some things to do that are unique to you and your family's lifestyle. Feel free to add them to this list so you do a thorough job of securing your home.

Checklist—Before leaving home:

1. Stop delivery of mail and newspapers, or ask a neighbor pick them up. Get "hold mail" forms at your local post

office, and keep a few extras on hand to use if you have to travel on short notice. Write the phone number for your newspaper's circulation office and the neighbor who helps you on your checklist so you don't have to look for it when the time comes.

2. Make sure your passport is valid for at least the next six months. Most countries won't let you enter if your passport is due for renewal in six months or less.

3. Make sure your emergency contact plan is in place. (See chapter 9.) This is especially important when you're traveling.

4. Double-check that everything is turned off. It may sound like a no-brainer, but have you ever been at the airport and wondered if you turned off the coffeepot? Talk about stress-producing! This is worth putting on your checklist.

5. Close your blinds at an angle that won't let outsiders see in, but isn't completely closed. Blinds closed up tightly during daylight hours can be a clue that no one's home. But if they're open just slightly, a potential intruder can't be sure and will probably move on to easier pickings. Alternately, see if a neighbor can come into your home to open your blinds in the morning and close them at night for a real feeling of occupancy.

6. Ask a neighbor to park in your driveway. A car coming and going from the driveway daily really makes it look like you're home. Neighbors are usually happy to oblige, especially if you live in an area with a shortage of off-street parking. Write these neighbors' phone numbers on your checklist, too.

7. Use timers to turn your lights on and off. Some computer systems allow you to program your lights remotely. I like them and they work well, but they're still a bit expensive, so I do it the old-fashioned way, with timers. You can be really creative with this. I have timers set to come on at different hours of the day and night in different rooms of the house. You can get timers that let you program more than one setting in twenty-four hours, so the lights coming on and off can appear to be random. My timers are always ready to go, but I use a type that's activated and deactivated by a switch. When I'm leaving, I simply push one button on each timer and it's activated. Consider putting your television on a timer if it's possible—not all TV sets can be turned on and off by a timer at the outlet. Think of a way to put a bathroom light on a timer.

8. Get someone to do routine maintenance work around your house. This can include mowing the yard, shoveling snow, feeding the cat, and watering houseplants. You want your house to look "lived in" while you're away.

9. Gather your passport, tickets, and travel information and put them where you won't forget them. I know people who've gotten halfway to the airport before finding out they had forgotten their ticket or passport. If you put this item on your checklist, you won't forget.

10. Leave a copy of your itinerary with your office, a friend, or a family member, including contact numbers if possible. If you don't have such information before you leave, relay contact numbers as soon as it's convenient. In case of family emergency, you want someone to know how to reach you.

11. Lock all doors and windows, and activate your security alarm system. Placing this seemingly simple item on the checklist can keep you from standing in the airport wondering, Did I shut that bathroom window?

I've written my checklist in the back of my combination address/appointment book for several reasons. One is to remind me to take my appointment book with me, as well as to check my schedule and appointments before I go. Second, my address book contains helpful numbers like the newspaper circulation department, neighbors, house sitters, and so on. Last, I always know where to find my checklist. If I have to rearrange my life on the run, the book and checklist make it much easier, whether I'm traveling for business or pleasure.

Packing

What does packing have to do with security? Plenty! Packing properly can keep you from standing out as a target for crime. In order to do that, keep these in mind:

Four Key Concepts :

1. Be low-profile. Flashy and expensive draws attention, sometimes the wrong kind.
2. Look travel-savvy. Even if you're a tourist, you don't have to look like a caricature of one.
3. Less is more. Less stuff, more awareness. Too much to deal with distracts you.
4. Still, be prepared. A few extra items for security purposes won't take up that much room.

Your goal is to pack as light as possible while still covering your needs. Naturally, the easiest way to avoid theft is to not have anything with you worth stealing, but at the same time, you simply can't travel empty-handed. I'm suggesting you be a "minimalist" packer rather than taking every little item you like, or "might use," or "probably won't use but it's nice to have it around anyway." I try to carry about five or six days' worth of clothing, no matter how long I'm planning to be away. Any-place I've ever traveled, I've found a way to do laundry, and usually the hotel had a laundry service. This lessens the need to take more clothing. You can always pack some Woolite or a gen-tle liquid hand or dish soap to wash out some of your things in your room's sink, if you wish. It's really much easier to do that or have someone else do your laundry than it is to lug around a massive suitcase filled with clothes. Don't worry about wearing the same piece of clothing more than once—nobody in the next city will know you wore that shirt two days ago.

Lugging that luggage can make anyone tired, and a tired tourist with both hands full sure makes an easy target. Lighten up, and take extra security precautions:

Top Ten Tips for Packing

1. Use covered name tags. This prevents crooks from seeing your name and address, and knowing that your house is probably unoccupied, ready to be burglarized. Use your last name and initials, and an office address and phone number if you can.

2. Carry as few pieces of luggage as possible. Tired-looking travelers who can't handle their luggage become targets for

crime. Choose suitcases that are easy to handle. I try to carry only two bags—a rolling suitcase like the ones used by flight attendants, and a small easy-to-handle bag that always stays with me. The smaller bag can be strapped onto the rolling suitcase, and the whole setup is easy to handle. When traveling by plane or other common carriers, I check the rolling suitcase (which contains mostly clothes and no valuables); the small bag is a carry-on. In the carry-on bag, I pack things I can't afford to lose, like my laptop computer, or things I'd need if my larger bag got lost, like prescription medicines, extra shirt, socks, underwear, and my shaving kit. Then if my checked baggage is lost or delayed, the first day of my trip won't be ruined.

There's another advantage to packing light: At some hotels, a traveler struggling with an overload of baggage may get charged more. Why? If you don't like the price you're quoted, you're less likely to pick up your whole mess and walk out the door. But if you're in control, you can leave as easily as you walked in. This makes price gouging less likely.

3. Consider using good but unassuming luggage. Expensive designer luggage stands out, and in fact is meant to be recognized. It also can mark you as someone with money. Not everyone will consider doing this, however, and if you do have expensive luggage, I suggest always having luggage handlers help you with it—and don't let it out of your sight. If you feel the need, hire extra security.

When choosing inexpensive luggage, avoid olive-drab, especially for large cloth duffel bags. You might be marked as military personnel and become a target for attack. For this reason, most military personnel no longer carry olive-drab luggage.

4. Pack a small first-aid kit. Mine holds a few Band-Aids, antibiotic ointment, aspirin, antidiarrhea medication, a few Q-tips, and some iodine. You can care for minor discomforts and not have to go looking for these simple items at what may be a bad time or place (late at night, the wrong part of town, and so on).

5. One more piece of emergency gear to pack is a small flashlight. This can be a lifesaver in a fire or other emergency by guiding you through the dark or signaling for help. A tiny flashlight that operates on AA batteries won't take up much space.

6. Carry traveler's checks for security more than convenience. Traveler's checks protect you against loss, but they're not universally accepted. Most companies issuing traveler's checks don't protect the establishments that accept them against loss. That's good for you, however, because those places that do accept them are usually pretty strict about asking for proper ID. I usually take the majority of travel money in traveler's checks, and I get them free through my bank. I carry enough cash or use my credit cards to pay bills in small businesses; I cash the traveler's checks in banks, hotels, and larger establishments that are used to handling them.

7. Take a cheaper camera. Expensive cameras are a target for thieves, and if you own one, you know that. Before you travel, think about how much you might actually use your

camera and for what purpose. If you can leave it behind, do so. If you can't, then be prepared to take extra security precautions. I use a small Olympus camera recommended to me by a professional photographer. It wasn't cheap, but it's easy to carry in my shirt pocket, and it takes great photos. For many purposes, an inexpensive or throwaway camera will do just as well.

8. Carry no more than three credit cards if possible. Leave a list of card numbers and their cancellation phone numbers at work or home, where you can easily get them if you need to. Don't leave expiration dates or the four-digit security numbers.

9. Don't forget vital personal health items, like prescription medication, vitamins, extra glasses or contact lenses, and phone numbers for your doctor, optometrist, and drugstore. If you wear corrective lenses, it's a good idea to carry a copy of your vision prescription with you. If you lose all your contact lenses or glasses, local optometrists can replace them for you.

10. Check the weather before you go and pack accordingly. The Weather Channel lets you know weather conditions worldwide; it's now easy to know what the weather will be like anywhere in the world.

What to Carry in Your Wallet

Just as you have a packing checklist, you should also remember to empty your wallet of items you don't want to lose and are better off not taking with you, such as department store and buyer's club credit cards and IDs, voter's registration card, and similar items. When I travel, I carry only my auto club card, AARP membership (yes, I'm over fifty, and I like the discounts), three credit cards (Visa, MasterCard, and American Express), health insurance card, driver's license, and one other photo ID. I can't think of much else a person would need when traveling.

Ladies, I want to mention purses again. If you carry a large one, it's a good idea to downsize when traveling. Sort through your purse before you leave and retain only necessary items. Put them in a smaller bag that's easy to handle, possibly a fanny pack.

Give Yourself an Edge

You're packed and ready to go. What else can you do to give yourself a security edge when traveling? Here are some additional tips and tricks for deflecting crime and staying safe when you're on the road.

More safety advice:

1. Make use of travel information and maps. It's always easier to get around if you know something about where you're going. If possible, go through this information before you leave, rather than walking the streets or the airport with your head buried in a map or book.

2. Don't broadcast your travel plans. Imagine you're riding a shuttle bus and your friendly, talkative driver asks you questions like these: "Do you live here or are you on vacation?" "How's the weather where you're going?" "Do you have to travel a lot? It must be rough on your family at home."

"How long will you be gone?" "Do you have any kids? I'll bet they miss you." At first, this may sound like friendly conversation. But your answers to the questions are extremely revealing. One quick look at the luggage tag bearing your name and/or address, and the missing information is filled in. I'm not implying that every person you encounter is potentially a crook. I'm simply suggesting that it's bad security to let too much personal information out.

3. Dress casually when possible. I like to dress up a little when I travel, but I never go overboard. As an undercover cop, I learned that if you want to go unnoticed, buy your clothes in a thrift shop. You don't have to go that far, of course. Just keep a low profile and don't draw attention to yourself with expensive clothing and jewelry items.

4. Consider carrying a dummy wallet. This is what cops call a "throw down" wallet, which means it's nearly worthless, and you can throw it down and run if you have to. It's made up to look real and contains credit cards, but they're all expired or canceled. The ID is false, and the billfold holds fake money with a couple of one-dollar bills on the outside. If you get into trouble, you can toss it a short distance away from you and the attacker. When he goes for it, you run in the opposite direction.

5. Use a money belt or inside wallet. I've used both when traveling overseas. My inside wallet loops around my belt and tucks inside my trousers. I don't care for the ones that go around your neck because of the possibility of being choked if someone grabs it. You can find these products in specialty shops, luggage stores, spy shops, and on the Internet.

6. Sew a button or some Velcro to your jacket's inside pocket. It's much harder for pickpockets to "bump and pick" you if you can button or seal the pocket. If you enjoy a challenge, you might install a zipper.

7. Consider carrying a "tool box" in the form of a Swiss army knife (in your checked luggage, please). Anytime you can do a fix-it job yourself, it keeps you from seeking help on your own in a strange place. I carry a little knife that has a magnifying glass, tweezers, screwdrivers, scissors, and corkscrew, and I've used it for everything from getting a splinter out of my finger to opening a bottle of wine. If you need a hiding place in your hotel room, you can use the screwdriver to take the cover off a light switch or cable TV outlet. (I prefer the cable TV outlet, and so should you, so you don't electrocute yourself.)

The "Go Bag"—And What's in It

I use a small bag in my travels that I call a "go bag." That's because it's always packed and ready to go—packed with my valuables and important items, that is. It's about the size of a woman's cosmetic bag, and it packs easily in my suitcase. Before I go to bed each night, I put my wallet, passport, money, and other small valuables into it. I then slip the bag under the mattress all the way to the center of the bed. If an emergency occurs and I need to flee my room, I grab my pants, the go bag—and go! There's nothing to gather up. I'm just out of there. It's an old habit, and one that makes me feel organized, too. Every night, I check my credit cards and traveler's checks before I put them into the go bag, just to make sure everything's there and accounted for. It's not uncommon for thieves to steal just one credit card, or to take a couple of traveler's checks from the back of the packet. If you don't notice for a while, they'll have a longer spending spree.

I'll probably have to find another place to hide my go bag now that I've told the whole world where I keep it.

Staying Healthy

It's easier to be alert and aware if you feel well. Criminals prey on the weak because it's easier. If you're tired, sick, or just a little under the weather, you may suffer lapses in your attention—and security. When you're away from home, it's important to try to follow any regular health routines you may have. If you take vitamin, mineral, or herbal supplements, make sure you bring enough along for your whole trip. Active types, you might plan ahead to partake in your favorite sports or other recreation. If you love tennis, stay at a hotel with tennis courts. Gym addicts should find a place to work out on a regular schedule. If you're concerned about jogging in certain neighborhoods, try running the stairs in your hotel.

You should try to drink plenty of water when traveling. Dehydration from dry airplane air and other causes will keep you from feeling your best and leave you more open to infection. Look for bottled water in areas where you're not sure about the cleanliness of the local water supply. Doing this, along with keeping up your regular health and fitness routines, gives you an edge by keeping your mind clear and your body healthy.

Jet Lag

Jet lag is that tired, run-down, general all-over blah feeling you can get when you travel across time zones. It happens when your body's circadian rhythms, or internal twenty-four-hour clock, get confused by the time zone changes. Symptoms including insomnia, disorientation, swelling limbs, fatigue, headaches, bowel irregularity, and lightheadedness are dictated not by the length of your flight, but rather by the number of time zones you've crossed. Recovery can take as much as one day for every zone crossed.

To get over jet lag and be alert again, here are some quick tips:

- Drink lots of water and juices, and skip the alcohol. Dehydration contributes greatly to jet lag, and alcohol is dehydrating. I drink a couple of glasses of water before getting on the plane, and four or five more during the flight.

- Book flights that arrive at night. You'll likely be tired anyway, so you can go right to bed and wake up refreshed the next morning, and in sync with the time zone. I like this because I don't have to arrive in the morning tired and be stuck with my luggage for several hours while I wait for my room to be ready.

- Don't think about what time it is at home. Mentally put yourself in the new time zone. The less you think about the changes, the better you'll adjust.

- If you feel you must take a nap when you arrive, keep it short. If you sleep too much, you'll be giving in to your home time zone and delay adjustment to your new one.

- Eat protein and avoid fatty and high-carbohydrate foods. Protein provides energy and stimulates you awake, while carbs and fats can make you sleepy.
- Drink caffeine beverages to help you stay awake until bedtime.
- Get some exercise. Before the flight, skip the moving sidewalks and walk to your gate under your own power. Move around any chance you get in the airport and on the plane to keep blood circulating and help you feel awake.
- Ask your doctor about the supplement melatonin. It may help you reestablish normal sleep patterns. Melatonin isn't a sleep aid—it's a hormone that's produced naturally in the pineal gland, a small gland inside the brain. Melatonin governs our biological clocks, such as our sleeping and waking cycles. Consult your doctor before using melatonin, and never give it to children.

Everyone's different when it comes to jet lag. I've seen people suffer for days with symptoms, and others show no symptoms at all. If you take reasonably good care of yourself, you shouldn't have too much of a problem.

Medical Emergencies

Few things can be as scary as needing medical care when traveling in unfamiliar territory, especially in foreign lands. This is why it's so important to do your homework ahead of time to learn what your options are should you need emergency medical care.

Call your medical insurance company before your trip to find out where you're covered, and how much. There may be medical facilities at your destination that are covered by your medical plan. You'll probably have at least some coverage if you're traveling within the country, but coverage may not extend to foreign lands.

If it doesn't, you may consider purchasing a travel medical insurance policy that will offer coverage within the country you're visiting.

Some sources to check:

- Your medical insurance company may offer such coverage or recommend other companies.
- Your regular insurance agent.
- Your travel agent.
- Your credit card companies may offer such insurance. Some cards, such as American Express, offer medical emergency assistance to cardholders.

Be sure to carry important phone numbers with you—doctor, pharmacy, dentist, and optometrist.

Transportation Security

Transportation hubs are high-crime areas where victims are often chosen based on their dress, what type and how much luggage they carry, and their personal demeanor. This is true in the United States as well as abroad. Whether you're in an airport, train station, or bus depot, you need to be alert for a number of potential problems. Theft is usually the biggest concern, but recently, possible terrorist activity has come to the forefront.

Keep these tips in mind:

- Don't let your bags out of your sight, especially your laptop computer or other valuable gear. Don't let a stranger watch them for you.

- Never let anyone but uniformed transportation personnel handle them.

- Keep a record of what's in your checked luggage. Keep valuables and things you must have, such as prescription medicines, in your carry-on bag.

- Don't accept gifts or other material when traveling unless you are absolutely sure of the person giving them to you and you've inspected them prior to boarding.

- Be careful of the "helpful stranger." One of his biggest scams is to help you put your luggage in a locker. He's already got a key in his hand similar to the one for the locker you're using; he simply palms your key and gives you either a fake or a key to an empty locker.

- Watch out for tourist traps: An "Oops!" is a common pick-pocket or luggage thief tactic. He spills something on you and, while you're distracted, an accomplice steals your luggage or picks your pocket. A variation of the "Oops!" is when an assailant does something mean but not injurious to you, like deliberately squirting chocolate syrup on you. Another member of the gang comes to your rescue, and a "confrontation" occurs between the "assailant" and the "rescuer," which may escalate into a fake fight. You're distracted by all this commotion, allowing a third member of the gang to swipe your luggage, camera, or purse.

- Always pack your own bag, and check through it if it's been out of your sight. If the bellman takes your bag down and puts it into the cab for you while you're checking out, you need to look through it because it's been out of your sight. It takes only a few seconds to plant drugs or a bomb in your luggage.

Air Travel

Air travel security starts in the airport, where procedures are changing rapidly and will likely remain fluid for years to come. One thing is sure—security has been increased, and you're likely to be much safer than in previous years. During these times of evolving airport security procedures, it's wise to ask your airline how long before your flight departure time you should arrive at the airport. Most airlines recommend arriving two hours ahead of time for domestic flights, and earlier for foreign flights.

You'll need to be more patient than ever, because lines and waiting times are longer. But you can make use of this extra time to increase your security awareness. In the terminal or on the plane, it's more important than ever to be alert and aware.

Go over this checklist of air travel security tips:

1. Throughout the terminal, look around and take a mental snapshot of your surroundings, noting all exits near you. Know your exits at the security check point, in a restaurant, at the ticket counter, even in the rest rooms.

2. Secure your luggage with locks or other sealing devices. This helps deflect pilferage and keeps someone from easily slipping something into your bag. I prefer plastic wire or

cable ties like electricians use instead of regular luggage locks. I want airport security to be able to open my bags if they feel it's necessary. The only way to get wire ties off after they're sealed is to cut them off, however, and I fear wire ties may be harder to use now. A small pair of scissors will easily break the seal, but bringing those scissors in your carry-on bag may no longer be permitted. If you can wait until you get to your hotel to get into your bags, or feel you can always find something to cut them open if you need to, go ahead and use wire ties.

3. If you hear a disturbance—loud noises, arguments, yelling—move toward an exit and wait there until you've identified the problem or the disturbance has passed. If it poses a real threat, use the exit and get to safety. This is a good idea anywhere you travel, including restaurants and bars.

4. When you get on the plane, sit in or near an exit row. There's more room, and in an emergency you can be one of the first ones out of the plane. Children aren't allowed to sit in the exit row.

5. Fly nonstop whenever possible. Every time your plane takes off or lands, it incurs one more risk.

6. Trust your instincts. If you see anyone who's suspicious or doing anything that looks suspicious at the airport, tell authorities. There are documented hijacking incidents in which passengers said they knew something was wrong and knew the hijackers were behaving oddly before they took over the plane, but no one reported it because they didn't want to offend anyone.

7. Make sure all of your luggage has your name inside as a backup to your covered name tag on the outside. Place a copy of your passport inside luggage if you're traveling outside the country.

8. Go directly to the gate after you check your luggage. Only ticketed passengers are allowed in the gate areas, and this keeps the casual thief away from you. Upon arrival at your destination, go immediately to the baggage-claim area to get your luggage. Don't stop to eat or dawdle in any way. That gives thieves a chance to pick up an extra bag. Have your claim stubs available.

Trains and Buses

Traveling by train or bus requires extra vigilance—you face many of the same risks as you would traveling by plane, but without a high level of security in the depots. Waiting areas usually aren't secure, nor are there strict security checkpoints. The transition zones between your point of arrival at the station and the spot where you board your train or bus are places of increased travel-related crime. Use your streetwise techniques, along with the strategies outlined earlier for all transportation hubs.

At bus and train depots, the most common crime theft is of luggage. If you sleep on a train or bus, sleep with your bags under your feet or in your lap. I've seen more than one person lose everything he had by dozing off, allowing a thief to easily grab his bags and get off at the next stop.

Security for Hotels, Motels, and Hostels

Your hotel, motel, or hostel is your "home away from home" when you're traveling. The transitional time you spend getting there from the airport or other transportation hub, however, can be the most vulnerable part of your trip. Crooks seek out newly arrived tourists who may be tired and unaware, so there are dangers lurking in crowded areas of airports, depots, and hotels. Pay special attention at this time, and follow your streetwise techniques.

Make security your top priority when you arrive at your hotel. You may want to make a quick check of the hotel's security measures. There are some simple tests you can conduct, and if you don't like how the hotel measures up, you may want to stay somewhere else. Try these tests:

- When you check in, the clerk shouldn't speak your room number out loud. Look at your room key—is it a computer-coded access card? If it's an old-fashioned key, is the room number visible on it or attached to it?

- Call the switchboard from a house phone and ask for yourself. If they give out your room number, then it's obvious the hotel isn't too security-minded. If they simply connect you and won't give out the room number even if you prod them, the security is good in that area at least.

- Look at the front desk in the morning—is there a pile of keys sitting there from guests who've checked out that morning? Lax treatment of room keys is a good clue to bad security.

You can't possibly know quickly how the rest of the operation is run, however. So once again the rule is to take your personal security into your own hands. Be your own security guard wherever you go.

Top Ten Tips for Secure Hotel Stays

1. Get a room on a floor between the second and the seventh. The ground floor is most susceptible to burglary, and most fire departments' ladders don't reach higher than the seventh floor.

2. Request a room at least a few doors away from the elevator and stairwell. This keeps someone from coming out of these areas unexpectedly, and it's also more quiet.

3. Avoid using the make up my room sign. It tells everyone you're not in your room. Call the front desk to request maid service, or call the maid to the room and stay while it's made up, if you don't mind a short wait.

4. Use the do not disturb when you leave the room. This gives the impression that you're in the room.

5. Know where exits, stairways, and public phones are located. Anytime you go into a building, and especially if you check into a hotel or motel, the most important piece of security information is the location of fire and emergency exits and stairs. You must know how to get out of the building quickly in an emergency.

6. If your hotel has several buildings, request a room in the main building. Security's hub is generally in the main building. Out buildings are more likely to be crime targets since they're usually away from most of the activity.

7. Don't open your door to anyone unless you're sure of the person's identity. Call the front desk and ask them to stand

by while you answer the door. It's especially important to do this if someone claiming to be a hotel employee shows up at your door unexpectedly and says he needs to get into your room. Call the front desk immediately to verify the person's claim.

8. Use the bellman to take your luggage to the room, even if you have only one bag. Ask him to check the room for you—this offers a great degree of safety during this transition period. Examine the room completely, including closets and bathroom, while he's still there. Bellmen are also good sources of information. Ask how late restaurants are open, if there are any crime problems in the area, and more. Find out the bellman's name, and don't forget to tip him—he can give you good information during your entire stay. Such "invisible people" love it when you ask their name and use it.

9. Check all the locks. If any of them are broken, don't accept a room. If you have a bellman with you, he will help you change rooms.

10. When you go in and out of the hotel, use the main entrance and make sure to stay in lit areas with lots of people and activity. This transition area is one of the most vulnerable spots in any establishment and where a lot of hotel crime occurs.

BYOS (Bring Your Own Security)

I've stayed in a lot of budget accommodations over the years. There's nothing wrong with low-cost hotels and motels, but they often have more security risks: rooms may lack phones, doors may not have security chains, they may be lax in locking the access doors after dark, and so on. In case you do end up at an establishment with less-than-perfect security measures, you may want to bring along some security of your own. Here's how:

- Buy portable travel locks for the door. There are several types, ranging in price from about seven dollars on up. Most of these locks wedge between the door and the frame. Use them anytime you're in the room, especially when showering or sleeping. Buy locks at luggage or travel shops, spy shops, or many outlets on the Internet.

- Use door alarms. One type is essentially a motion detector that hangs on the doorknob and sounds a loud siren when activated by the motion of someone trying to open the door. It costs less than twenty dollars. Another type is a small doorstop wedge—slide it under the door, and it sounds an alarm if someone tries to open the door, while preventing the door from opening. This is also priced under twenty bucks. You can buy these alarms in the same outlets where you'll find locks.

- Make your own security lock. A screwdriver and a pair of pliers can fix a door so that no one can open it. Use a long, slender, flat-head screwdriver and pliers with rubber-coated grips to fashion this improvised lock. Place the point of the screwdriver under the door and lift the handle with firm pressure until you feel the door shift slightly upward. Open the pliers and place them under the screwdriver handle, wriggling the pliers until you have a tight fit and have created a wedge (see illustrations). This will keep the door from opening inward. It works great; I've used it a number of times.

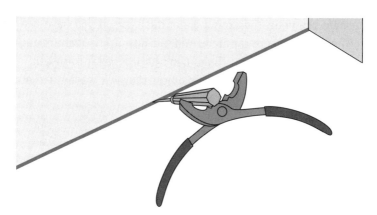

Pliers and a screwdriver can make a security door lock when you're traveling.

- Create a do-it-yourself door alarm. Put flat metal objects like keys, coins, or ballpoint pens between the top of your door and the doorjamb. Place them so that they'll fall if anyone

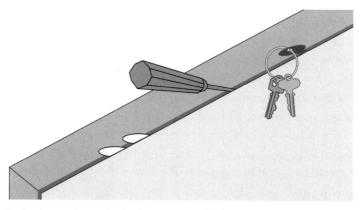

Placing keys, coins, and other items on top of a door can serve as an alarm when the door is opened.

opens the door. Then put a metal trash can, if you have one, by the door where the items will fall into it and make enough noise to wake you up. If you don't have a metal trash can, use a nightstand or any other object that will make a racket when struck by falling keys.

Fire!

No matter where you are, you should always have an escape plan in case of fire. One of the first things you should check after arriving at your hotel is the location of fire extinguishers and emergency exits. Some hotels have a fire escape route posted on a floor plan on the back of your door. Study this, then go into the hallway and follow the route to make sure you know exactly where to go if you hear a fire alarm. Don't just take visual notes—mentally record the "directions" to the exit, such as "up the hallway and turn right at the next hall . . ." Count how many doors you pass between your room and the exit—this can help you find your room again if you try to get out but have to retreat to your room. Remember that you may not be able to see if the hallway is filled with smoke or it's night and the power is out. You'll have to trust your directions to help you find your way out or back. After you've found your exit route, locate a second exit in case the other one is blocked off.

The most important thing to remember is to get out when you do hear an alarm. Don't waste time wondering if it's a real emergency or a false alarm. It's always better to exit the building and learn later on that it wasn't really an emergency than it is to stay inside and become trapped. Fire is always a danger. Plan for it when you check into your hotel room. It bears repeating that you should try to stay between the second and seventh floors: You are more likely to be a target of burglary on the first floor, and most fire department ladders don't reach past the seventh floor.

Top Ten Tips in Case of Fire

1. Keep calm and don't panic. Grab your go bag (see above) and room key.

2. Feel the door before leaving your room to see if it's hot. If not, ease it open and stay low—both heat and smoke rise.

3. If you don't see anything in your hallway, proceed to the nearest exit (which you noted soon after your arrival). Close your room door behind you. Keep your room key with you in case you do run into fire or smoke that forces you to retreat to your room.

4. Don't ever take the elevator in case of fire. It may break down and leave you stranded between floors, unable to escape. Also, the shafts may fill with smoke and toxic gases quickly.

5. If there's smoke in the hallway, cover your face and head with wet towels or a wet washcloth. Stay low and crawl if necessary toward the exit.

6. Feel the exit door before opening it. The fire could be in the stairwell. If it's cool and you don't see smoke coming from under the door, ease it open, then proceed out the exit or down the exit stairs.

7. If you must retreat to your room, or if you can't leave it in the first place, fill your tub and sink with water, wet all

your towels and sheets, and put them around the door to keep smoke from entering. Use wet towels over your nose and mouth or your face mask to filter smoke. If the bathroom has an exhaust fan, turn it on to help remove smoke from your room.

8. Let someone know where you are. Try the phone to call for help. If the room's windows don't open, you must decide whether or not to break them. Sometimes outside air can feed the fire.

9. Hang or wave something colorful out the window so rescuers can see you.

10. Don't take risks by trying to fight a fire alone. Firefighters are trained professionals. Your safety is best served by getting out or getting to a temporary refuge until you can be rescued.

Hotel fires are survivable. Be sure to keep your flashlight and other safety items readily available on your bedside table. Don't keep them packed away. In a fire emergency, every second counts.

Foreign Travel

International travel can be a real trip, literally. Visiting countries with different cultures, learning new languages, and meeting exotic peoples are just the start. Whether you're new at traveling abroad or a seasoned pro, there's always something different to do, new places to go, and new things to learn. From a personal security standpoint, traveling in foreign countries isn't much different from being at home. As always, your security depends on being alert and aware, and having a plan for any possible situation.

Language and culture are two important issues when traveling to foreign lands. It's helpful to learn a bit about the culture so you don't inadvertently do something to offend people or draw undesired attention to yourself. Learning at least a little of the country's prominent language is a security measure, as far as I'm concerned. Especially try to learn phrases asking for assistance and directions.

I've given the following advice and information to corporate executives and other business travelers. While they are often targets of crime, the truth is that *anyone* can be a target, simply by standing out as a foreigner.

Executive advice:

1. Travel with a copy of your passport photos and a certified copy of your birth certificate in your carry-on bag. Make several copies of your passport ID page. If you ever have your passport stolen or you lose it, it's much easier to obtain another if you have these items.

2. If you think you'll be driving in a country where English isn't the primary language, get an International Driving Permit. They're an excellent additional form of identification; you might consider buying one even if you don't think you'll be driving. You can buy them through your local AAA office for a nominal fee.

3. Respect local laws and customs—remember, the U.S. Constitution doesn't protect you in a foreign land. Try to learn some of the language of the country you're going to visit.

No matter where I'm going, I always learn a few words of the local language before I arrive. Learn at least enough to ask for a police officer or a doctor, and enough to tell people you don't speak their language well. I've always found that people are happy to help, and I think that once you start learning another language, it can be really fun.

4. Don't let your guard down just because someone approaches you who speaks English. Crooks know this can make you feel an immediate "kinship" and make you feel comfortable, and they'll jump to take advantage of that.

5. I've advised you to not read maps in the streets, but sometimes you may have little choice. If so, try this trick: Place the map in a copy of the local newspaper in the local language. Anybody watching you may be thrown off track.

6. Take your cell phone with you. Even if it doesn't work, you can pretend to call someone if you think you're being followed or feel you're in danger. It's a good ploy and may well deflect a crime.

7. Know where the U.S. embassy or consulate is located, as well as embassies and consulates of friendly nations (Canada, Great Britain).

8. Spread your money to several different pockets and your hidden inside wallet. Never keep all your eggs in one basket. Keep just enough money in one spot to pay the current bill. That way you don't pull out all your money at any given time. Don't forget to put a rubber band around your wallet to alert you to pickpockets. If I'm in a crowded street situation, I never keep my wallet in my back pocket—instead I button it in my jacket pocket or front side pocket.

9. As soon as you arrive at your hotel, take their business card, a piece of letterhead stationery, or a pack of matches with the hotel's name and address on it and put it in your wallet or purse. This way you can always get back to the hotel. I know this works—when I was ten years old, I showed a pack of hotel matches to a cab driver and got back safely to my hotel after I became lost in New York City.

10. Don't change money (or buy art or antiques) on the black market. It's not that anyone can just walk outside and easily find the black market, but in many countries, the black market will often find you. The exchange rate is higher, but since these people are already lawbreakers, there's a good chance some of them would rob or cheat you just as easily as they'd do "business" with you. Another risk: You might get caught up in a sting and end up being arrested, which you don't want to do (see "If You're Arrested!" later in this section). It's not worth a couple of dollars' difference. Change your money in the bank, hotel, or with a licensed dealer.

11. Learn to use the local pay phones and public transportation systems. Ask your hotel bellmen or concierge how much calls are, and how to use calling cards. They can also help you with local public transportation schedules, which are worth using because it's fun and interesting to travel with the locals.

12. If you have any problems or lose your passport, notify the local police immediately to make a report, then contact the nearest U.S. embassy for a replacement passport. This will be easier if you have extra passport photos and a copy of your birth certificate, as I mentioned earlier.

13. If you need a taxi, have the hotel concierge or the restaurant manager call one for you. It's still worth an extra tip to know you're getting a legitimate cab and not a"gypsy cab." These unlicensed cab drivers can charge you double or triple the regular fares.

Extra Precautions in Countries with Political Unrest

In these uncertain times, it's best to avoid traveling to countries that are experiencing political unrest. I don't want to overstate any risks or make travelers paranoid, but the current world climate makes it necessary to take extra precautions when traveling in general, and when visiting foreign lands in particular. If you do travel to areas of unrest, it's a good idea to go with a tour group, especially one that's been in operation in the area for a long time. They're in tune with the local problems and know where it's safe to go and what areas to avoid. They'll usually pick you up at your hotel, take you directly to what you want to see and back, often providing extra security. A big plus is that such groups use the same drivers, guides, and hotels all the time, and they know all the people involved.

Many journalists and businesspeople I've known often had to travel right into some of the world's more dangerous places as part of their jobs. They're experienced at keeping a low profile, but the casual traveler probably isn't. Here are some tips for extra security in troubled times:

When extra security is needed:

1. Before you go, contact the U.S. Department of State for travel advisories. Call the department's Office of American Citizen Services at 202-647-5225; it's staffed 24/7.

2. If you have any concerns for your security in the country you're visiting, let the closest embassy or consulate know you're there and what your plans are.

3. Avoid becoming involved in local politics, and don't voice your opinion, even if asked. Make that especially if asked—someone may be trying to bait you. Avoid all disputes; if an incident occurs, leave the scene immediately.

4. Vary routines whenever possible. Those seeking to commit crimes often key on the habits of their potential victims. Terrorists who would prey on foreigners may stake you out and learn your habits.

5. Keep business associates and family members informed of your whereabouts and arrival times. Make sure they have the Office of American Citizen Services' number.

6. If you don't speak the local language fluently, speak softly so you don't call attention to yourself.

7. Be constantly vigilant when driving. Practice the defensive techniques discussed in the carjacking section of this book. Don't leave maps or rental agreements in plain view—stow them in the trunk or glove compartment. Be sure to rent a car that's common in the country you're in, and if possible, don't take one with a license plate that's different from what native residents have.

8. Be careful what you photograph. You could be accused of espionage if you take photos of police without their permission, or of the military, bridges, or communications facilities.

9. Watch what you wear—don't dress in clothes that might be mistaken for military uniforms, and avoid patriotic

displays. While you may be proud, you also want to be safe, because corporations have more ransom money than ordinary citizens.

10. Avoid large crowds or anywhere anti-American sentiment is being displayed. If you see any demonstration, turn and go the other way. If you can't easily escape, go inside a restaurant, hotel, or other establishment. Shop, eat, and spend money until it passes. There's a certain amount of safety in most retail businesses—shop owners around the world seem to want to protect their customers.

11. Are you being watched? Apply the same techniques used to recognize a stalker (chapter 8) to recognize surveillance. If you feel that you're being followed, don't try to slip away or lose them. It could be the police, who in some countries may watch the activities of foreigners. If you try to lose them, they could take this the wrong way. Go to your hotel or office and contact your embassy for advice.

12. Carefully scrutinize anyone who wants to practice his English or any other language with you. Any accidental encounter with a friendly stranger needs to be analyzed. If you're a business traveler, the person could be trying to learn business secrets, or may be targeting you for kidnapping. If you're a tourist, he may wish to involve you in some political scheme. It's best to keep your distance from anyone who is trying to become too friendly and too close too fast. Be especially careful of repeated "coincidental" contacts with anyone.

13. Be careful of any mail or packages from unknown sources. You never know what they may contain.

If You're Arrested!

In difficult times or in politically unstable countries, there's a risk of being detained by foreign police or intelligence agencies for any number of reasons. If you should be detained or even arrested, try to stay calm, be polite, and act confident. Follow these tips:

- Remain calm. Admit nothing and volunteer nothing. Don't do anything to provoke the officials.

- Ask to contact your embassy or consulate. This doesn't mean you'll be allowed to do so, but stay calm and keep repeating your request.

- If an embassy representative arrives, ask for identification. The person could be a plant to get you to discuss your situation. If you don't believe it's really an embassy representative, keep repeating your request.

- Don't agree to anything your detainees may propose. They may try to bargain with you for your release, which is a common interrogation technique. Wait for a representative from your embassy before agreeing to anything.

- Don't sign anything. Your detainers may explain that it's simply procedure for you to sign a report, but don't do it. Wait for your embassy representative to arrive and examine any such documents.

My advice is that if you don't have to travel to an unstable country, don't. There are so many other places you can go where your safety and security won't be so compromised.

Chapter 7

The Secure Workplace

Eight hundred **workplace homicides** occur each year.

Workplace homicide accounts for 12 percent of all workplace deaths.

You probably don't work at Fort Knox, so security at work should be a concern. For many years, workplace security was my professional duty. The employees at my company were lucky enough to have management who were concerned about their safety and were willing to do what it took to protect them. Many people, however, work for smaller companies that may not be able to afford a security department, or even a security director. The idea of security at the workplace may simply not be a big concern to management. The law, however, does require companies to provide at least a measure of security and safety to employees, and for good reason. A look at the statistics can be scary. In a 1999 survey of human resource departments, 57 percent of those that responded reported at least one violent incident at their workplace between 1996 and 1999. Workplace homicides account for 12 percent of all fatal workplace injuries and are the second leading cause of fatal workplace occupational injuries to women. That's not to mention petty crimes such as theft, which occur at work as often as anywhere else.

If you're an individual with little or no control over how security is designed or managed at your workplace, it's up to you more than ever to take responsibility for your own personal security while at work. This means being aware of the possible dangers, remaining alert for the signs of impending trouble, and having a plan to deal with any situation.

Violence in the workplace is the biggest concern of employees and employers alike. Let's look at where it comes from, and how you can reduce your risk of being caught up in it.

Workplace Violence Defined

The phrase *workplace violence* can conjure up images of post office employees going berserk from overwork and using firearms to take their frustrations out on supervisors. The truth is, "going postal" can happen to anyone, anywhere, in any line of work, but it's only one component of what is technically defined as workplace violence, which is: *any* violence in the workplace, whether perpetrated by employees or outsiders, whether directed at employees or outsiders visiting the business premises. It's not limited to postal employees or to corporate offices, but rather reflects every imaginable workplace, from police officers in their patrol cars and taxi drivers in their taxis to CEOs, farmers, dentists, bus drivers, and teachers. Some of the jobs most at risk for workplace violence are performed by people you come into contact with every day.

In fact, according to the U.S. Justice Department, the top ten most dangerous and violent workplace situations occur in occupations where people have the most interaction with the public, and include some jobs that may surprise you. In order, they are:

1. Police officers.
2. Private security guards.
3. Cab drivers.
4. Mental health workers.
5. Prison guards.
6. Teachers (from special education and elementary school through college).
7. Bartenders.
8. Gas station attendants.
9. Convenience store clerks.
10. Bus drivers.

This list encompasses violence from all sources, internal and external. It makes you stop and think when you see that teachers are considered to be in nearly as much danger at work as prison guards, and in more danger than convenience store clerks, bartenders, and bus drivers.

Internal Violence

In all the years I was a corporate director of security, the only incident of internal violence I can recall occurred when one employee hit another employee with his umbrella. There were times when potential incidents were nipped in the bud, but in general the biggest threats my company faced came from external sources, everything from threats of rattlesnakes in the parking lots to death threats purportedly made by Charles Manson to executives and reporters.

Conflict in the workplace is the source of many violent incidents, be it conflict between one employee and another, between an employee and a manager, or stemming from problems an employee has at home or elsewhere outside the company.

Many people mistakenly believe there are only two ways to deal with conflict: fight it or ignore it. In the workplace, either choice can be a recipe for trouble. If companies don't strive for good management of conflict in the workplace, umbrella-wielding incidents or worse can occur. Your goal is to avoid being involved in such incidents, or being caught in the vicinity of them and being harmed innocently.

Toward that end, you should know the danger signs of potential violence in fellow employees. Look for these signs:

Top Ten Signs of Potentially Violent Behavior

1. Bringing weapons to work or flashing a concealed weapon. This is a big one—immediately report any weapons brought into your workplace. Don't assume the person is "just kid-

ding," and don't try to convince yourself that the person would never use it.

2. Thinly disguised threats. Such casual comments as, "One of these days someone's going to shoot that guy" may be said in jest—and may indeed be harmless. But use your intuition. If it sounds like a possible threat that this person could carry out, discreetly report it to your security people, management, or a supervisor.

3. Constant and often petty conflicts with supervisors. The person may simply be frustrated and dissatisfied with his job, but if it seems to escalate with no relief in sight, it may indeed be a sign of potential violence.

4. Depression or mention of suicide. Such deep psychological problems may be cause for concern.

5. Drug or alcohol abuse. People struggling with substance abuse may lose control and do things they wouldn't normally do.

6. Groundless or exaggerated complaints about the job or coworkers. Once again, this doesn't always mean you should head for cover, but if it turns into an attitude of "everyone's out to get me," it could be a danger sign.

7. Bullying or intimidating posturing. Someone who normally isn't very aggressive but suddenly starts behaving this way could mean trouble.

8. Paranoia or exaggerated secretive behavior. For example, the person gets panicky if you try to borrow something from his desk or wish to open one of his desk drawers,

or the person goes to great lengths to not let anyone see inside his locker or vehicle. You have to wonder what he's hiding.

9. Sudden displays of hopelessness. Use of despairing phrases such as, "What's the use?" "Nothing ever works for me," or "There's no point in trying," should raise a red flag.

10. Any sudden negative change in behavior, such as bad grooming, sloppy dress, suddenly dressing in black every day, even excessive neatness to the point of obsession might be a clue to a psychotic change in personality.

If you spot any of these signs in a coworker and have an instinct that they're part of a larger, possibly dangerous picture, report them to a supervisor immediately, or your company security director if you have one.

External Violence

There has been an increase in recent years of incidents of stalking and domestic violence being played out in the workplace. It used to be limited to the home, but it's a fact that domestic violence and stalking behaviors often spread into the workplace environment. Think about these facts:

- More than 45 percent of all stalking cases involve disruption within the workplace, with devastating effects on the company and the quality of life of employees.
- The U.S. Department of Justice estimates that boyfriends and husbands commit thirteen thousand acts of violence against women in the workplace every year.

You may not have considered that dangers to you at work may come from the spouse of the person sitting next to you. But that's only one concern. No matter where you work, you face the same dangers of robbery, assault, violence, and other crimes as you do at home. You spend a lot of hours at your workplace, and you should know its safety and security weaknesses and strengths as well as you know your home's. This information can help save your life in the event of major incidents, whether they come from violence or even disasters.

In the same way you've assessed your home with security planning in mind, you should now turn an eye to your workplace. Creating a plan of action to deal with workplace violence is similar to the process you went through in the section on home invasions. Take a few seconds to consider what you might do at various locations in your workplace in a number of situations:

Consider this:

1. How secure is my overall workplace? Is access to the facility controlled? Can anyone from the outside come in at any time? Are there unguarded entrances?

2. How easy would it be for someone to surprise me in the parking lot? During the transition from the lot to my building? Inside the building? In my office or work area? In the lunchroom, rest rooms, or other locations I frequent?

3. If I was trapped in any of those locations, how might I escape?

4. Is there a safe room or some other location I can retreat to and summon help?

5. Can I summon help easily in any of these places? Are there phones, fire alarms, panic alarms, windows to yell out of? Can people in nearby offices hear me if I scream? Are there other creative means available to either escape or draw outside attention to my situation? (For example, grab a fire extinguisher and start shooting it off; jump over a desk and be out the door; shout to anyone to call 911.)

6. What if I'm working alone late at night and someone breaks in or my security is otherwise compromised? What would I do?

7. Is there anything of value in my workplace that someone might want to steal? Does the office look like it contains valuables, even if it doesn't?

As with home invasion scenarios, your goal is to escape harm without escalating violence. Determining escape routes throughout your workplace is one of the most important security actions you can take. Whether the threat is violence or disaster, knowing how to get out safely and in a hurry doesn't make you paranoid—it makes you prepared. By now, you've probably become aware of at least one or more situations at work that could pose security risks to you or others. Think your options through now, before you *have* to do it.

Your workplace is a unique combination of public and private space. In a public building, there are many things you have no control over, such as fixing any security breaches you may discover. You do have some control over your private space in the building. In the end, your personal security at work is your own responsibility, and you need to make a plan for any possible situation. Here are some tips:

Top Ten Tips for General Security in the Workplace

1. Don't be a theft target—keep valuables and money with you at all times, or locked up and out of sight. Theft of the information in your purse or wallet is a big concern, as is the risk that your keys can be copied.

2. Always verify the identification of any vendors, repair persons, or delivery service personnel who wish to enter restricted company areas. Guard against divulging any proprietary information to such people.

3. Watch what you say and to whom you say it. Openly discussing the social plans of a coworker may be overheard by an eavesdropping ex-spouse who has come to your workplace. Other information to keep quiet: vacation plans, your social life, personal appointment schedule.

4. Park in well-lit and well-traveled areas. If that's not possible when you first get to work, go out later in the day and move your car closer to the building, especially if you plan to work late at night.

5. If you're working late, have a "check-in" plan with fellow employees who also work late. The idea is to check in with each other at regular intervals. If you have a security department, request that someone check in on you regularly.

6. When you leave work alone at night, be alert and proceed slowly. Take a quick look around. Don't walk outside fumbling for your keys or reading the newspaper. If you notice

any suspicious people or vehicles, notify security personnel. Ask someone to walk you to your car.

7. If possible, lock rest room doors when you use them at
   night. If they don't have locks, suggest to management
   that locks be installed for nighttime security.

8. If you have your own enclosed office, consider installing a
   deadbolt lock and possibly a "peephole" if you can't see
   who's at the door when it's closed.

9. Trust your instincts and never hesitate to report anything
   that makes you feel uneasy.

10. Discuss safety and security planning with fellow employees
    and friends. Consider forming a business watch group
    among surrounding businesses.

If you have security concerns at your place of employment,
bring them up with your management. If you don't get the satisfaction you're looking for and you still feel threatened, consider calling the U.S. government's Occupational Safety and
Health Administration (OSHA) for advice.

Chapter 8

Stalking and "Dating Crimes"

One in twelve women are stalked at some time in their lives.

Last year an estimated 371,000 men were stalked. Nearly 1,007,000 women were stalked.

Eighty percent of all restraining orders attained against stalkers are violated.

The majority of stalking victims know their stalkers well.

Most violent crimes begin with stalking.

Millions of innocent citizens are secondary targets to stalking.

An astounding 1.4 million Americans are victims of stalking crimes every year. As you can see from the statistics, the victims aren't just women. I can attest to that. I've been stalked. Despite my background, knowledge, and coping abilities, I found it to be a truly disturbing experience.

In our society, we're taught that if at first you don't succeed, try and try again. Stalkers take this old adage to heart. It can be surprising who stalkers are—they come from all backgrounds, all ages, all walks of life, and both genders. Often, stalking victims have had a prior relationship with the stalker—maybe a long and intimate one. But at other times, the victim has barely spoken to the stalker, if at all, as when fans stalk celebrities. In fact, romantic relationships or obsessions don't have to be involved. Some stalking cases arise from the workplace, as former employees become obsessed with the loss of their jobs or the people they perceive were involved in doing them wrong.

No one can be sure what makes a person turn an obsession into a prolonged nightmare for another person. When I heard the following story, I learned just how much of a nightmare it can be.

A Case Study

A woman I'll call Helen told me her story and asked for advice. She was scared and didn't know what to do. She wasn't sure how it had started, this little problem she had with Carl, a man she worked with who had turned into an unwanted suitor. Now he threatened to ruin her life. Maybe it was their first conversation in the office lunchroom, or the time she sat beside him at the boss's birthday party at the local pub after work. She wondered if it could it have been the dinner invitation she rejected, or the subsequent four invitations she also turned down. That's when the flowers started arriving at home and at the office, and not long afterward, she saw him driving slowly down her street.

Not long after that, the phone rang. It was Carl, and Helen didn't know how he had gotten her carefully guarded phone number. He talked with her as if they had been sweethearts since high school. That was the start of daily multiple phone calls, and the more Carl called, the angrier Helen got. No matter what she said, he wouldn't stop. She complained to the boss, to the phone company, and to the police. She had her phone number changed three times, but somehow Carl kept getting the new one. The boss talked with him, but it did nothing. Carl began sending Helen things—cards, packages, long letters— and Helen was afraid to go to her mailbox. She was also afraid to be alone at night, to go to her car, to even walk out her door at one point, because it seemed that no matter where she went, Carl was there.

Helen was a wreck by the time we talked. Her skin crawled, and she was having panic attacks. She lived in constant fear, and had lost her sense of security, her peace with the world and herself. She felt vulnerable, and even became angry at herself for allowing this to have happened. She somehow felt responsible for the misery the stalker was inflicting upon her.

It's a horrifying story, but it's typical of what serious stalking cases can become. When does unwanted attention become stalking? Helen missed the early warning signs that Carl's attentions had moved beyond being interested and turned into full-blown obsession. In retrospect, the signal were there.

Stalking signals:

1. Overly attentive behavior. Helen could barely move without Carl wanting to make sure she was "okay," that she didn't need anything, that she was comfortable, and on and on.

2. Expressing anger when a date is declined. Carl didn't do this at first, but when he persisted and Helen kept gently rejecting him, he started to openly show his anger.

3. Placing heavy emphasis on casual commitments. Helen tried to remain friendly with Carl (a mistake), but when she would agree to meet him at coffee break, she completely missed how important that was to him. He wrote it in his calendar, told everyone he could about their big "date," and even brought flowers to the break room one day.

4. Making future plans early in the relationship—far too prematurely. This was one of the earliest signals Carl had given Helen. At the boss's birthday party, Carl began talking about houses and children, commenting on how beautiful their children together would be. Helen had laughed heartily and chalked the comment up to a beer too many. She thought Carl was being funny. Little did she know how serious Carl was.

5. Constantly inquiring about whereabouts and activities. Casual chitchat about Helen's interests and schedules soon became intense grilling. His casual questions made her uncomfortable, but his obsessive interrogations terrified her.

6. Extreme jealousy. This first raised its ugly head when Helen met with a visiting vendor at the office, and the man took her to a business lunch. Carl followed them, unnoticed, and went into the same restaurant, getting a seat where he could see them but not be seen by her. At one point he couldn't contain himself any longer—he became so upset, he marched over to the table and demanded to know how long the two had been seeing each other, behind his back.

7. Manipulative behavior designed to get an immediate response from you—for example, threatening suicide or other harm to himself. Carl hinted often that he had a gun at home and might want to "end it all."

8. Bad-mouthing to friends and coworkers. Stalkers sometimes talk ill of their victims to others. Carl told coworkers how Helen had led him on, was unfaithful to him, and broke his heart.

These are the primary warning signs that Helen missed. Interestingly, it turned out that in the early stages, Carl had spent a lot of time following her, but Helen was completely unaware of it. Even as she told me how he seemed to just show up at odd places, it never struck her that the "coincidence" was too great.

Are You Being Followed?

Being followed by the stalker is one of the earliest signals, and one of the easiest to spot. If you're questioning whether someone's attentions are moving beyond casual interest and turning to obsession, ask yourself if perhaps you're being followed.

Are you being followed?

1. Does the person show up at places where you wouldn't normally see him? Does the person appear shortly after you arrive? Is the person already at your destination, seemingly waiting for you?

   If so, the person is either familiar with your habits, or has some inside knowledge about your plans.

2. Does the person leave notes on your car, in many different locations? Does the person leave notes at your workplace, or at your home?

   This says the person is probably following you, or has other means of knowing where you're going to be.

3. Do you have regular meetings, gym workouts, or other habits the person knows about? Do you encounter the person at these locations?

   You should make a change in your habits. If you have control over the location of a regular meeting, change it one time and see if the person shows up at the new location. If you usually go to the gym early in the morning, switch to lunchtime. If the person still shows up, you know you're being followed.

4. Do you ever feel as if you're being followed in your car by a suspicious vehicle? Some stalkers may actually hire a private investigator to follow you, or enlist others to help keep track of you. If you think there's a suspicious car behind you, try diverting from your regular route and see if the car follows. A good way to do this is to make a complete circle by making four right turns or four left turns. Anyone still behind you after that is definitely following you.

At night, be sure to not take deserted roads where you may become trapped. Try entering a busy fast-food parking lot, a movie theater lot, or other place where it would be easy to tell if you're being followed, but there are lots of people around.

More things to look out for:

- Letters or cards written in red ink—this is usually a sign of anger and may be a clue to escalating emotions.

- Damage to vehicles. Flattening tires, scratching paint, and otherwise damaging vehicles—yours or a friend or relative's—is common in stalking behavior. Remember, cars are considered extensions of our personalities. A stalker may take great pleasure in attacking your car, or even your friends' cars, and feel like he's attacking you personally.

- Tampering with vehicles. A stalker may tamper with your car so you'll break down and he can come to your rescue. Or his motives may be worse—to injure you. Look for anything suspicious: Check that lug nuts are tight and note any missing hubcaps; listen for slow leaks in tires; look under the hood to see if battery cables are connected or if anything else looks out of place. When inside the car, test your brakes by pumping them, then look under the car to see if brake fluid leaks out. If you do find something wrong, call police immediately from a safe place, and don't try to drive or fix the car.

- Other types of threats include sending dead flowers or flower stems with the blossoms cut off; leaving photos of you with your image crossed out or otherwise defaced; threatening pets or family members; threatening friends or coworkers. All types of threats should be treated with urgency. Threatening words, whether spoken or written in letters, can develop into behaviors. Some stalkers escalate to terrorizing you to try to scare you. Others will turn to physical terror such as trying to run you off the road, and are a real threat to do you physical harm.

What Victims Must Do

Helen went through a pattern many stalking victims go through. It starts with denial, which leads to frustration, fear, depression and self-blame, then intense anger. It's usually at this point—where Helen was when she first came to me—that most stalking victims finally decide they've had enough. She might have been able to nip the situation in the bud if she hadn't denied the problem in the first place.

If you think you're in the early stages of a stalking, it's very important that you admit this fact to yourself right now. Stalking victims who deny the problem only give the stalker time to escalate his behavior. By admitting that you're in a stalking situation, you've taken your first step toward cutting off a potentially dangerous situation. Here's what else you must do:

- Trust your instincts. If you think something isn't right, it probably isn't. Helen ignored her gut instincts about Carl. She had actually picked up plenty of signals that he wasn't the average guy, but she ignored them, thinking the thoughts too fantastic.

- Be firm about not being interested in a relationship. When Carl became persistent in asking Helen out, she tried not to hurt his feelings. She thought it was understood that she wanted nothing to do with him in that way, but Carl apparently understood her words and actions quite differently. So be very clear and don't say anything that can be misconstrued.

• Cut off all communications with the stalker *now*. Don't respond to the person in any way, shape, or form. Response to the stalker's attempts at communicating with you only reinforce his behavior. Don't talk, make eye contact, or even acknowledge the person if you pass him on the street. Not responding can decrease the stalking behavior or end it altogether, as the person's number one goal—attention from you—is being denied. Stalkers often focus their obsessions elsewhere (once again, deflecting the situation away from you).

If the situation doesn't end here, you must take further action. Here are more tips:

Top Ten Tips—What to Do If You're Being Stalked

1. Don't try to reason with the stalker. Several times, Helen tried telling Carl to "get real," something she herself should have done far sooner. At this point, neither she nor anyone else could talk reasonably with Carl. If anyone tried, Carl only felt everyone was ganging up on him.

2. Take basic personal security precautions at home, at work, and on the streets. If the stalker doesn't know where you live or what your phone number is, protect that information as I've described in earlier chapters of this book. Change your phone number if you have to. Carl got into Helen's house once. Despite what was happening to her,

she hadn't taken even simple security precautions, not believing—or wanting to believe—that things could possibly get any worse.

3. Tell everyone you know that you're being stalked, including friends, family, coworkers, bosses, office or apartment security personnel. Show his picture around if you have it. Create a support system for yourself so that you not only have some strong shoulders to lean on, but also enlist many pairs of eyes and ears to help you keep watch. Helen's neighbors knew about Carl and were known to have reported him to the police as a suspicious person driving through the neighborhood. More than once, alert neighbors prevented Carl from being on Helen's property.

4. Keep a diary of every attempted communication by the stalker—phone calls, letters, notes, and so on. Record every time the person drives by your home, noting date and time. Save phone message tapes and any gifts the stalker may send. If possible, take photos or video of the person driving down your street or on your doorstep. Go into your memory to record what happened from the very first incident.

5. Make a police report. Stalking is a crime in all fifty states. A lot of people may not be aware of this, and are hesitant to call police. Victims may also be reluctant to involve police if they know the stalker and don't want him to be arrested or have a police record. The problem is, the stalker can make things much worse if the behavior is allowed to continue.

6. If you have children, tell the school authorities or day care personnel that there's a potentially dangerous situation ocurring. If you have a photo of the stalker, give it to them, or give them a description. Make sure they don't let your child leave with anyone but you or someone you designate as safe. Instruct everyone to not answer questions from strangers about you or your child.

7. Ask law enforcement to periodically drive by your home. There's nothing wrong with asking for extra help. If you've filed a police report, they know it's a legitimate concern. I repeat: Stalking is a crime in all fifty states. Don't forget that fact.

8. Keep your cellular phone with you at all times. You'll always be able to call for help, even if you're not near a regular phone, or if for some reason your home phone is out.

9. Always remember that it's not your fault. If you feel powerless, isolated, that you're not in control of your life, anxious, afraid, or depressed, seek counseling. You aren't and never were responsible for what the stalker is doing or thinking.

10. Prepare an escape plan. Always be ready to leave your home for a safe place if you need to. For tips on creating an escape plan, see "Top Ten Tips for Escaping an Abusive Situation" on page 98 in chapter 3.

Helen's ordeal lasted nearly a year. I believe the most important thing she did to end her situation was to stop all responses to Carl's behavior. Once she did that, she turned the tide. Carl's behavior lessened in intensity and frequency, and he eventually gave up. Helen was lucky—not all situations turn out that well.

Let me make one thing crystal clear: *Never* underestimate the dangers a stalker can pose. You can't know what's going on inside that person's head, and the world that exists in there may be a completely different and unrecognizable world from the one you actually live in. In the stalker's world, "No" can mean "Yes." He hears "Go away" as "I want you to stay." A complete reversal of word and action meanings can occur. Stalkers convince themselves that others are influencing you to behave the way you are, or that you're simply shy and can't express your "true feelings." A stalker's mind is a place you really don't want to go. But you do need to understand enough about it to try to counteract it, and know that you absolutely can't reason or bargain with this person.

I can't say this enough: There are laws against stalking in all fifty states. Call the police. The law is on your side. You don't have to face the behavior of a stalker alone.

What About Restraining Orders?

Helen considered getting a restraining or protective order against Carl several times, but stopped short of doing it on advice of friends and family. There's a lot of controversy on this subject. In the days before stalking laws, restraining orders were one way a victim could have a stalker arrested, since clever stalkers could carry out a stalking without really breaking any laws. Yet all too often, this one act could push an already unbalanced person over the edge and cause him to respond violently. Stalking laws now give the victim a legal weapon that should cover things restraining orders used to. Statistically it's been shown that if violence is present in the situation from the start, a restraining order can have the effect of prompting more violence nearly half the time. If violence isn't involved, a restraining order may be effective in preventing further contact between stalker and victim. It's not an easy decision to make, so the decision should be informed. Consult legal advisers and others before deciding to go this route.

Still Need Help?

While I've never seen it myself, I've heard and read horror stories of how victims of stalking weren't taken seriously by authorities. TV is filled with based-on-a-true-story movies about women whose cries for help went unheard. I'm not saying it happens a lot, but it has been known to happen.

If you feel you're not getting the attention your threats deserve, or that you're not being taken seriously, I suggest you call local crisis hot lines, domestic abuse centers, rape hot lines—any such service that advocates for victims of crimes. Even if you've not been abused or raped, I can tell you that these groups are filled with activists who really understand the system and can work within it. They likely can guide you or offer assistance.

Date Rape

Seventy-five percent of men and 55 percent of women are intoxicated during date rape, and only 23 percent of all date rape cases are reported.

Rape is an ugly crime of violence most people don't want to think about, let alone discuss. Date rape can be more difficult to talk about and is less understood because it takes anonymity out of the equation. The attacker is known to the victim because the rape occurs in a dating situation or setting. It's still rape, however, and date rape is claiming more victims every year.

Many incidents go unreported for several reasons:

- Victims fear they won't be taken seriously. Since victim and perpetrator know each other, claims that the sex was forced are often viewed skeptically by others.

- Since alcohol or drugs are almost always involved, there are often legal hangups over whether the sexual relations that occured were truly rape or consensual. Victims don't want to be placed in that position.

- Since victims know their attacker, they may feel somehow responsible for the attack, or feel they don't want to ruin the man's life.

Date rape happens in two different ways. One is spontaneously, with no premeditation on the part of the perpetrator. He finds himself in a situation where his date is intoxicated, exhausted, or her defenses are down for some other reason. It's likely he's much stronger than her. He takes advantage of the situation. Otherwise, date rape is premeditated by a perpetrator who essentially stalks his victims and uses drugs or alcohol to force a situation he can take advantage of.

If you are alert and aware, and have the knowledge of what to look out for, you can avoid becoming a victim of date rape. There are two things to look out:

- Identify potential perpetrators.
- Avoid circumstances favorable to the crime.

First, let's examine how you might spot a potential perpetrator of date rape. It's too bad that they, along with those who prey on children, don't just glow in the dark. But those who would perpetrate date rape may give themselves away by their behavior, which can stand out just as much. Be alert for any of the following behavioral clues that can help pinpoint this type of personality. They don't all point directly to a potential date rapist. They may simply indicate someone you may end up not wanting to spend much time with.

Danger signs:

- He gets into your personal space beyond what is acceptable, and may even enjoy your discomfort. Anytime someone gets closer than the norm of what is acceptable is a big hint.

- He doesn't listen to you, or constantly interrupts your talking, especially to talk about himself, his exploits, how wonderful he is, and so on. This doesn't always mean the guy's a date rapist; he may just be a boor.

- He shows anger toward women. This isn't always done in a serious way. He may make jokes about abusing women, their intellectual inferiority, how they're only interested in money, or whatever his particular pet peeves are.

- He calls you derogatory names or uses terms you find belittling. This can be pretty subjective when it comes to what individual women might find belittling. "Hey there, little lady" may not bother some women, but I know several who would be put off by it and would view the person who said it quite differently from that point on. On the other hand, some terms are unmistakably meant to be derogatory.

- He tends to do what he wants, with no thought to your wants. Be alert for any violent physical behavior, such as pushing or grabbing you to get his way. Such behavior is a *major* clue.

- He exhibits possessive or territorial behavior, even if he doesn't know you very well. This might indicate a tendency to take liberties due to perceptions of "ownership."

- He acts as if he knows you more intimately than he does. Once again, he's taking liberties.

- He drinks often. Alcohol lowers inhibitions—yours and his.

Next, let's examine where and how date rape begins. The where is easy—almost anyplace people congregate to party and drink, because it makes it easy to give the person drugs or take advantage of alcohol use. The 1990s saw the rise of using drugs with the intention of commiting date rape. Here are the most popular drugs used in date rape:

Most common date rape drugs:
Rohypnol (registered brand name for flunitrazepam).

Also called roofies, ruffies, roche, R2, rib, rope, and Mexican Valium, this potent tranquilizer is used legally in more than fifty countries to treat sleep disorders and for psychiatric cases. It's illegal in the United States. It's colorless, tasteless, odorless, and, when combined with alcohol, can produce disinhibiting effects within twenty to thirty minutes. The effects of a commonly used two-milligram dose can last from six to eight hours, even as long as thirty-six hours. Effects are sedation, impaired concentration, driving impairment, sleep, and, when mixed with alcohol, impairment of psychomotor skills and, most importantly to this discussion, amnesia. Not remembering the date rape incident is what makes prosecution of the crime so difficult, and what makes Rohypnol so popular to use. The drug is inexpensive, usually five dollars or less per pill. It's commonly slipped into a woman's drink at a crowded bar, nightclub, or college fraternity party.

Gamma hydroxybutyrate (GHB).

Also known as "grievous bodily harm," Georgia Home Boy, liquid ecstasy, goop, gamma-oh, or simply "G," this drug was banned by the Food and Drug Administration (FDA) in 1990 except under FDA-approved, physician-supervised protocols. GHB comes in liquid or powder form and produces almost immediate relaxant effects. Other effects include vomiting, dizziness, and drowsiness. Proper medical care is required to recover from the effects of this drug, and emergency room treatment is often necessary. Though GHB has a salty taste, it is virtually undetectable when diluted in sweet liquids.

"Fry cigarettes."

These have emerged as a date rape drug. Also called amp, water-water, drank, and wetdaddy, they are tobacco or marijuana cigarettes dipped in embalming fluid (a compound of formaldehyde, methanol, ethyl alcohol or ethanol, and other solvents). Occasionally, fry cigarettes are laced with PCP, which makes them extremely dangerous—even deadly. A study conducted by the Texas Commission on Alcohol and Drug Abuse quoted men who used fry cigarettes in date rape as saying, "You can control a girl more than you can with Rohypnol." The cigarettes are easy to detect, however, since they smell like gasoline when they burn, and can taste like rubbing alcohol.

How can you avoid these drugs? Here's a plan that can greatly reduce the chances of accidentally ingesting them. At first look, you may think some of these suggestions are a bit paranoid. Remember to put the suggestions into context—I'm not talking about doing these things when you're with your usual network of people. I'm saying to use common sense and your sixth sense whenever you're in a situation that makes you suspicious in any way. The point isn't to be suspicious or afraid of *every* party or bar you go to, but rather to be alert to what's going on around you, no matter where you are.

Top Ten Tips for Avoiding Date Rape Drugs

1. BYOB—bring your own beverages if you're going into a situation you're unsure of. If you bring your own, you know it's safe if you keep tabs on it. If you drink alcoholic beverages, bring something you don't need to pour out into a glass, like beer or wine coolers. Putting drinks into open glasses makes them more vulnerable.

2. Go to the bar yourself, even if someone offers to buy you a drink. Watch it being made, and don't let anyone but the bartender, waiter, or waitress handle it before you do.

3. Don't leave your drink unattended. Always carry it with you, even into the rest room. That's when many women are tempted to hand a drink to someone and say, "Would you hold this for me until I come back?" Wrong move. Take it along.

4. Don't dip into the punch bowl or drink from a container or flask being passed around the crowd. Essentially, don't drink from anything you haven't controlled from the start.

5. Be alert to anyone who keeps refilling your drink without you asking for more. Once again, it's a situation where you aren't in control of what's being poured into your glass.

6. Create a "buddy plan." You and your friends watch out for each other, and may want to have a "designated sober person." (Hint: This could also be your designated driver.) If anyone shows signs of becoming overly intoxicated in an unusually short amount of time, get them to a safe place immediately. Don't let them out of your sight!

7. Always have a way to get home on your own. If you're not with friends and can't use a buddy system, you might pre-arrange with someone to come and pick you up. Or make sure you have cab fare and the cab company's phone number with you so you don't have to accept rides from anyone. Someone else's car is a vulnerable place to be.

8. If you smoke, bring plenty of your own cigarettes so you don't have to accept any from strangers. If you do, be alert to any odd aromas or tastes, and don't be afraid to stub it out quickly if you sense either of these things.

9. Have something to eat before going out. Drugs can be put into food, too, though I've never seen it happen. But it's

not beyond the realm of possibility, so use your instincts. Judge each situation on its own. If you have a good support group at the party and know everyone, enjoy yourself.

10. If anything or anyone is suspicious to you or makes you feel uncomfortable, take action. Get away from people you aren't sure of. Avoid becoming trapped in secluded places or rooms. Don't be afraid of refusing a drink, asking for another one, or spilling one out if you didn't see how it was being made or are suspicious of it in any way. Your mind can make things like this bigger than they really are, so don't worry about being embarrassed. At parties, leaving a drink, dumping it out, or not finishing it will hardly be noticed, if at all.

It's time to play "What If . . . ?" Suppose you find yourself in a date rape situation. What would you do to get out of it immediately?

What If?

- First and foremost, trust your instincts! If a situation feels uncomfortable or causes you concern, remove yourself from it immediately. Don't be afraid to ask someone for help.
- Try to stay calm. If you've thought about this ahead of time and have a plan, you already know your options.
- Be assertive, even abrasive if you have to. If you perceive things getting out of hand, pull out all the stops. Be rude, get angry, scream and shout—do whatever it takes to alert others to your plight and to send a clear message that it's *over*. Don't be afraid to call the police if you have to.
- Say no *forcefully*. Keep saying no.

- Use escape tactics: Scream loudly, push the offender away, make an attempt to run, kick and flail to keep the person away from you. The best time to escape is at the beginning of the attack, so do whatever it takes to get away.

- Consider a counterattack. Fighting back is a tough decision; I'll talk more about making such a decision in chapter 10, on self-defense.

Defensive options:

1. Poking the attacker's eyes, biting his finger or ear as hard as you can, grabbing and twisting his genitals, and scratching at his eyes. Kicking and kneeing in the groin isn't as effective as you might think, mostly because it can be difficult to hit the mark in the first place. Leaving scratches, however, can make a date rapist rethink his actions—often he'll convince himself that what he's doing isn't really rape. But if he starts getting injured, it can jolt him back to reality. Plus, it can help the victim prove that sex wasn't consensual.

2. Pretending to pass out or faint. Wait for him to drop his guard and loosen his hold on you, then run or fight to get away.

3. Try a ruse on your attacker that would make him want to stop:

   - Tell him your father or brother is a cop or an attorney, if he doesn't already know what they do. Fears of a relentless investigation by the "boys in blue" or humiliating, crushing lawsuits may wilt his ambitions, so to speak.

   - Claim you have a venereal disease. Pull out all the stops

here—make it so bad that he simply won't want to take the chance that you might be lying. Start spitting on him and ask him if he wants AIDS.

- Claim you've recently had a serious operation, are menstruating, or are pregnant.
- Pretend to be sick—start gagging or choking, or pretend to vomit.

If You Become a Victim

Should you become a victim of date rape, get medical attention immediately. Seek support and counseling to help you through the trauma. Contact organizations and support groups, some of which are listed in the resources section.

"Rolling" and the Mickey Finn

This is the place to discuss "rolling" because it's done with the help of "Mickey Finn." This robbery crime is common, but most often goes unreported. You'll understand why in a moment.

Here's how it works: The victims are men, usually married, and generally businessmen on a trip. The female perpetrator, usually beautiful and young, searches for the perfect target in upscale hotel bars and lounges, and upscale clubs known to attract tourists or business travelers. She looks for a man who's alone. He may obviously be a traveling businessman, and may obviously be married. If he's not wearing a wedding ring, she may determine if he's married through conversation. Now, there's no easy way to say this, gentlemen, but the most important thing she looks for is a man who isn't used to having beautiful young women lavish him with attention—which is then exactly what she does. After she's totally captivated the victim and has him eating out of the palm of her hand (or he's bought dinner for her), she gets invited to his room, where she has no problem separating him from his wallet, his watch, and his jewelry. Why is it so easy? Because she's "slipped him a Mickey"—Finn, that is. She's spiked his drink, and he never stood a chance.

There are plenty of drugs to choose from, including the date rape drugs described earlier. But often these criminals use veterinary tranquilizers or other colorless, odorless pills, deftly slipping them into the man's drink at the first opportunity. She chooses traveling businessmen as targets because they're often alone, and they have to leave town as soon as their business is over. She does really well to find a guy with a morning flight the next day. Married men are much preferred because, even if one had the inclination to press charges, he probably wouldn't—that would require admitting in court that he had a woman in his room. So as you can see, it's fairly foolproof, and the victim is usually the fool.

Incidentally, it's not certain where the term *Mickey Finn* comes from. It's generally associated with "knockout drops" or any spiked drink designed to knock a person out. Allegedly, Mickey Finn was a notorious Chicago tavern owner who ran several criminal enterprises from his Lone Star Saloon and Palm Garden on the South Side. He supposedly spiked customers' drinks with "white stuff" that may have been chloral hydrate, which knocked them out cold. Later, the unconscious customers were dragged to a back room where all their valuables were taken before they were dumped—often naked—into an alley. As with Rohypnol, the victims remembered nothing when they woke up. Other tales describe a Mickey Finn as a purgative, a laxative given to an obnoxious bar customer to give him a reason to leave without the bartender having to throw him out. Whichever it is, the end result is the same.

The best advice I can give on how to avoid being rolled is: Be alert, be aware, and be as honest as you can with yourself. Guys, that means that if you're wondering why such a beautiful young woman is paying so much flattering attention to you, then you're probably right on target. That's your instinct talking, your "reality check," so listen to it. Go back and read the advice to women on how to avoid date rape and its associated drugs, particularly the advice on avoiding drugs in drinks. Then always be alert to what another person's real motives might be.

Chapter 9 # Natural Disasters and Terrorist Attacks

The Federal Emergency
Management Agency
responded to forty-three declared
disasters in 2001.
These disasters covered
twenty-nine different states plus
Puerto Rico and the District of
Columbia. The disasters
encompassed ice storms, terrorism,
floods, earthquakes, tropical
storms, tornadoes, windstorms,
and a hurricane.

General Preparations

Our lives were changed overnight by the September 11, 2001, terrorist attacks. Faced with new threats, it's more important than ever to think ahead and have a plan. Our imaginations can create some pretty difficult scenarios, but visiting those thoughts is what makes them less scary, even if it's only a little less so. We fear the unknown, and by at least contemplating the unknown, we can make some measure of preparation for dealing with it, should it ever become reality. We may find ourselves so bolstered by the planning that we not only see the possibility of survival, but embrace the possibility of emerging from the ordeal stronger than ever.

I got into a discussion about disaster preparation with some of my friends, and I asked them what they planned to do if a disaster struck. They told me they were all coming over to my house. That was both flattering and frightening to me. I was glad to hear that they thought my preparedness was thorough and viable. But living in south Florida, where hurricanes are a way of life, it surprised me that these people hadn't taken some very basic measures to help get themselves through a disaster. I told them they really need to make their own plans, because there's not room for everybody at my place.

Years ago when I was a cop, I was the civil defense liaison between the police department and other city services. I attended regular planning meetings for man-made catastrophes and natural disasters, the latter of which is a big topic in south Florida. I learned that preparations for various disaster scenarios are very much the same, because the aftermath of many such disasters is similar. A large tornado, a natural gas explosion, a bomb detonating in a building—if you've seen news images of these occurrences, think about how much alike they look in the aftermath. Destruction of property, injuries, utilities going out of service, inability to reach victims, lack of supplies—all these things happen. With this in mind, a good place to start your disaster planning is with some basic measures that can provide for your safety and security in more than one possible situation.

Disasters, either man-made or natural, often put you in a position of being isolated in your home for a period of time, either by choice or by necessity. Whether it's earthquakes or tornadoes, winter storms or hurricanes, floods or even volcanic eruptions, the basic preparations you make should be geared toward that scenario of isolation and shelter.

What about the new disasters everyone currently fears? Terrorism, biological attack—our country has already been a victim of these. Going through that difficult period has made everyone think about preparedness. Just as basic personal security practices can help you in many situations, you can also extrapolate basic disaster preparations to cover scenarios of terrorism and chemical or biological attack.

First, a word about survivalists and disaster preparation: Being prepared for major disasters does *not* automatically make you a survivalist. I bring up this point only because the term can have negative connotations, and I don't want people to think negatively about being prepared. You're not crazy, kooky, nutso, or "out there" because you're thinking ahead, gathering a few supplies, and making plans in case of disaster. To me, it doesn't make you a survivalist, but it does go a long way toward making you a *survivor*.

I couldn't ever call myself a survivalist, even though I certainly put survival high on my list of things to do in case of disaster. I'm not cut out for the survivalist lifestyle—I like restaurants, pizza delivery, movies, friends, and bookstores too much to live in the wilderness. But I do like to think I'm a survivor, so I definitely have a disaster plan.

Think the Unthinkable

Some of the topics covered in this section used to be unthinkable. You still may not want to think about them. But remember that if you think things through and have a plan, decision making at the time of a disaster can come easier, quicker, and with more confidence. Training and mentally planning for possible situations must go hand in hand. Well-trained people can still freeze up if they haven't made a mental plan to cover whatever might occur.

When I make my plans, I start with an assumption that has proved itself out over and over: that people in this country are pretty resilient, and they pull together when disaster strikes. Whether it's a natural disaster or a terrorist attack, people in one part of the country immediately begin working to help those in the stricken area. With this in mind, my basic disaster plan covers the survival of my loved ones and me for at least one week *without outside assistance,* and does so as comfortably as possible. This basic plan assumes that we will "shelter in place," which is take shelter at home rather than to evacuate, and that outside help will come within one week.

Start by identifying what emergencies you are most likely to face. This can help you in assembling your emergency supplies. I keep certain emergency supplies on hand at all times. There's nothing wrong with stocking up on a few things, and not having to rush out to procure supplies when a threat approaches. In fact, as you go through this list, you may find that you already have a number of these items on hand and, in fact, use them in your everyday life. This can make disaster planning easier.

Top Ten Disaster Supplies

1. Camp stove with fuel.

A portable camping stove with an emergency supply of fuel is easy to store, and an absolute must if you have to shelter in place and utilities are out of service. I have two small single-burner camping stoves—one that burns white gas and the other, propane. Any good-quality portable stove will do. I like propane because it's safer to store extra fuel than having cans of gas around. But I have one of each because in an emergency, you can't be sure which fuel might be easier to obtain. Better to cover all bases. Avoid charcoal stoves—you can't use them in a closed space because they generate deadly carbon monoxide.

2. Water-storage containers.

I have three plastic five-gallon jugs stored empty and out of the way in the back of a closet. When a hurricane is approaching, I fill them up—along with my bathtub—and don't have to run out to buy bottled water. Additionally, I've stored a couple of filled gallons of water, just in case a disaster strikes suddenly, with no warning. The rule of thumb on water rationing is one gallon of water per day per person. I drink a lot of water, so I plan on two gallons a day per person.

Along with water, I keep at least one gallon of unscented bleach. It's an inexpensive and reliable disinfectant that can also be used to purify water in an emergency. It's generally advised to use sixteen drops of bleach per gallon of water, and never more than thirty-two drops per gallon. If you plan to measure anything in drops, it helps to keep an eyedropper around, too.

3. Food.

Emergency food should consist of items that store easily and have a long shelf life. Better yet, consider foods you have around the house all the time and consume and replace regularly. I've never stashed away canned meats or other strange items I don't ordinarily eat. I figure if a disaster strikes, why force myself to eat lousy food? A lot of foods I eat regularly are easily stored and cooked, so I include them in my emergency food stores. The list consists of: pasta, tomato sauce, smoked oysters, cereal, beans, rice, coffee, tea, and the few canned vegetables and soups I do like. With a stove, water, and fuel to cook with, I can eat pretty much as I usually do. When storing canned goods, don't forget to include a manual can opener!

4. Duct tape and garbage bags.

Duct tape is a wonderful product that has a multitude of uses. It can help keep your windows from shattering in a strong wind, or help to seal a room in the event of a chemical attack. Garbage bags are for garbage. You don't know how long it might be until trash pickup resumes, so having good, sturdy garbage bags can help make life much less smelly. They have many other uses as well, such as sealing off openings or serving as makeshift ponchos in bad weather.

5. First-aid supplies.

My medicine cabinet is my first-aid kit. A lot of the things you keep around on a daily basis can also serve you as a disaster first-aid kit. I always have the following items on hand: adhesive bandage strips, antibiotic ointment, aspirin, gauze, iodine, hydrogen peroxide, eyedrops, antidiarrhea medication, tweezers, and other items that people should probably have on hand anyway. If you have those basic items, you don't need a separate first-aid kit.

Additional items I like to have include a package of two-part temporary tooth cement, a brand my dentist recommended. This stuff has saved members of my family a painful weekend on several occasions. I also keep several surgical masks, which are useful if I ever have any sanding to do as well. I try to not run low on the items I do keep, and therefore I don't feel the need to have a first-aid kit. I do have a small travel first-aid kit, however, with fewer items; it's reserved for travel use.

6. Custom-need items.

Everyone has certain specific needs that will have to be met during an emergency. You'll need to have a week's supply of these items on hand as well. These might include pet food, toiletries and personal hygiene items, prescription medications, disposable contact lenses, vitamin supplements, baby formula and diapers, denture products—anything that might be important to you. For things like this, take time to figure out how much lasts you for a week. Then, when you have that week's supply on hand, you simply buy more. That way you'll always have enough.

By the way, I also keep a few extra rolls of toilet paper stored in the closet. It's just one of those things I don't like to run out of. If you're a smoker, you might put away a week's worth of cigarettes—one of the worst disasters I've experienced was going through a crisis with a smoker who hadn't planned ahead.

7. Battery-powered radio and batteries.
That boom box you take on picnics will do just fine if it can be run on batteries. No need to get something special. Just be sure to have plenty of extra fresh batteries on hand.

8. Flashlight with batteries.
I keep a big flashlight near the door, probably one of those habits I have left over from being a cop. I also keep a few mini flashlights around the house, and one in every car. I get the type that use the same batteries I put in the TV, stereo, and VCR remote controls. When I have to replace the batteries in my remotes, I use the ones from my flashlights. This way I'm always putting fresh batteries into the flashlights.

9. Sleeping bags.

I have one for every person in the house. They're useful even if it's just a case of the electricity going off on a cold night. Treat it like a camping trip—fire up the camping stove, make some hot chocolate, and crawl into the sleeping bags.

10. Cash.

I try to keep a few dollars around—not thousands, but enough to tide us over in case banks are closed or ATM machines don't work. If you have a week's worth of food on hand and a real emergency strikes, you probably won't need too much money anyway.

It's not that difficult to stock up with these supplies. You probably have most of them in your home already—you just never thought of them as "disaster supplies." The most you may need to buy is likely a camping stove, fuel, and some extra batteries. Quilts and comforters can substitute for sleeping bags if you don't have them. Increase your supply of unrefrigerated foods to last at least seven days, wash out and put away the one-gallon milk jugs for water storage, and you're covered.

Safe Rooms

I discussed safe rooms in chapter 3, but this same room can be put to several uses. In this case the basic safe room suggestions apply, but the room you retreat to in an emergency now is part of your disaster plan.

If you haven't chosen a safe room yet, consider an interior bathroom. This is what I use for a safe room. It has a toilet, the tub can be used for water storage, and it's where my medicine cabinet—aka first-aid kit—is located. It's an easy room to get to in case an intruder invades, it can be sealed off against chemical attack (using duct tape and the shower curtain or garbage bags), and it's a good room to take refuge in if the roof happens to blow off during a hurricane. I don't necessarily think I'll ever need to use it for any of those reasons, but it's in my plan because of the remote possibility that I *might* have to use it.

Vehicles as Places of Refuge

Unless you have a convertible, your vehicle—car, truck, SUV—may be an excellent place to take refuge in a number of emergencies. You can put up the windows, close the vents, and turn off the air conditioner to keep chemicals and dust out. It offers safety from lightning in a storm, as long as flying debris doesn't break a window.

Vehicles also offer some protection against fire. I know this firsthand. Someone once threw a Molotov cocktail onto my police car. It broke, igniting gasoline and spreading flames over the hood. I figured it was safer to stay in the car than to jump out and possibly get burning gasoline on my clothes, or have another Molotov cocktail thrown at my head. I rolled the window up, turned off the air conditioner, and kept driving. Even though wind fanned the flames, they quickly burned themselves out as the fuel was spent. It actually caused very little damage to the vehicle. But that flaming police car driving down the street must have been quite a sight!

Family and Loved Ones Contact Plan

Being separated from your loved ones during a disaster can cause a lot of anxiety and worry. When Hurricane Andrew hit south Florida in 1992, one of my employees went through such an ordeal. His parents lived in Homestead, in the heart of the storm's devastation. He had no idea if they were alive, injured, or unharmed—their telephone was out, and he had no other way of contacting them. Therefore he had little choice but to try to drive into the stricken area to find out if his parents were safe. He didn't get far—the roads were blocked and the National Guard turned him back. Meanwhile, his parents were equally anxious to let him know they *were* all right. They had no phone or electricity, and their car had been destroyed, but otherwise they were safe and uninjured. They needed some supplies and hoped he could bring them these things as soon as the roads were open. In an effort to contact him, they walked several miles and eventually found a working pay phone. They tried to call him, and were surprised to find they could actually make a call out of Homestead. But they were unable to reach their son—though his home was far enough away from Miami to be undamaged, it was close enough to the storm that his phone lines were down as well. The result was a family in the dark about each other's whereabouts, frantic to make contact but unable to leave word anywhere.

If we happen to be separated from our loved ones when disaster strikes, it can be a nightmare trying to find out if they're safe and where they are. This doesn't have to happen. Putting a family emergency contact plan in place can give everyone peace of mind.

Here's how it works: You set up a contact hub, usually a close friend or family member who lives in another city or state. You want someone who lives far enough away that a disaster in your area isn't likely to affect that person. Now he's your emergency communication center. If you're separated from your family and can't reach them during a disaster, you direct your communication efforts toward this person, as does everyone else in the family. The contact person can pass messages among you, and everyone can know each other's whereabouts. You can reciprocate and serve as the contact person for your contact as well. Exchange all important phone numbers with each other—home, office, pagers, and cell phones for every member of your family. Don't forget e-mail addresses. Interestingly, after the World Trade Center attack, it was nearly impossible to get a phone call into or out of the New York City area due to extreme call volume. Yet I exchanged many e-mails all day with friends who live in Manhattan. The Internet was still accessible, even though you couldn't place a voice phone call.

The contact plan would have worked nicely for my friend and his family after the hurricane. If they had agreed on an out-of-town contact person (*way* out of town in the case of Florida and hurricanes), they could have left messages for each other and eliminated a great deal of anxiety. The parents might have also gotten their much-needed emergency supplies a lot faster.

Speaking of New York, I want to mention another recent case of a couple who live in New Jersey and were in New York on business at the time of the terrorist attack on the World Trade Center. They were supposed to meet at the World Trade Center for a late lunch, then take the train back home together. The couple have two grown children—a daughter who lives in

California and travels as part of her job, and a son in the military. (You might already see where this is going.) At the time of the terrorist attack, all four people were on the road, trying to call each other to find out if everyone was all right. Luckily they were all okay, but they spent a rather frantic day worrying and trying to contact each other—a day that could have been avoided if they had prearranged an out-of-the-area emergency contact person to call.

Communication Plans

What else can you do to plan for limited communication during a disaster? Here are some suggestions:

1. Carry your out-of-town contact's name and phone number in your wallet or purse. Use an "In Case of Emergency" card. Be sure your children have one as well. The out-of-town name and number offers added security in case your child loses the card—there's nothing a potential predator can use. But if police or other emergency personnel need to find you, they can still locate you through your out-of-town contact.

2. Set up an in-town contact person for emergencies, as well as a meeting place that's not too close to your home. If something localized separates you, it may still be easy to make contact within your area. The plan can be as simple as saying: "If for any reason you can't go home, go to Aunt Sara's house across town."

3. Set up a "fire" meeting place near your home. I've seen parents rush back into a blazing house because they thought a child was still inside. The child was outside and

safe all along, but the parent couldn't find him in the confusion. As part of a complete fire safety plan, select a place to meet. It could be a neighbor's house or the big elm tree half a block down the street. It may sound overly simple, but lives have been saved by designating such a meeting place.

Children and Disasters

When I was a small child, my father took me by the hand and showed me where we would all meet if there was a fire, or if we had to escape our house without warning for any other reason. He talked to me about what to do in a hurricane—I'd heard the story plenty of times about how my mother's family home was completely blown away in the 1926 hurricane. I wasn't scared when my father told me things like this, though. He spoke calmly and gave me a sense that what he was saying was important. But most of all, his talk assured me that we were all in this together, and he needed my help to make planning work. That's what made me feel better.

Disasters can be frightening for adults, but they can be traumatic for children, who will look to adults for guidance on how to act. Fear is normal, even healthy—fear is what motivates us to action and helps keep us safe. When making family plans for hurricanes, fire, or any possible disaster, it's important to talk with children and understand something about how they perceive scary events and react to them.

I asked David Walsh, Ph.D., a psychologist and the president of the National Institute on Media and the Family in Minneapolis, to tell me about children and fear. Dr. Walsh is the author of seven books on children and parenting, and he offered the following facts:

- Fear is an intense concern or worry caused by real and/or imagined danger.
- Fear is a natural and normal reaction to a scary event.
- Children younger than five years old cannot always tell fantasy from reality. Media depictions of attacks and disasters can be as scary as the real thing.
- Some children will exhibit fear through behavior, not words. Examples might include a lump in the throat, crying, abnormal fussiness, or agitation.
- Sensitive children with vivid imaginations are more prone to intense fear reactions.
- All children, even the very young, have a sixth sense that enables them to be aware of an adult's fear and anxiety.
- Children will respond differently at different ages.

To help children with fear, Dr. Walsh advises this overall strategy: Acknowledge their fear while simultaneously reassuring them.

"Take your cues from the child," he says. "Don't assume they are more afraid than they may be. Conversely, don't assume that they are unaware of what has happened."

Dr. Walsh gives the following advice on dealing with children in the event of a disaster, or if you're making your family disaster plans:

- Take children's fear seriously. Don't try to talk them out of it.
- Respond calmly. Don't exaggerate their fears by using extreme language or by overreacting.

- Answer their questions directly, but don't give them more information than they are asking for or than they need.
- Provide physical reassurance with lots of hugs and touching.
- Make sure they know that it's okay to ask questions.
- Manage the media diet according to their age.

    Remind children of other national tragedies (for example, the bombing of Pearl Harbor, the *Challenger* space shuttle explosion, the World Trade Center attack) and explain that life goes on, and the United States does overcome these tragedies.

How to Handle Children

Children of different ages need to be handled differently, since their perceptions of events vary. Here are Dr. Walsh's guidelines:

In early childhood:

Even though very young babies and toddlers may not know what's going on, they may pick up a parent's worry and anxiety with their "sixth sense."

Try to stay calm around babies and toddlers.

Maintain normal routines as much as possible. Routines are reassuring for babies.

Shield babies and toddlers from media reports as much as possible.

Preschoolers:

Preschoolers will be more tuned in to what's happening. They probably hear or see media reports, and have likely heard others discussing events. Preschoolers are most concerned about their own safety and the safety of their parents, relatives, and friends. They're not always able to distinguish between fantasy and reality.

Acknowledge that something very scary has happened or is happening, but you and other adults are making sure they'll be safe; the adults will figure out what's going on.

Give them lots of hugs and physical reassurance.

Try to maintain the child's normal routine.

Don't let preschoolers watch nonstop scary news reports on TV. They can't control what's happening, and watching the reports will only scare them.

Preschoolers will need more comfort, especially at bedtime.

School-age children:

These children will be more aware of what's going on and the reactions of other people. They're also most concerned about their own safety, and that of family and friends.

Be honest with them. Tell them what you know about what's happening without exaggerating or overreacting.

Acknowledge that something very scary is happening or has happened.

Emphasize that they're safe and that adults will find out what's happening.

Limit their TV coverage.

Continue normal routines as much as possible.

These children will need more comfort and lots of reassurance.

Make sure you talk to the child. Don't assume that kids are too young to know what's going on.

Middle school children:

Children this age will be very aware of what's going on. They may be prone to exaggeration. Jokes or humor can mask fears for this age group.

Talk to the middle school child and answer any questions.

Acknowledge any feelings of fear, horror, and anger.

Provide comfort and reassurance.

Children this age will be more interested in details. Share what you know but don't overwhelm them.

Some children may act out scary feelings or become more withdrawn. Ask them to tell you about their feelings.

Use historical examples to explain that bad things happen to innocent people, but as people and as a nation we go on with our lives and resolve bad situations.

High schoolers:

High schoolers may have already talked about events with friends. Be honest with them and tell them what's going on. This age may be glued to TV, eager for news and details.

Talk about what's happening. Discuss both your and their feelings.

Acknowledge fear, sadness, and anger.

Some teens may just block out the whole thing and refuse to acknowledge that anything big has happened, or that they care. This often masks real fears and feelings of being overwhelmed.

Some teens may make jokes. Let them know it's not funny without lecturing them.

Some teens may be very interested in discussing issues that events raise. Be willing to engage them in serious discussions.

In the case of terrorism, be careful to avoid blaming a whole group of people or targeting particular groups.

Use historical tragedies as a basis for conversation. Talk about how the situation may be resolved in terms of rescue workers, governmental responses, foreign policy changes, and so on.

Knowing how to appropriately handle children of all ages in a disaster is important for their security, as well as the whole family's.

Evacuation Plans

I've seen specific areas evacuated for a hurricane emergency. I estimate that 80 percent of the residents heeded the call to evacuate, while the rest stayed to ride it out at home. Since it was a hurricane, there was plenty of time, and the evacuation was orderly and efficient. Even traffic moved fairly well in most places. Only areas with two-lane roads moved a bit slower.

I've often considered what it would be like if an entire city, county, or region had to evacuate quickly. There are plans to cover such scenarios, created by planners at all levels of government. But no one can possibly know how such evacuation plans will play out in reality. There are too many variables, and those variables also affect your personal emergency evacuation planning.

Consider these questions:

- Why is an evacuation order being given?
- Are you leaving for a few hours? For days? Will you *ever* be coming back to your home?
- Where will you go in any case?
- If forced to evacuate, how much time will you have to plan? Days? Hours? Minutes? Seconds?

Most of these questions will be answered when an event happens, but in some cases you won't learn answers until much later. The likelihood of an immediate forced evacuation is remote, but it can happen, and sometimes for reasons you may never have considered.

Several years ago, my mother was awakened in the early-morning hours by a police loudspeaker announcing that there was a chlorine gas leak in the water treatment plant across the street from her apartment complex. All residents were to evacuate immediately. She did as she was instructed, and managed to make the most of it by going to visit her sister in the next town. Though we had gone over emergency plans together, she never called me to let me know where she had gone. Her excuse was that she didn't want to wake me so early. I figured out where she was pretty quickly, though, since she and her sister were so close. But I did have a few anxious moments when I first heard the news that morning—and she was having coffee with her sister.

The moral of that story is: If you have an emergency plan, don't be afraid to use it.

I'd never really thought about the water treatment plant near my mother's home as a potential source of danger that might require leaving home in a hurry. It's time to ask yourself: What possible dangers lurk in *my* neighborhood or surrounding area?

Think of the possibilities:

- Do you live near a nuclear power plant? How close is it?
- Is there a water treatment plant that uses chlorine nearby?
- Is your area subject to hurricanes or floods? When was the last time you had such an event, and how serious was it? What did you do?
- Do you live near railroad tracks? Do railcars on the line carry hazardous chemicals? Has there ever been an accident or chemical spill nearby?
- Do you live near an interstate highway with lots of truck traffic? Have you seen any tanker trucks that may carry hazardous materials?
- Do you live in or near a wooded area? Is the area prone to fire? When was the last fire in the area?
- Have there ever been riots or civil unrest in your area? How long ago? How serious were they?

If you're unsure of potential dangers near your home, you can find out more by contacting your local emergency planning office or emergency operations center. Usually this task is done by your local government, either county or municipality. It's not usually a state or federal function at this level, so look for the correct agency in the local government pages of your phone book. If you can't find the proper agency, contact the fire department (nonemergency number, please!) or your city hall and ask for advice. When you reach the proper emergency planning agency, ask about potential dangers, as well as what planning has been done for such emergencies, including official evacuation routes. All this information is vital when forming your personal evacuation plan.

Depending on the nature of the emergency, it may be safer to stay in your home. In Florida, coastal areas are routinely evacuated when hurricanes approach, but most inland areas aren't. Nevertheless, people in storm areas are generally aware of official evacuation routes, as well as some of their own devising—because you just never know. If you've thought ahead of time about how you might clear out of your area, you can act quickly and calmly if you're ordered to evacuate, or if you choose to go on your own.

Evacuation plan checklist:

When making your evacuation plan, go through this checklist of important things to remember:

1. Know where you'll go if you have to leave your home in an emergency. Depending on the cause of the evacuation, you may need to consider high ground (flood), going inland (hurricane), a rural setting if you live in the city (terrorist attack on a heavily populated area). Next, will you go to a public shelter? A friend or family member's home? To a hotel? If you'll be going to a friend or relative's, be sure you can get there on a tank of gas (about 150 to 200 miles away).

2. Know what travel modes you might use. You could travel by foot, car, motorcycle, horse, boat, or combination of several if necessary.

3. Locate important documents. Have a safe place at home to store documents so you always know where they are if you need to grab them and run. Social Security cards, deeds, life insurance policies, and homeowner's/renter's insurance policies are all important.

4. Plan your evacuation routes. Take into account things like bridges and low-lying areas that may be flooded or otherwise block your route.

5. Don't forget your family emergency contact plan. Make one if you don't have one already. You need this in place if an evacuation is called and you are separated from your loved ones.

6. Know how to turn off gas, electricity, and water. Make sure everyone in the family knows how, too. You don't want to return from an evacuation to find your home burned down due to a gas leak, or discover that broken pipes have flooded your entire house.

7. Learn about your community's emergency alert systems. If you live in an area near a nuclear facility, there may be sirens to warn of an accident. Many communities have warning horns and sirens for other dangers, such as chemical spills, fires, and more.

8. Have a family meeting to review and understand the evacuation plan. This is to ensure everyone's safety should an evacuation be called when you're not with them. A frank

discussion about everyone's fears and worries can help develop confidence during a crisis. Don't wait for the hurricane to approach or the tornado to be sighted before talking about what everyone should do.

9. Find out what emergency evacuation procedures are in place at your children's schools. See how you might coordinate them with your own.

10. Think about what alternate evacuation routes you might take if you anticipate serious traffic jams. Depending on the reason for the evacuation, you may be seeing a mass exodus of the entire population (this might be the scenario after a nuclear plant accident, for instance). If you've thought about alternative routes, you might dodge traffic jams. Consider alternate modes of transportation as well. If your gut tells you to abandon your vehicle and try to get out on foot, be prepared to follow your instincts.

11. Consider what you'd take with you if evacuated by car. Now consider what you'd take if you had to evacuate on foot. Don't forget the possibility that you may go partway by vehicle and need to switch to another mode of transportation.

12. Make a plan for pet care. Pets are family, too, so consider possible needs such as extra food, water, tranquilizers to help them cope, sturdy pet carriers, ID tags, and more. Talk with your veterinarian for more advice specific to your pets.

13. Don't forget to check that your insurance is adequate. This part of your plan is for your peace of mind later on. I've noticed that people who have excellent homeowner's insur-

ance tend to be less concerned about leaving things or being "wiped out" by losses, and hesitate less to flee their home in an emergency.

14. Take a first-aid class. I firmly believe in doing this. I've taken refresher courses and had nurses and paramedics as classmates, there to brush up on their skills. If you've never taken such a class, you may be surprised at the extra boost of confidence it gives you to be so prepared.

15. Go over your emergency evacuation plans at least once a year. I review mine each year before hurricane season, checking that all supply items are on hand and adding to any stores that need replenishing.

On the subject of what to take with you, I remember the first time I heard an evacuation order. I thought, *What do you mean, evacuate? I can't leave all my stuff behind!* Let me tell you, if you really have to evacuate, you can easily leave that stuff behind. I know I developed a whole new perspective on "stuff" and evacuations after Hurricane Andrew. Since then, I've bought more insurance and put my irreplaceable items (photo albums, family treasures) in a place I can easily grab them to take along if I have to hit the road. I believe the most important thing, worth far more than any "stuff" I have, is the safety and security of me and my loved ones.

I have a checklist of the limited number of items I plan to take with me if I have to evacuate. I can probably gather those things plus my emergency supplies and be out the door in less than fifteen minutes. When seconds can count, being prepared to flee quickly is what's really important.

Final hints and ideas for your evacuation plan:

1. Back your car into the driveway. If you feel threatened by approaching disaster, whether it's a wildfire, hurricane, or other danger that you have forewarning of, pack your car ahead of time, make sure it's filled up with gas, and back it into your driveway. This is part psychological and part practical—it can give you a feeling of confidence to know it's ready to go and headed in the right direction, because it really is!

2. Leave a contact number on your door. Consider leaving your out-of-town contact's number. Tape it to the door with clear plastic tape, which will protect it from the elements.

3. Consider wearing several layers of clothing when evacuating, depending on the type of danger. Chemical spill or attack, nuclear hazards, even biological attack can contaminate clothing. Wearing extra layers allows you to shed the contaminated clothing as you move farther from the danger. Additional clothes can also help protect you from fire.

4. When it's time to go, gather what you're taking, plus a change of clothes or two, turn off your air-conditioning or heat, shut off any utilities you can, lock your doors and windows—and you're out of there.

Natural Disasters

Floods

I'm sure you've seen the spectacle on TV—massive flooding, cars swept into streets turned into roaring rivers, people clinging to the vehicles for dear life, awaiting rescue as rain pours down in torrents, fueling the floodwaters even more. It probably took only a few minutes for the victims to find themselves in that situation. They aren't called "flash floods" for nothing.

Floods are the second most common natural disaster, next to fire, and flash floods are the number one weather killer in the United States. Hard to believe, but when thinking about the forces of nature, consider this: The power of floodwaters flowing against a stalled car can be as much as five hundred pounds! Not only that, as water rises, cars become more buoyant, and it can take as little as two feet of rushing water to sweep most cars away. Even more surprising, just six inches of fast-moving water can sweep people off their feet.

Floods can be caused by broken dams or levies, spring rains, thunderstorms, hurricanes, or melting snow. They can happen in a short period of time or develop slowly over a period of days. Fast-moving water only a few feet deep can destroy buildings, rip out trees, and carry dangerous debris. Once flooding starts, you may have precious little time to get to safety.

Remember the following tips when making your flood preparedness plan:

Top Ten Tips for Surviving Floods

1. Evacuate if you're ordered to do so. Don't assume you'll be safe. You don't know what conditions may have prompted the evacuation order.

2. Review your emergency evacuation routes for high ground. Floodwaters could block your way if you haven't checked for low-lying areas. Use one of your alternative routes if necessary.

3. Secure any propane or gas tanks near your home so they don't float. Ripped gas lines can cause explosions.

4. Install septic tank backup valves or check valves in your water and sewer system to keep sewage from backing up into your home during a flood.

5. If your car stalls in floodwaters, abandon the vehicle if you can do so safely. Get to higher ground immediately. Remember that two feet of water will sweep away almost any vehicle, and it takes only one foot of water to take away a small car.

6. Avoid downed electrical wires. Dangerous currents can travel as much as a hundred yards in water.

7. Stay out of floodwaters if you can. They can carry silt, filth, waste, and disease. Make sure children don't play in the water.

8. Watch out for poisonous snakes. Floodwaters can force snakes out of their natural habitat and, just like you, onto higher ground, or bring water snakes right to your door.

9. Stay away from storm drains, and the edges of rivers, ditches, ravines, or culverts. Flood-soaked areas may give way unexpectedly, causing slides that can sweep anyone standing nearby into floodwaters.

10. Don't go near flooded areas until the all-clear is given. You can't tell if floodwaters are rising or falling just by looking at them.

Floods can be quite dangerous, sweeping away even houses if the current is swift enough. So the most important thing to remember is that if an evacuation order is given, follow it. Right now, you might want to check your homeowner's insurance and see if you have a flood rider. Insurance won't automatically cover flood damage. You might consider spending a few dollars to gain this extra coverage. Once again, knowing you can replace your possessions can make abandoning your home an easier decision when danger strikes.

Tornadoes

The power of tornadoes can be awesome. These rapidly rotating columns of air attached to thunderstorms can last anywhere from a few seconds to more than an hour. Sometimes, storms can spawn families of tornadoes that can last several hours. The funnel storms can be nearly stationary, or move along rapidly, destroying whatever stands in their paths. They can move at speeds as high as 70 miles per hour, and produce wind speeds of 100 to 250 miles per hour.

Tornadoes can give you little time for decision making, so have your plans in order. Be alert to changing weather patterns, and know the difference between a tornado watch and a tornado warning:

- A *watch* means the weather conditions are right for a possible tornado in the area.
- A *warning* means a tornado has been spotted in the area.

In addition to your disaster plan, be on the lookout for blowing debris and the sound of an approaching tornado—many people say it sounds like an oncoming freight train. If you're in a tornado emergency, follow these tips:

Top Ten Tips for Tornado Emergencies

1. Have a designated safety area in your home, which may or may not be your safe room. For tornado threats, a basement is preferred. If not, try an interior room with no windows, a closet, a center hallway, a bathroom, subbasements, or root cellars.

2. If you're not home, seek shelter in a steel-reinforced building, tunnels, underground parking facilities, basements, interior corridors, and subways.

3. Keep away from windows. Avoid the upper stories of multistory buildings, house trailers, and parked cars.

4. Take cover under heavy furniture such as desks or coffee tables. If your home has an interior stairway and there's a space or room underneath, go in there. Stairways are strong structures.

5. If driving, never try to outrun a tornado. Trying to do this has resulted in many deaths. Abandon your vehicle and take shelter immediately, even if you simply jump into a ravine or ditch.

6. If you're in a mobile home, leave it immediately and seek appropriate shelter, or lie in a ravine or ditch a safe distance away from the mobile home.

7. In a room with windows, close curtains or blinds, then crouch under something strong like a sturdy table, a desk, or under a stairway.

8. Wrap yourself in blankets, overcoats, anything to help protect you from flying debris.

The duck and cover is a strong position that can help protect you from falling debris.

9. After the storm, be careful of fallen power lines. Call utility companies to report outages or line breaks.
10. If you live in an area prone to tornadoes, conduct regular tornado drills with your family to make sure everyone knows what to do.

Incidentally, there's always been a question about whether or not to leave a window open just a crack when a tornado passes by. Recent research from Texas Tech says that all windows and doors should remain closed when a tornado is approaching.

Earthquakes

Until there's a way to predict quakes before they happen, you must be prepared for one to strike at any time if you live in an earthquake-prone area.

I was in an earthquake in San José, Costa Rica. It happened in the middle of the night and nearly tossed me out of bed. It was one heck of a way to wake up, and after the shaking stopped, I got up from underneath the table, threw on my clothes, grabbed my "go bag," and went outside. There were alarms going off all over the city; fire engines were wailing.

There wasn't much damage to be seen, and it appeared the danger had passed, so I went back to my room. I was amazed to see how much water had been splashed on the floor from the toilet tank. The locals later said the quake was quite mild in comparison to others they had experienced. Even so, it sure got my attention.

So far, science hasn't found a way to predict when an earthquake will occur. They'll always catch you off guard. If it happens to you:

Top Ten Tips for Earthquake Emergencies

1. During the quake, stay indoors! Power lines may be coming down outside. Also, taller buildings tend to topple outward in an earthquake.

2. Get into a doorway, if possible. Doorways are strong. Or get under heavy furniture like desks and big tables. If you happen to be outside when a quake hits, get away from buildings, large trees, and power lines. Drop to the ground and cover.

3. If you're in an interior hallway, crouch against the wall. Watch out for doors swinging open and shut.

4. Stay away from windows and heavy objects, like TV sets. A friend in Los Angeles went into her debris-strewn living room after the Northridge quake and discovered that her thirty-one-inch TV set had been thrown all the way across the room!

5. In your safest place, duck, cover, and hold—crouch low to the ground and protect your head with your arms. If there's

something to hold on to, grasp it with the hand of the arm that's covering your eyes and hold on.

6. Watch out for swinging doors and smaller moving objects. Glasses and dinnerware in the kitchen can fall on you; cabinet doors fly open.

7. After the shaking stops, evacuate the building. Don't use elevators; they may be damaged.

8. Outside, beware of broken gas lines. If you're at home, turn your utilities off if you can before you leave.

9. Keep away from power lines and buildings to avoid falling debris.

10. If you're in a car, get away from bridges, overpasses, and underpasses. Slow down and find a clear place way from buildings, power lines, and tall trees. Stay in your car until the shaking has stopped.

It may not be over when the shaking stops—after the initial quake, expect aftershocks and be prepared to take the same cautions. Don't go into damaged structures. Be alert for electrical wires and steam, gas, or water leaks.

If you live in an earthquake-prone area, you should have your emergency supplies ready at all times and take some extra precautions:

- Keep your drinking water jugs filled.
- Bolt bookcases, china cabinets, and any tall furniture to wall studs to keep them from falling over.
- Strap your water heater to the wall.
- Put strong latches on your cabinet doors to keep tableware and glasses from flying out.

- Avoid placing heavy items like TVs on upper shelves of entertainment centers or wall units—they can become heavy missiles in a strong quake.

Fire and Smoke

Please educate your children about fire. They're often the ones who become victims because they haven't been taught what to do. Make it a family project to come up with a plan and practice it.

Fire is the most dangerous and most common of all disasters. A building can be completely engulfed in flames in a matter of minutes. Thousands of people in this country die in fires each year, but many of those deaths could have been avoided if time was taken to plan.

Whether the fire is in your home, where you work, or wildfire outdoors, the biggest dangers can come from smoke. In fact, most victims die of smoke inhalation or from toxic gases rather than burns. This is why firefighters wear breathing apparatuses. Many of the synthetic materials found in offices and homes are compounds containing poisonous chemical agents, such as arsenic and cyanide, that can be released in a fire. Some of these chemicals are similar in composition to chemical warfare agents.

You can take precautions in your home, or any building you visit, to increase your chances of surviving a fire. If you are caught in a fire, your planning can help you escape. Here's how:

Car Fires

The most common causes of car fires are poor maintenance or electrical problems, not crashing or rolling over, as you see in movies and TV shows. If you're driving down the road and see smoke or steam coming from under the hood, your car may be overheated or on fire. In either case:

1. Stop the car as far off the highway as safely possible and put the car into PARK. Don't turn the engine off until you've done this—it will lock the steering wheel in vehicles with automatic transmission.

2. After you are safely off the road and stopped, turn the engine off. In cars with electronic fuel pumps, this will stop the flow of fuel.

3. Get out of the car and move away from the road and traffic. Your biggest danger is being run over by rubberneckers. There's a natural tendency for drivers to steer in the direction they're looking, so don't stand in front or in back of a burning vehicle.

4. Don't open the hood. Light-colored smoke that diminishes after a few minutes could be steam, meaning the car was overheated. But it could also be smoke in the early stages of a car fire. Darker smoke indicates burning of plastics and petroleum products, but don't open the hood in either case. You may burn your hands, and additional oxygen from opening the hood may cause the fire to burn more intensely.

5. Don't stand near the burning vehicle. The smoke caused by a vehicle fire is full of toxins and carcinogens from the burning components, and breathing these toxins can affect your health long after the fire's out.

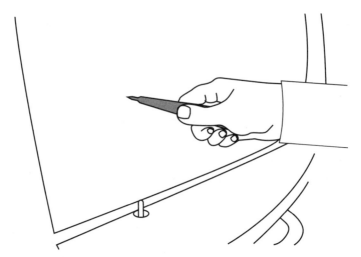

Use a spring-loaded center punch to break a car window if a car fire renders your electric windows inoperative. You can also use it to escape from a vehicle submerged in water.

Stay at least one hundred feet from the vehicle. Unless there's a fuel leak, cars fires don't immediately explode, as films would have you believe. It can take quite a while to burn to that point, and the fire department will usually put out the blaze before then. If a car continues to burn, the tires will usually blow first, then the drive train, which is filled with oil, and finally the gas tank explodes. This may take more than twenty minutes. If there's not much fuel in the tank, it will contain more highly explosive vapors and have a greater chance of an explosion.

Some people carry a spring-loaded center punch in the car, just like the tool carjackers sometimes use to break a window. In this case, you would use it to break the windows in a fire if it caused the electronic door locks and windows to short out, trapping you in the car. You can also use it to escape a car submerged in water, or any other reason your windows and doors might short out.

Fire Survival Tips

In your home:

- Develop your family fire escape plan. Find two exits from each room. Windows are okay as exits.

- Install good smoke detectors—they more than double your chances of surviving a fire. If you have a home security system, they should be part of it. Check them once a month and change batteries once a year. Install a detector in each bedroom corridor, at the top of stairwells, and along your main escape route.

- Keep your fire extinguisher near the door. You never want to be moving away from your exit during a fire, so if you're going for your fire extinguisher, you're at least heading toward the exit.

- Use rope ladders or hook-on fire escape ladders for upper-floor windows.

- Designate a meeting place outside the home so you can account for everyone in the household if there's a fire.

- Practice your escape routes. Hold a family fire drill.

If a fire occurs:

- Don't panic. Wake everyone in the house by yelling, "Fire! Everyone out!" Get outside as quickly as possible—don't stop for valuables. Smoke and heat rise, so get on the floor and crawl quickly along a wall to your exit. This is called the "fire crawl."

- Feel doors before opening them. If they're hot, take another exit. If not, open the door carefully. If smoke or heat rushes in, quickly close the door and take your second exit route.
- If you can, cover your nose and mouth with a cloth or wet towel to keep from inhaling smoke and gases.
- If you need to exit through a window, make sure the door to the room is closed before opening the window. Draft from the open window can draw flame and smoke into the room you're in.
- If you can't exit through the door and need to wait for rescue, place wet towels or sheets into the cracks around the door to keep smoke from entering the room.
- If your clothing catches fire, *stop, drop, and roll.* Drop to the ground, and cover your mouth and face with your hands to protect them from the flames. Then roll over and over to smother the flames.
- When you get out of your home, stay out. Don't go back inside for any reason.

In high-rise apartment buildings or any public buildings away from home:

- Learn the location of fire alarms, escape routes, and fire extinguishers.
- Never take an elevator to escape a fire. Go to stairwells.
- If you can't get to an escape stairway, find a room with a window to the outside.
- If you find a working phone, call 911 and tell the dispatcher

where you are, even if you see emergency vehicles at the scene.

- Stay where rescuers can see you. Wave something out the window.
- Once you get out of the building, stay out. Don't go back inside for any reason.

Winter Storms

I've visited the frozen North during winter, and it never fails to remind me why I'm more than happy to keep living in my native Florida. Snow, freezing rain, ice, blizzards—severe winter storms cause a surprising number of deaths each year. Everyone is potentially at risk of death due to conditions related to winter storms, such as:

- Exposure to cold. This affects mostly people over age sixty, usually male. Some of these deaths occur in the home because power is often lost during severe storms.
- Ice and snow. Being caught in the storm, particularly in an automobile, is a danger, as are accidents. If you know a storm is coming, don't plan on traveling by car. Stay home, if possible.
- Carbon monoxide poisoning. Starting your car in the garage to warm it up can increase this risk. Cold cars run "rich"— that is, they make more carbon monoxide than usual, and can fill your garage within minutes. If the garage is attached to your house, that gas can seep into the house, especially once you leave and close the garage door. To be safe, you must start the car, back out, close the garage door, and move the car away.

Winter storms can last for days, knocking out power and trapping people in cars or in their homes. It's important to have emergency supplies on hand if you live where winter storms occur. Being "snowed in" isn't much different from "sheltering in" when it comes to being prepared. The disaster supplies list at the beginning of this chapter is a must for those who reside in cold climates. Add to those precautions:

- An alternative heating source. If power is lost, it may not come back for days. You must have another way to stay warm if you can't leave your home to go elsewhere. If your home has a fireplace, stock up on firewood before winter. Be sure your chimney and chimney flue are checked and cleaned before the season. Use space heaters with care, and don't use them in the bathroom or around water.

Frostbite and hypothermia are two more dangers during severe winter storms:

- Frostbite occurs when the skin is exposed to cold so severe that there is permanent damage. Fingers, toes, noses, and earlobes are most prone to frostbite. Symptoms include loss of feeling and a white, pale appearance to the skin. You should seek medical help immediately, but if you can't do so, *slowly* rewarm the frostbitten parts of the body.

- Hypothermia is a condition in which body temperature drops below 95 degrees Fahrenheit. Normal body temperature is 98.6 degrees. Symptoms of hypothermia include slow slurred speech, disorientation, uncontrollable shivering, memory loss, drowsiness, and apparent exhaustion. Seek medical help immediately if body temperature is below 95 degrees. If you can't do so, then begin warming the victim *slowly,* starting with the trunk, or core of the body. *Don't* warm arms and legs first—doing this can drive cold blood toward the heart and cause heart failure. Don't give the victim hot liquids to drink, or any alcohol, drugs, or coffee. A little warm broth is okay.

If you have to go outside in extremely cold weather:

- Wear layered clothing.
- If you absolutely have to travel, be sure to keep blankets, sleeping bags, extra clothing, and even some food and water in your car, in case you get stuck.
- Try to stay on the main roads.
- Carry nonclumping cat litter, sand or rock salt, and a snow shovel in the trunk of your car to help generate traction if you become stuck. The extra weight in the trunk can provide more traction as well.

If you do become stuck:

- Stay with your vehicle. Don't go for help unless help is clearly visible. It's easy to become disoriented and lost in blowing snow.
- Be careful running the car's heater if you get stuck. It's a carbon monoxide risk without proper ventilation. Make sure the exhaust pipe is clear of snow and ice. Run the car for ten minutes per hour, opening the windows a little for ventilation.
- If you're very cold, don't go to sleep unless you're not alone. Then, take turns sleeping and making sure the other person wakes up after a short time. Huddle together and share body heat if necessary.

- Make sure rescuers can see you. Open the car hood if you can, or tie a brightly colored cloth to the antenna or door.

   Just as I check my emergency supplies every year before hurricane season, residents of colder climates should check theirs before winter.

Hurricanes and Typhoons

I have more experience with hurricanes than any other natural disaster, and the worst one I've ever seen was Hurricane Andrew, which killed scores of people and ran up damages in the billions of dollars in August 1992. I did some disaster relief work immediately after the storm, and I can tell you that I've never seen such destruction in my life. The entire town of Homestead, Florida, was devastated. There were no street signs, and house numbers were literally blown off homes. Utilities were out, public transportation wasn't running, debris and devastation were everywhere. People had no way of knowing where relief supplies were being distributed unless they had a radio, which was the only way people could receive news. Even cellular phones didn't work, because all the towers had been blown away.

   The first few days were pretty rough. I saw a lot of heartache and loss. But virtually everyone I talked to who rode out that storm told me the same thing: If they had it to do all over again, they would have evacuated. Hurricane Andrew was a category four storm, extremely strong, and I'm quite sure that I'd leave if a storm that big and powerful was bearing down on my home. I'd put the shutters up on my windows and doors, pack my most valuable possessions, and leave. There's nothing I have worth dying for in a storm like that.

Hurricanes (in the United States, Central America, and South America) and typhoons (in the South Pacific and South China Sea) are tropical cyclones. These large, dangerous storms can be four hundred miles in diameter and pack winds in excess of two hundred miles an hour. They can push a wall of water, called a storm surge, in front of them that's more than twenty feet high. This surge can devastate coastal areas as the storm sweeps in from the sea, and is actually more dangerous than the wind. Torrential rains generally accompany the storms, and most deaths related to these storms are due to flooding from rain or surge.

That's the bad news. The good news is that the National Weather Service is quite good at predicting hurricane paths, and getting better every year. Though hurricanes are some of the most dangerous storms around, they're also one of the easiest to prepare for. Unlike earthquakes, hurricanes give plenty of warning before they strike. There's time to make preparations if you aren't already prepared by the time one forms.

Follow all the rules for general disaster preparedness. In addition:

Additional thoughts:

- Bring in outdoor objects such as lawn furniture, toys, and garden tools. Anchor objects you can't bring in, like storage sheds and doghouses.
- Secure your house and other buildings by closing and covering windows. Put up hurricane shutters, or use plywood to board up windows. Take down any outside antennas.
- Turn your refrigerator and freezer to the coldest settings. Open the refrigerator only when absolutely necessary and

close quickly. If the power goes out, your food will stay cold longer.

- Store drinking water in clean jugs, bottles, and cooking utensils. I like to fill the bathtub with water to use for toilet flushing, if the water has to be turned off.

- Review your evacuation plan, just in case you have to leave.

- Move boats to a designated safe place, or moor them securely. If transporting, tie the boat securely to the trailer with rope or chain. Use tiedowns to anchor the trailer to the ground or house.

If a hurricane warning is announced:

- Listen to radio or television for official news and instructions regarding possible evacuation.

- If you live in a mobile home, check that your tie-downs are secure, then evacuate *immediately*.

- Store valuables and personal papers in waterproof containers on your home's highest floor. If you evacuate, take them with you, if possible.

- Make arrangements beforehand to take any pets to a shelter that accepts them, just in case you must evacuate. Your veterinarian or the humane society can help you. Check on this information at the start of every hurricane season.

- Stay inside, away from windows, skylights, and glass doors.

- If power is lost, turn off your major appliances to reduce the power surge when the electricity is restored.

If an evacuation order is called:

- Secure your home by turning off the electricity, unplugging appliances, and shutting off the main water valve.

- Leave as soon as you possibly can. Follow the official evacuation routes, or the routes you've personally planned, if they're not closed by officials. Watch for flooding and washed-out bridges.

- Call your out-of-town contact person right away and tell him you're evacuating, where you're going to be, and how to reach you, if possible.

- Make sure your pets have everything they need to go with you. If you're going to a public shelter that doesn't accept pets, take them to their prearranged shelter place.

- Bring your own emergency supplies, clothing, blankets, and sleeping bags to the shelter.

- Lock up your home and leave.

After the storm:

- Tune in to local radio for official information, and to learn when you can return home.

- Go home only after you're advised by officials that it's safe.

- Be careful of downed power lines.

- When entering your home, beware of snakes, insects, and animals that may have been driven to higher ground by floodwaters.

- Open all windows and doors to ventilate and dry out your home.

- Check for spoilage in your refrigerator and freezer.
- Immediately photograph any damage to your home, contents, and grounds for insurance claim purposes.
- Use your telephone only for emergency calls. Let your contact person know that you're back home and safe.
- Check for gas leaks in or near your home. If you hear hissing or blowing noises, or smell gas, open a window and leave quickly. Shut off the gas at the main valve outside and contact the gas company. Don't go back inside until the situation is rectified.
- Check for electrical system damage, and sewer and water line damage. Contact the appropriate utilities if necessary.

Lightning

Lightning kills an average of eighty people every year and injures thousands. Meteorologists call it the "underrated killer." No wonder—the temperature of a lightning stroke can reach 50,000 degrees Fahrenheit! The sun isn't even that hot.

An average stroke of lightning is six miles long. But lightning can have an extreme range of more than twenty-five miles. Thus the expression *a bolt out of the blue,* which refers to a bolt of lightning from the edge of a cloud next to a blue sky.

You can use lightning and thunder to roughly calculate how far a storm is away from you. Thunder travels at the speed of sound, which is about one mile every five seconds. Lightning travels a lot faster, at the speed of light, so you see a lightning bolt before you hear the accompanying thunder. The farther away the storm, the longer the time interval between seeing the lightning and hearing the thunder. When you see the flash, start counting seconds. If it takes five seconds until you hear thunder, then the storm is about a mile away.

I think lightning is also underestimated. People seem to take a lot of chances in lightning storms unnecessarily. Follow the tips below to avoid becoming a victim of lightning strikes:

Top Ten Tips to Survive Lightning Storms

1. Stay inside. Don't go out unless absolutely necessary.
2. Avoid open doors and windows, and anything inside that may conduct electricity if your house gets hit, such as sinks, stoves, pipes, and plug-in electrical items.
3. During a storm, don't use the telephone, electric razors, electric toothbrushes, or hair dryers.
4. If you're outside, get inside. If you can't, lie low in a ditch, gully, or cave. Avoid the highest object in the area, and hilltops. If isolated trees are nearby, you're safer to crouch in the open. Stay twice as far away from trees as they are tall.
5. Don't work on anything that can draw lightning, like power lines, fences, pipes, or anything made of metal.
6. Get off the golf course—clubs and (especially) those metal cleats in your shoes are good lightning rods.
7. Get out of the water—that includes the bathtub and the shower. Get off small boats.
8. If you're in your vehicle, stay there. Generally cars provide good protection during lightning storms.

9. Stop work on farm equipment and get off. Lightning often strikes metal farm equipment in contact with the ground, such as tractors.

10. If your hair stands on end, or your skin tingles, or you feel an electrical charge, drop to the ground immediately. Lightning may be about to strike you. Crouch down on the balls of your feet—this makes you a smaller target and places a smaller portion of your body in contact with the ground, which may become electrified.

Tsunamis

Tsunamis, or tidal waves, aren't very common. They strike the United States on the average of once every nine years, but they can occur at any time of day or night, and in any season. The most likely places for tsunamis to strike in this country are Hawaii, Alaska, and the west coast of the mainland.

Technically, tsunamis are a series of waves that are produced by earthquakes, volcanos, underwater landslides, or even meteorites. They travel at an average speed of 450 miles per hour across the open ocean, and wave height by the time they reach shore can range from ten feet to more than one hundred. Interestingly, because the waves have almost no amplitude at sea, ships rarely feel them, and they're nearly impossible to see from the air.

Tsunamis can originate hundreds, even thousands of miles from shore. They travel so quickly there is often little time for a warning. There's more than one wave, and the first one isn't usually the largest. The waves can occur from five minutes to ninety minutes apart. One sign of an approaching tsunami is when coastal water suddenly recedes. This indicates that a huge wave is sucking the water away from shore as it builds in height. People have been known to walk onto this newly bare ocean floor, only to have the tsunami crash in on them.

There's a general rule regarding tsunamis: If you're close enough to see it, you're *too* close. Here are more tsunami survival tips:

Tsunami survival:

- Know if your home is in a danger area. Know your home's "altitude" above sea level, and the distance of your street from the coast. Evacuation orders are usually based on this data.

- Know the warning signs. Tsunamis can be caused by an underwater disturbance or an earthquake, so quakes or sizable ground rumbling can be a warning signal, as are rapidly receding—or rapidly rising—coastal waters.

- Have your evacuation plans in order, including more than one evacuation route. Quakes and flooding may block off your typical evacuation route. Evacuate to an elevated inland location.

- Make sure your emergency contact plans are clear. Since tsunamis strike with little warning, you and your family may be separated when one occurs.

- Never go to the beach to watch the tsunami come in. If you can see it, you're in danger.

- Don't return home until authorities say it's safe to do so. Remember, tsunamis are a series of waves, and later waves may be larger than the first ones.

Man-Made Disasters

As scary as natural disasters can be, those made by humans can be far more frightening. I'm talking about terrorism, chemical warfare, and biological attack. Industrial chemical spills and leaks qualify as well, because though they're accidents, they can be of such proportion that they're indeed disastrous.

We don't like to think about such disasters. Anyone who is old enough to remember the Cuban missile crisis and the Cold War era probably recalls, perhaps with some humor, the "duck and cover" drills and the bomb shelter mentality brought about by a constant threat of nuclear war between the superpowers. In the past decade or so, those threats essentially vanished, resurfacing only slightly during the Gulf War. We more or less all went about life with a great feeling of worldwide security. That came to an end on September 11, 2001, when the potential for disasters caused by humans was made real once again.

Let's examine what preparations can be taken in different terrorism and man-made disaster scenarios. If you've followed emergency preparedness planning in the book so far, you're about 75 percent prepared for these types of emergencies as well. You'll see why shortly. But first, let's look at a current trend to acquire gas masks, hazardous materials suits, and other gear that might—or might not—serve to protect you in case of an extreme emergency.

The Truth About All That Fancy Protective Gear

There was a rush on purchasing all kinds of protective gear after the September 11 attacks. Fears of chemical or biological warfare, increased by the discovery of deadly anthrax in several locations, made owning gas masks a priority for many people.

Some purchased protective suits, even portable environmental rooms—but will any of these things actually help you?

I believe owning such protective gear is a personal choice. I don't own any myself. Since most attacks occur without warning, you would pretty much have to wear your gear 24/7 for it to be effective. I like my khaki shorts, boat shoes, and tropical shirts too much to start wearing hazmat suits and gas masks all the time. I did my homework and learned as much as I could in order to make that choice, and learning more is something I always advise. As I said, the choice is yours, and if you want to learn more about protective gear, read on.

Face Masks

Your local drugstore or hardware store can supply you with simple filtering face masks that cover your nose and mouth and will filter out particles from the air. The finer the filter, the more expensive the mask. These won't do much good, however, if a biological attack occurs right in your neighborhood. But if you live more than twenty miles away, they can be of some use. It doesn't hurt to have several in your emergency supply kit.

Gas Masks

At first, having a gas mask sounds like a good idea. The problem is, there are only a few, very specific circumstances in which one would be helpful, and frankly, those circumstances aren't likely to occur. Basically, you would have to know exactly when a biological or chemical attack was going to occur, and we know from recent experience that biological agents are usually discovered when the first symptoms appear in the victims, long after they've been released. Chemical agents, on the other hand, cause symptoms immediately, which may be too late to put on a mask. Plus, many of these agents enter the body through the skin. Clearly, having a gas mask wouldn't help in either those circumstances.

If you do have warning, however, gas masks require a snug, airtight fit, so they must be properly fitted to your face. An improperly fitting gas mask can be dangerous, not only because it won't work right, but because you can actually suffocate yourself if you don't know how to wear it properly. *New Scientist* magazine has reported that gas mask filters have a limited lifetime, sometimes a matter of hours, so if you're buying a used mask, you may not know if it's even viable. Also, the filters when new are covered with a protective plastic seal. If you don't know this and don't remove it before use, you can suffocate yourself. During the Gulf War, it was reported that more Israelis died suffocating from improper gas mask use than did from scud missiles.

Many people advocate saving your money and not purchasing gas masks. At the same time, some psychology experts have suggested that if buying a gas mask gives you peace of mind and helps reduce a condition of chronic anxiety, then go ahead and do it for your mental health. In the end, the decision is always yours. Personally, I don't have one.

Other Gear
Supplied air respirators completely cover the head and feed air to you through a tube connected to an oxygen tank. If you've got about five hundred dollars, you can get one. You can get more information about these respirators from the Environmental Protection Agency (EPA). The same problems apply here as with gas masks.

Vaporproof suits, along with an air respirator, offer full body protection. Be prepared to spend another thirteen hundred dollars or more for one of these suits, which are worn by the brave souls who enter leaky nuclear power plants or anthrax-tainted buildings. The truth is, you'd probably never get such a suit on in time in the vast majority of cases.

Chemical Accidents and Spills

Earlier in this chapter, I mentioned a water treatment plant chemical leak that required evacuation of a section of my hometown. Such man-made accidents don't occur every day, but they're hardly rare. You've probably seen stories on TV or read about such incidents in the newspaper: A tanker truck carrying hazardous chemicals overturns on an interstate highway; a train derails, sending a hazardous material tanker car crashing, causing a major chemical leak; industrial accidents force workers to flee the plant—and sometimes nearby residents to evacuate. The simple act of mixing chlorine bleach with ammonia can technically be called a chemical accident, as it will release deadly chlorine gas that can overwhelm a person, even seriously injure or kill. But we're concerned with preparing for chemical accidents on a grand scale.

The largest industrial disaster ever to occur was the 1984 Union Carbide chemical accident in Bhopal, India. A tank containing a dangerous chemical used in manufacturing insecticide began to leak. Nearly twenty-five hundred people were killed, and a hundred thousand were injured.

Police, fire, and medical personnel are trained to respond to chemical emergencies. In the event of a major chemical accident or spill, you will be required either to evacuate your home if you're too close to the disaster site, or to stay put if it's safer to do so. If you're to leave, follow your evacuation plan; if you'll be sheltering in place, you may need to be prepared to use your safe room. You'll be notified by local authorities in some way, whether they phone you, knock on your door, or drive through the neighborhood using sirens and loudspeakers. Be alert for the following information:

What to know:

1. What type of hazard, and how soon it's expected to dissipate.

2. What area is contaminated and what evacuation routes are advised. You may be far enough away that you won't have to implement your disaster plan if the contaminant is dissipating rapidly. If you must evacuate, however, you don't want to run directly into the contaminated area or anywhere near it.

3. Whether you need to stay in your home or evacuate. If the contaminant has already enveloped your area, you will probably want to stay indoors—close windows, turn off all fans and air conditioners, close vents and fireplace dampers, and seal windows and doors with duct tape, or by placing wet towels around openings. If you're in a multi-story building, go to the highest floor.

4. Locations of shelters. If you must evacuate, you may need to know shelter locations.

5. Phone numbers to call if you need help evacuating. If you're disabled, elderly, or otherwise need additional help, don't hesitate to call for it. Call 911 if you don't hear other emergency numbers to call.

6. Radio and television coverage. Most stations will stay on

top of an emergency, and provide important information such as which areas must be evacuated and when you can return home.

7. First-aid treatment instructions. If you think you may be contaminated, wash yourself and your clothes with cool water. In an emergency, jumping into a swimming pool, fountain, or any clean water can help dissipate contaminants quickly. Don't use hot water—you'll open your pores further to the contaminant.

8. Which medical facilities are open to handle the emergency. Locations other than hospitals may be designated as emergency treatment sites if emergency rooms are full.

Terrorism

Terrorism has come to the forefront of everyone's minds worldwide. After September 11, 2001, we ask ourselves how anyone could possibly have been prepared for what happened at the World Trade Center. The truth is, if everyone inside those buildings had been armed, it wouldn't have helped a bit. If every person had a gas mask, nothing would have changed. What did help the people who survived was an awareness of what was going on, despite what they might have been told. I believe that listening to gut instincts probably offered more protection than any piece of gear they could have had.

I know that if a bomb drops right on top me, all the survival training in the world won't help. That's when I might remember the old saying, "When your number's up, your number's up." But if you haven't taken a direct hit and there's even a chance that you can survive, then trusting your instincts, being alert and aware, and knowing how to react—because you've thought about it beforehand—can make all the difference in the world. Even in the most disastrous of circumstances, if you have the *slightest* chance, the basics can get you through.

When dealing with man-made terror, there are mental adjustments to be made. Terror weapons are used not only for their physically destructive value, but for their ability to cause psychological damage. They cause feelings of terror, and underscore the fact that we're not in control. Yet who can control a hurricane, tornado, or tsunami? You can't, but the fact that such disasters come to us from nature seems to make them a bit more "okay," and mentally we deal with them differently. Still, the decision-making process for disaster, natural or man-made, is much the same. You recognize the danger, then determine if it's safer to leave the area or shelter in place and ride it out. The preparations you take for possible man-made disasters are the same as for coping with natural ones, with a few added precautions particular to the type of disaster.

First, we'll look at what to do in the event of an explosion or shooting, and then we'll discuss the two most feared terrorist attacks: chemical and biological.

Explosions

Let me share with you the information on bombs and bullets that's taught at police academies and basic training on explosions and firearms—or at least a very condensed version. The hope is you'll never have to use it.

The first terrorists I ever prepared for were the ones who used hand grenades and submachine guns to blow up airports and hijack airplanes in order to make demands and a statement for their cause. Today they almost seem tame, but there's nothing tame about explosives. It's unlikely that you'll ever find yourself in a situation where you would face the possibility of explosions. Still, if you are caught near an explosion of any type:

Explosive advice:

- Hit the dirt, fast! When you see the flash of an explosion, don't wait for the bang. The concussion occurs somewhere between the flash and the bang, and that's what you're really concerned with. You may have a second or two, so get down fast.
- Get as low as possible as quickly as possible to avoid being hit by flying shrapnel. If you're indoors, stay low to avoid smoke and poisonous gases, which tend to rise toward the ceiling.
- Dive behind something solid that offers protection, such as furniture or a car. Hedges or bushes might provide some pro- tection, but debris can still get through.
- Beware of secondary explosions after the first explosion. Don't go into an area until you're sure it's clear. Terrorists sometimes detonate a bomb, then wait for rescuers to arrive before setting off a second explosion.

Should you become trapped in the debris of an explosion, stay put and try to remain calm while waiting for rescuers. Move as little as possible in case you're injured, and to prevent kicking up dust, making breathing difficult. If you're out of view, tap on something so rescuers can hear where you are. Don't shout unless you absolutely have to in order to draw attention, as it can cause you to inhale too much dust.

Firearms

It's also unlikely you'll ever be caught in the middle of gunfire. I've faced gunfire because I chose law enforcement as a career, but even then, most cops go through their entire careers without firing their weapons except on the practice range.

I've always felt that if someone is shooting at you, it's better to be a good ducker than a good fighter. Survival all comes down to your ability to make yourself a difficult target. Shooters will usually go for the easiest targets first. After all, when you play a video game or practice target shooting, do you try to shoot the smallest, most difficult targets first? Probably not.

How to be a difficult target:

- Move fast. It's harder to hit a moving target than a stationary target. Television makes it look easy, but it's quite difficult in reality. The faster you move, the harder you are to hit.
- Stay low and make yourself as small a target as possible.
- Don't lie down on hard surfaces. Bullets don't bounce like pool balls or basketballs do on a hard surface—instead they'll rise a few inches off the surface and follow it. If you lie down on asphalt, concrete, or another hard surface, all your attacker has to do is shoot in front of you. The bullet will strike the surface, rise a few inches, and ricochet right into you.
- Do lie down on grass, sand, or other soft surface to make yourself a smaller target. Bullets don't usually ricochet off these surfaces, so they'll offer some protection.
- Launch yourself in unexpected directions. It's harder to hit a target that moves unpredictably than one that can be followed in the sights. Make your moves when your assailant

isn't ready—at the beginning of the attack when there's more chaos, when he's reloading, distracted, or looking the other way. Don't just run, but *burst* from cover and get to safety.

- Put something between you and your attacker as soon as you can. After you do, keep moving. Bullets don't go around corners, but you don't want to give your assailant time to walk up on you.
- Don't stop moving until you reach safety.

Chemical Attacks

In June 1994, a Japanese terrorist cult known as Aum Shinrikyo drove a converted refrigerator truck to the city of Matsumoto, Japan, northwest of Tokyo. In the early-morning hours, they activated a computer-controlled system that released the truck's cargo of sarin, a deadly nerve agent. The neighborhood was targeted because it was home to three judges sitting on a panel that was hearing a lawsuit against the cult. The deadly gas killed seven people and required nearly two hundred people to spend at least one night in the hospital. Then in March 1995, the same cult released packages of sarin on five different trains in the Tokyo subway system. This attack killed twelve people and sent nearly a thousand to the hospital.

You hear a lot about the possibility of terrorist chemical attacks. Some experts say the death toll would be vast; others point to how difficult it is to make and disperse these weapons in a mass-casualty scenario, noting that the Aum Shinrikyo attacks, while injuring many, killed few. As a police officer, I've used and trained with both CS and CN gas—also known as tear gas—and with pepper spray. I know that they're difficult to predict and control in use, especially on windy days.

Chemical agents are inhaled or absorbed through the skin, and generally cause immediate symptoms. Nerve agents, toxins, mustard agents, and others all fall into this category. They are stable, easily dispersed, and highly toxic. Severity of injuries depends on the type and amount of the chemical agent used, and the duration of exposure. Two of the most well-known nerve agents are VX and sarin, which affect how nerve impulses travel in the nervous system. Depending on the dosage, symptoms can range from mild poisoning to death. Nerve agents affect how nerve impulses travel in the nervous system. Symptoms of exposure include one or more of the following: pinpointed pupils, stomach cramps, nausea, sudden headache, tightness in the chest, burning sensation or twitching skin on exposure to a liquid, dim vision, dizziness, drooling or excessive salivating, and runny nose.

There are antidotes to chemical agents, notably atropine, which can promote full recovery *if* treatment is immediate. But as of this writing, atropine is available only to military, hospital emergency room, and emergency response personnel.

What can you do in the event of a chemical attack? If these things are so difficult to detect, how might you know about one before feeling symptoms yourself? Look for these indications:

- If you suddenly see birds falling from the sky, butterflies or other large insects dying, or even small animals becoming sick or keeling over, take action. Be alert and aware of your surroundings. Look for other indications of a possible attack, and look for shelter.

- If you see lots of people falling to the ground with symptoms, take action. If one person collapses in the subway, on the street, or in the mall, it's probably a medical problem like a heart attack or seizure. But if several people go down, you may have cause for concern.

In the case of chemical attack:

- If you're outside and see indications, go inside. Once inside, turn off air conditioners and any other device that brings outside air in. Shut the windows to keep the contaminated air and chemicals out. Call authorities. Go to an interior room. If you have a safe room, seal it with duct tape or put wet towels around the edges of the doors and windows. Taking these precautions can increase your protection tenfold.

- If you're inside and see indications, go outside. Get into the fresh air. Move as far away from the contaminated building as you can.

- Move to a higher floor if inside, and higher ground if outside. Chemical agents are manufactured to be heavy, to fall close to the ground and linger in the air. This is why such agents are so deadly to soldiers in trenches.

- In either case, take your clothes off. Don't be bashful—you need to get this stuff off you as soon as possible, and you can remove 80 percent of contaminants by removing clothing. Discard clothing in a plastic bag or covered container.

- Rinse your skin with cool water immediately—don't use hot water, because it will open your pores to the contaminant.

- Remain as calm as possible. Increasing your breathing rate will increase how quickly and deeply you might breathe in a contaminant.

- If you've been outside, call authorities once you've sheltered in and taken care of yourself and your family as outlined above. Tell authorities you believe a toxic gas may be present outdoors.

If a chemical attack occurs near you and you're not immediately affected, authorities will advise you to either shelter in where you are and seal the premises, or evacuate immediately. If you're sheltering in, your general emergency preparedness will serve you, along with the tips just discussed.

Biological Attack

The use of biological weapons isn't new. In the sixth century B.C., the Assyrians poisoned their enemy's wells with rye ergot, a plant fungus that caused muscle contractions. In 1797 Napoleon tried to infect the residents of the besieged city of Mantua with swamp fever during his Italian campaign. In the French and Indian Wars, the British gave blankets used by smallpox patients to Native Americans they were fighting. And in Oregon in 1984, the Rajneesh cult used typhoid to contaminate salad bars in local restaurants, hoping to incapacitate enough people to influence an upcoming local election. They managed to sicken 750 people.

Despite worldwide efforts to curtail biological weapons manufacture, the threat seems to always be there. We were all reminded of that recently when anthrax became the latest weapon of terror in our own country. In many ways, the scenario hasn't played out to match the extreme nightmare visions experts have warned us of, or that our own imaginations would conjure, but that doesn't make the threat any less real—or deadly. Personal security in times like these requires extra vigilance and knowledge of the threats.

There are many diseases that have potential as bioterror weapons. Most are difficult to manufacture and disperse. The good news is that decades of research have failed to develop practical means of distributing many of these diseases as weapons of mass destruction. Recent experience, however, has shown that mass distribution doesn't have to occur for biological strikes to take place, and for the resulting terror to spread. Vigilance is still the order of the day, particularly in these troubled times.

Some diseases hold more potential as weapons than others. Here are the top seven candidates.

Potential Bioagents

Anthrax

The name comes from the Greek word for coal, *anthracis,* because the cutaneous (skin) form of the disease causes coal-like black sores. Anthrax is a bacterium; before it became a bioweapon, it was contracted mainly through contact with infected animals or their hides. It's highly infectious and often lethal when inhaled. It is *not* contagious—that is, it's not spread from person to person. Its spore form can be inhaled, ingested, or contracted through the skin. Viable anthrax spores can live dormant in the ground for decades.

The United States, the former Soviet Union, and at least fifteen other countries have experimented with anthrax as a weapon. The possibility of mass spreading of anthrax—or something else—was raised by the fact that the 9/11 terrorists had investigated crop duster planes. But tests conducted over the years by the U.S. government on the possible release of anthrax via plane have shown it to be extremely difficult to do effectively. This quashes the validity of a nightmare scenario making the rounds of the rumor mills and the Internet, which states that about one hundred grams of anthrax spread effectively over Washington, D.C., would kill between 150,000 and 3 million people in surrounding areas. According to those in the know at the Johns Hopkins Center for Civilian Biodefense Studies, it would actually take a hundred *kilograms* of spores, and the number of infected would be much smaller, limited to those who were exposed directly.

Symptoms of anthrax vary according to its form:

- Inhalation: Symptoms are upper respiratory and similar to colds and flu, deteriorating to severe breathing problems leading to death for those left untreated with antibiotics.
- Cutaneous: Characterized by redness, irritation, and black sores.
- Ingested: Severe gastrointestinal symptoms result.

A vaccine for anthrax exists, but is currently not widely available to the public. Anthrax is treated with antibiotics, but if treatment is not begun early the disease can be fatal.

Smallpox

Smallpox is a highly contagious virus, called variola, that's easily transmitted through the air from person to person. You need be only six feet away from an infected person to contract the disease, which can also be transmitted on clothing and bed-ding. The disease was eradicated through worldwide vaccination, and only the CDC and a Russian counterpart laboratory are officially storing virus samples. But it's feared some nations may have obtained samples and are currently using smallpox in biowarfare research.

Symptoms of smallpox include high fever, fatigue, head- and backache, and characteristic rashes and lesions on the face, arms, and legs, which turn to scabs and fall off during a four-week course. The death rate is about 30 percent. There's no proven treatment for smallpox, though the vaccine itself is effective and has been shown to help patients recover or lessen severity of the disease, even up to four days after exposure. (Incidentally, the vaccine was originally made from the cowpox virus, which is where the word *vaccine* came from—derived from the Latin *vaccinus,* meaning "of or from cows.")

Smallpox is considered a serious bioterrorism threat. In June 2001 U.S. antiterrorism authorities "played" a war game called Dark Winter to determine the nation's readiness in case smallpox were deliberately released by aerosol methods in three states. The results weren't too encouraging: The smallpox spread to twenty-five states and fifteen other countries within only two weeks! Quarantine methods and the current vaccine supply of about fifteen million doses weren't adequate to handle the emergency. It was a wake-up call that spurred officials to action—at least forty million doses of a new vaccine have been ordered.

Botulism

This muscle-paralyzing disease is caused by one of the deadliest toxins made by a bacterium. Botulinum toxin occurs naturally in foodborne botulism, but it can also be inhaled. The toxin poses a terrorist threat because it's easy to produce and transport. Several governments are known to be developing botulinum toxin as a biological weapon. But direct exposure on a mass scale is considered difficult to achieve. Cooking will inactivate the toxin in food, and no cases of botulism carried by water have ever been reported. Still, an aerosol release of the toxin could be one of the most dangerous types of terrorism attack.

Early symptoms include double vision, blurred vision, drooping eyelids, slurred speech, difficulty swallowing, dry mouth, and muscle weakness. Severe botulism causes respiratory failure and paralysis, sometimes leading to death. Most patients do recover after an extended period. The death rate is about 8 percent.

The Centers for Disease Control (CDC) maintains a supply of antitoxin against botulism. A vaccine is available, but isn't widely used because botulism toxin actually has legitimate medical uses for treating migraines, back pain, and cerebral palsy. And let's not forget injections of Botox, a purified protein produced by *Clostridium botulinum* bacteria, used to eliminate those unsightly facial wrinkles.

Plague

Millions of people in Europe died from bubonic plague in the Middle Ages, so many that it's believed the world's population was halved as a result. Plague was called the Black Death because the bacteria, transmitted by flea bites or person to person, caused internal bleeding from burst blood vessels. Dried blood under the skin turned black.

The United States and the former Soviet Union developed aerosol (spraying) methods of releasing plague bacteria to produce pneumonic plague, a highly lethal and contagious inhaled form of the disease. Unfortunately, it wouldn't be difficult to do, and it's believed a spray bottle or a crop duster could be used. In a report by the World Health Organization (WHO) in 1970, it was estimated that fifty kilograms of plague bacteria dispersed over a city of five million could result in thirty-six thousand dead.

In pneumonic plague, the lungs fill with a frothy, bloody liquid. Other symptoms include fever and weakness. Plague is highly fatal if not treated within a day of onset of symptoms. Several antibiotics are effective, however. A bubonic plague vaccine is available, but work is ongoing to develop a vaccine to pneumonic plague.

Ebola and Marburg

These two diseases are viral hemorrhagic fevers from a family of viruses called filoviruses. They are highly lethal and contagious, but not easily spread for bioterrorism purposes. Ebola isn't carried by humans, and how the virus first invades a human isn't known. Once someone is infected, it can be transmitted through contact with bodily fluids, or with infected objects such as needles. So a potential terrorist would almost certainly have to infect himself and try to transmit the disease. Since most Ebola victims die within a week, it's not likely a terrorist would get very far with his mission.

Outbreaks of Ebola have occurred in Africa, and the disease

was generally spread among those caring for victims who had close personal contact. But the disease has never been reported in humans in the United States. Symptoms include high fever, fatigue, dizziness, muscle aches, and bleeding under the skin, in internal organs, and from body orifices. There's no known cure or vaccine.

Marburg symptoms include fever, chills, headache and body aches, along with nausea, chest pain, and body rash. In severe cases, massive hemorrhaging occurs. Marburg has a 25 percent fatality rate. There is no treatment or vaccine.

Tularemia
Japan and the United States experimented with using tularemia bacteria as an aerosol weapon during World War II. The United States destroyed its stockpile of tularemia in 1973, but continues defensive research on the bacteria. The disease is normally spread by mice and other small animals and is one of the more dangerous terrorist threats to untreated water supplies. While it's usually treatable with antibiotics, flu-like symptoms and pneumonia can occur and may be extremely debilitating. The mortality rate for outbreaks is usually about 2 percent. No vaccine is available.

What to Do—How to Handle Suspicious Mail
When I was a corporate security director, I made sure our mail facility was located in another building, away from our main offices. In those days, threats by mail consisted mostly of letter bombs and were explosive in nature rather than biological. It used to be that businesses paid more attention to the possi-

bility of threats in the mail than the average citizen did. Now the threat in the mailbox is biological, and everyone is eyeing their mail suspiciously, if only because of possible cross-contamination.

If anthrax scares have made you jumpy at your own mailbox, you're not alone. Here are some tips for handling suspicious mail.

You should be suspicious of mail if:

- It's unexpected or from someone you don't know.
- It's addressed to someone no longer at your address.
- It's handwritten and has no return address or bears one you can't confirm is legitimate.
- It's lopsided or lumpy in appearance.
- It's sealed with excessive amounts of tape.
- It's marked with restrictive words such as PERSONAL or CONFIDENTIAL.
- It has excessive postage.
- It contains a visible substance you can't identify.

If you get a suspicious letter or package:

- Don't handle it. Don't shake it, bump it, or sniff it.
- If you can, put it into a plastic bag that you can seal well, like a food storage bag or freezer bag. This is to keep contaminants from leaking out, as well as to preserve possible evidence.
- Wash your hands thoroughly with soap and water.
- Notify local law enforcement authorities.

What to Do—Surviving a Biological Attack

Being alert and using common sense are your best defenses in any disaster, and are especially important in a biodisaster, where your regular senses may not help. Unless terrorists announce that they've unleashed a biological agent, they're undetectable except in a medical lab. Bioagents aren't likely to be discovered until they produce symptoms in victims.

Should such an attack occur, you'll need to consider several factors before deciding on a course of action. Depending on these factors, you'll decide whether it's safer to shelter in place and keep the danger outside, or to evacuate to a safer area. If you leave the area, for example, will you leave the danger behind? If not, then sheltering in place is probably the best course of action. On the other hand, if leaving gets you out of a hot zone, and you can do so safely, then evacuation is the action to take.

You'll need to know:

- What is the agent? How infectious or contagious is it? If smallpox were found, for example, you would be facing a highly contagious disease and may need to stay home, quarantining yourself until vaccine was available in your area.
- Where did the attack occur in relation to your home? If smallpox were found two thousand miles from your home and appeared to be contained, you would need to be inoculated. The CDC and your public health department would quickly announce plans for giving vaccine to the public.
- How was the bioagent dispersed? If an aerosol was released in the atmosphere, it would be helpful to know if you're

downwind of the incident. This may require you to shelter in place, and perhaps go to your safe room and seal it off. Aerosol dispersal is a big concern—by going into your safe room and sealing it, you put a barrier between you and the germs touching your skin or entering your lungs. If you're in a building in which a bioagent was dispersed through the ventilation system, you'd need to get outside and away from the building as quickly as possible.

- Is your area at risk for a possible attack? You must consider if there's anything about where you live that would attract bioterrorists to make a statement. If there's a risk, be alert to possible mail contamination. You may consider protection for your ventilation system.

- Might evacuation be necessary? This is actually unlikely, except in localized situations. A building may need to be evacuated, but not a large area. Authorities would probably want to isolate the disease to make it easier to treat victims and curb the spread. But be prepared to evacuate anyway. Follow your evacuation plan. Keep in mind where the contaminated area is and modify your evacuation route if necessary. Take your emergency supplies with you.

You should have your emergency supplies already on hand. Add these items to it for biological attack preparation:

- Face masks. I discussed these earlier in the chapter. They can help filter some particles.

- Goggles to protect your eyes. These are a good idea to have in your emergency supplies anyway. You want something that you can wear along with the face mask, which covers your nose. The most likely candidate is swimmer's goggles.

However, ski or work goggles may be just as useful. Test them out before buying.

On this subject, one question always comes up: Should I keep antibiotics on hand? I can only tell you that some biological agents respond to such treatment and others don't. There are a number of medications used, and it's difficult to know which one might be the right one. The CDC and infectious disease doctors who are experts in bioterrorism advise against stockpiling antibiotics and self-treating. I've always listened to my doctor, so I'll tell you the same thing. If you're concerned and want advice, talk with your doctor. If you aren't satisfied with that talk, consider a second opinion.

Whether you shelter in place or evacuate:

- Wash frequently with soap and water.
- Listen for official information and instructions. If medications or vaccines are being distributed to the public, you'll need to know where to go and when.
- Stay as healthy as possible by eating right and getting plenty of rest. Your immune system will need all the help it can get.

Should you be concerned about your water supply? Contaminating public water supplies is much easier said than done. But if you have any reason to believe your water supply may have been compromised:

- Use your emergency water until you hear official instructions from authorities.
- Ask your local emergency operations personnel about boiling the water or using filtration. Follow their instructions.

Chapter 10 **Self-Defense**

One in three women and one in four men will become a victim of violent crime in her or his lifetime.

Physical confrontation should always be a last resort. Throughout my career, I've usually been able to avoid or end confrontation without employing violence. But there have been times when I've had to take aggressive action against criminals to defend myself or to protect others. I've used personal weapons such as mace, pepper spray, a nightstick, and firearms, as well as hand-to-hand fighting methods. I'm five feet nine inches tall and weigh 160 pounds, and most of the time my adversaries were larger and stronger than me. Yet I was able to use these techniques to protect myself and accomplish my goal, which was to defeat the criminals and take them into custody with the least amount of violence.

If you find yourself in a dangerous situation, your goal is quite different—to defend yourself and to escape from the situation safely. You may be able to do that without taking aggressive action. But if not, you can use many of the same self-defense techniques I've used—with minimal training and practice—to accomplish your goal. The more you practice, of course, the better you'll become.

Is Resistance Futile?

At some point, you may have to decide whether or not to resist an attacker, and how to make that decision is at the root of a lot of controversy. Law enforcement top brass often say, "Your wallet isn't worth dying for," and recommend that people simply not resist any robbery attempt, while they themselves would resist in certain situations. We sometimes hear of a robbery victim who was killed or injured, and are told, "He resisted for *just twenty bucks!*" I don't believe that's what happens. I believe that when people resist, it's not always for the twenty dollars or for the wallet; rather, it's a rebellion. The victim has decided to not be bullied or intimidated by a thug. It has little to do with the money, but it has everything to do with personal dignity. *How dare you!* the victim thinks. The holdup or attack is a personal affront, a violation, and the victim is not going to let that thug intimidate him.

People are sometimes killed or seriously injured while resisting, and sometimes they're killed or seriously injured while fully cooperating with the assailant. There are no data proving that one way has better odds than the other, but to be on the safe side, we're often told to simply comply.

I believe the decision is more complicated, that there are too many variables involved. Each situation is different, fluid, and changing so rapidly that decisions must be made on the fly. A police officer can be in a restaurant and watch a robbery go down—and do nothing—because he knows it can create more of a danger if a gunfight erupts in a restaurant crowded with innocent people. He makes a decision at that moment based on the circumstances and on what he knows. But suppose a woman is attacked and being dragged into a dark alley, with no idea what the attacker has in mind? She wonders, *Is this guy just going to steal my purse? Is he going to rape me? Kill me?* She has to go by instinct, and there's absolutely no guideline in the world to tell her what to do.

Besides instinct, the decision is made by planning and thinking through possible attack scenarios. If you have a plan in your own mind, then you've made your decision about *how to make the decision* when and if the time comes. I know from my own experience that there are times when I would resist, and times when I would not. My general feeling is that I wouldn't resist unless I felt I was in more danger by not resisting, or that what I was in danger of losing was worth risking my life for. I would resist if I felt I could do so without escalating the violence, or if I could make a powerful first strike.

Ideally, you want to keep yourself from ending up in a situation where you have to make that choice, and that's what this book is most about. But I know that this isn't always possible. The people on the September 11 United Flight 93 chose to resist the terrorists who hijacked their plane, and they perished when the plane crashed in the Pennsylvania countryside. They made their choice, and it was a brave one. They're all heroes, but I'm saddened when I think of them, because being a hero doesn't bring them back.

You must make your own decision about resistance. Should you choose to resist an attack, your goal should be to escape without escalating the violence, rather than overpowering and destroying your attacker.

In resisting an attack, the first two or three seconds are the most important. This is the time when it's usually easiest to break free, but it's also the time when your mind is the most stunned and confused by the attack. For this reason, the most significant part of any self-defense is to train your mind and body to instantly respond together. How do you do that? After you've read and studied the following self-defense techniques, both armed and unarmed, you plan by picturing the possibility of an attack in your mind. Think about your transitional situations and where you're most vulnerable—at your car, in a parking lot, at the ATM, going into your office—and visualize an attack in these situations. What would you do? How would you respond? If you see an attack on a TV show, picture it in your mind and come up with a defense for it. Play these scenarios over and over in your head and plan your strategy, just as you pictured how to escape home invaders in each room of your house (chapter 3). Using imagery in this way can help keep you from freezing or panicking should a real attack occur.

If you train, but don't use imagery, it's likely you won't respond as quickly. I've seen highly trained people freeze in emergency situations—they're shocked by the situation, and to me that says they didn't have a visual image of the emergency beforehand. This idea of using imagery for preparation isn't new. Sports psychology today centers on using intensive visual imagery work to help players perform their best by seeing all possible situations in their minds first. Professionals play an entire tennis match or eighteen holes of golf in their minds first in order to do it calmly and smoothly when the time for the tournament arrives. Being prepared to defend yourself is much the same. It takes away the shock value of the incident and, in some ways, an attacker's element of surprise.

I routinely visualize situations. Combining it with security habits helps make you more aware of potential danger zones, which you can then avoid. I think that once you try visualizing, you'll find it's an easy habit to get into.

Unarmed Defense

You have several assets you can use against an attacker, even if you think you're at a disadvantage size- or strengthwise.

Your assets are:

- Your mind. It's a powerful weapon. Visualizing in advance leads to quick thinking on the spot.
- Your voice. This can be very strong when you want—and need—it to be.
- Your teeth and jaws. Believe it or not, these are the strongest parts of your body. You'll see shortly how to use them.
- Your legs. These are the second most powerful part of your body. They have tremendous strength by virtue of the fact that they carry you around all day.

I'm going to combine these four assets to teach you two simple self-defense techniques. To become proficient in these two moves, practice them with a friend, preferably someone bigger and stronger than you. It will build your confidence, and you'll know that you have the technique mastered when that stronger person can't overpower you. These two moves were outlined briefly in chapter 5, "Protecting Our Children." In this chapter, I'll give you more details on how they apply to adults defending themselves. But take note: Don't try these moves if the attacker has a gun! These aren't moves to disarm someone. They're mugger defenses with escape being your primary goal.

The Leg Latch

The purpose of this move is to get your body in a position that makes it difficult for your attacker to cause you serious harm while you scream for help. When someone grabs you, your first instinct is to pull away. The attacker grabs harder, and at the same time is bracing himself to hold you more firmly. He needs to keep himself in balance, and since he's on the offensive, he has the advantage at this point. Your job now is to throw him off balance. Using the leg latch move gives you the element of surprise, because you're going to do exactly the opposite of what your attacker expects you to do. Instead of pulling away, you're going to move toward him and latch on to his leg.

When grabbed from any direction:

1. Crouch down quickly and use your legs to drive your body in the direction you're being pulled—toward the attacker. This should throw the assailant off balance.

2. While driving toward him, drop farther to the ground, grab the attacker's leg, and hug it as if you were hugging a tree or a pole. You've probably seen little kids grab on to their parents' legs this way. Wrap your arms and legs around the attacker's leg.

3. Work your way behind the attacker, holding on to the leg and screaming at the top of your lungs, "Police! Help!"

4. Keep your head high and close to the attacker's backside to make it difficult for him to kick you with his other leg or strike you with his fists.

5. Your assailant may try to escape you at any time to this point. If so, let him go; you run to safety. If the attack continues, consider biting the inside of his upper leg, which is an extremely tender spot, or higher to even more tender spots. (At this point, he may be the one screaming for help.) Alternate biting and screaming until he tries to escape or help arrives.

I doubt that many attackers would persist in their attack once biting became involved. Most of the fun has gone out of the attack, and they didn't visualize being attacked themselves, and especially not in this manner. To find out where some tender spots are, feel the back of your own leg, or lightly pinch the person you train with.

If the attacker falls to the ground at any point during this move, you may have the option to run away *fast*. But don't stop screaming, even if that happens.

This move is *not* to be tried if your attacker has a knife or a gun. You don't want to stay close to someone who's trying to stab you with a knife or is holding a heavy weapon like a club. You want to get out of arm's reach.

Drop, Kick, and Scream

This technique uses your legs and voice as your primary defense.

When attacked:

1. Use the same technique as in the previous move to drive your attacker off balance.
2. Next, roll to the ground and lie on your back, keeping your hips and legs up in the air.
3. Kick your legs wildly and scream, "Help! Police!" Kick rapidly toward the attacker, but erratically so he can't get close and grab your legs, or get near your neck, mouth, and throat to stop you from screaming.

While an attacker doesn't feel physically threatened by a person in this defensive position, he'll feel threatened by the possibility of the police responding to your screams. So don't let up on the lung power.

Drop, kick, and scream is a good defense against an attacker using a knife. I want to note that there are two kinds of knife attackers—those who use a knife to intimidate in order to get something from you, and those who actually want to use the knife to cause bodily injury. If someone appears to be intimidating you with a knife to steal your wallet or purse, for example, you may want to give it to him and run in the opposite direction. But if the person is attacking you with the knife, stabbing at you, then dropping to the defensive position offers your assailant only your legs to stab at. Screaming is a powerful weapon as well, since attackers need to maintain stealth to avoid capture, and screaming draws lots of attention.

These two defensive moves are effective and easy to learn, and can be used by people of all ages, sizes, and strengths. If you're interested in learning more about unarmed self-defense techniques, consider taking a class at your local gym, community center, or martial arts studio. You can find many books and videos on the subject as well.

Guide to Personal Security Devices

The threat of becoming a victim of violent crime has created a huge market for personal security devices. You can purchase pepper sprays, tear gas, tasers, personal alarms, and stun guns at spy shops, gun shows, police supply houses, pawn shops, and specialty shops, as well as on the Internet. Laws governing ownership and use of these weapons vary from state to state, and sometimes from city to city. Be sure you know the laws pertaining to these weapons before buying or carrying any of them.

I've used all of these devices, and there are three reasons I sometimes prefer any of them to carrying a gun:

1. Nonlethal weapons are safer to have in a home where children are present: An accident wouldn't be fatal. It would be extremely uncomfortable, though, and you should of course teach children not to touch these devices and take safety precautions.

2. You can defend yourself from an attack that is not a life-and-death situation: for example, someone breaking your car window and reaching in to the seat next to you to steal your purse.

3. If you mistakenly use the weapon against an innocent person, you haven't killed anyone. You can't take bullets back.

Let's look at these individual devices and how to use them.

Tear Gases and Pepper Sprays

Many law enforcement agencies require their officers to experience the effects of tear gas or pepper spray before they're allowed to carry these weapons. It gives the officer a firsthand understanding of the weapon, and it reduces liability by allowing the officer to testify in court that he has had the weapon used against him with no lasting harm. I've used and trained with these weapons, and they're very effective when used properly. The range is up to twenty feet, so you don't have to get too close to an attacker. An added advantage is that they're easy to use against multiple assailants.

Gases and pepper sprays are available in easy-to-carry aerosol sprays. Some have key rings so you can always have them on hand. Make sure you get a product with a safety device to prevent it from discharging accidentally in your purse or pocket. I prefer products that make it easy to tell which way to hold it just by feeling it—for example, one product has finger indentations in the canister's holder that immediately tell you the correct way to hold it. This is critical if you're in the dark, or if you're in a surprise situation where seconds count and you don't want to waste time figuring out which way to point. Good-quality tear gas and pepper spray products with safety features are generally priced under twenty dollars.

Tear gas is a chemical irritant that causes a burning sensation of the eyes and nose that can last up to twenty minutes. It operates on mucous membranes and causes copious tears, thus the name. I've used it to great effect. If it didn't stop an assailant, it at least temporarily distorted his vision and limited his ability to fight back. Use of tear gas has decreased with the introduction of pepper spray products.

Use your thumb rather than your forefinger—it's stronger and gives you a more powerful grip for better control.

Pepper spray contains pure oleoresin capsicum, which is the hottest part of the habanera chili pepper. It's also called OC spray, but I call it assault with a dangerous vegetable. Unlike tear gas, pepper spray is an inflammatory and is effective against people who are feeling little or no pain, like psychotics, drunks, and drug addicts. It also works well on dogs and wild animals.

Since pepper spray works on the entire respiratory system, it can be more effective than tear gas. I certainly found it devastating when I was sprayed with it in training. I learned why—believe it or not, there's an actual unit of measurement for the heat felt by the human body when it comes in contact with hot peppers. A jalapeño pepper measures five thousand of these Scoville Heat Units. Most pepper sprays measure over five million on the same scale—that's a thousand times hotter!

When using pepper spray, more isn't necessarily better. A light spray can penetrate the membranes of the eyes, nose, and mouth more efficiently, and the propellant—usually alcohol—will evaporate quicker, causing the attacker to feel the effects of the spray more rapidly. Those effects can last more than an hour, but probably have no more long-term effect on the body than any hot pepper would have.

There are combination products that use tear gas and pepper spray with an ultraviolet marker. Besides incapacitating an assailant, it marks him with a dye that police can use to identify him. I particularly like this combination because the tear gas is felt immediately, followed by the pepper spray for a double whammy.

If you need to defend yourself with one of these weapons:

1. Grasp the container in your fist and press the plunger with your thumb while aiming the nozzle at your attacker's face or chest. Use your fist because it gives you a good grip on the canister, and your thumb exerts more constant pressure. This makes it harder for your assailant to grab the canister and take it away from you. If necessary, you could defend yourself with that closed fist, too.

2. Be careful that the wind doesn't blow the irritant back in your face. Remember, the effective range can be up to twenty feet. Try to keep your back to the wind to avoid stray spray. Still, even if the wind does carry some back into your face, your attacker will get the worst of it.

I believe you shouldn't own a weapon if you haven't practiced with it and don't know how to use it. If you're going to purchase pepper spray or tear gas for self-defense, I suggest you buy one container to carry and one for practice. Don't spray yourself, and don't spray it inside—trust me on this one. I know someone who tested pepper spray in the kitchen sink; he couldn't get near his kitchen for hours. Follow the product directions carefully. Take it outside and spray it against a wall or fence so you know what the range is, what the spray looks like, and how much pressure it takes to spray it. If you wish, you might take an unarmed self-defense class that teaches the proper use of pepper spray.

Stun Guns and Tasers

Stun guns and tasers are increasingly popular weapons that deliver a high-voltage shock—enough to incapacitate an attacker for five minutes or as long as twenty minutes. Weapons are available with varying voltage outputs, but a lower voltage will take longer to achieve the desired result. Both weapons daze and confuse their victims by scrambling their brains with high-voltage electricity. Medical experts say the chance of causing lasting injury to your attacker is extremely low.

Unlike pepper spray, close physical contact with your attacker is required in order to use a stun gun. You must press the contacts on the handheld device against your attacker's body and pull the trigger for two to five seconds. If the gun is used incorrectly, or if you're unable to keep the contacts pressed against the assailant, the shock may not incapacitate him, though it may cause severe pain. This can serve to really get him angry and may escalate the violence.

Tasers, however, can be used from about fifteen feet away from the attacker. Electricity is transmitted to the attacker through probes that are shot from the weapon into his body.

The probes are propelled by compressed nitrogen and travel about 135 feet per second, making it nearly impossible for the attacker to duck out of the way when you fire. When a probe hits, the attacker is felled in one or two seconds. You can fire the taser, then set it down and run because the weapon will keep electricity flowing to the probes and incapacitate your attacker while you flee.

Tasers and stun guns are effective nonlethal weapons, but they're larger and more bulky to carry than chemical spray weapons. Stun guns cost from twenty-five to fifty dollars or more. Tasers start at around two hundred dollars at the low end, ranging up to six hundred or more for the deluxe models with integrated laser sights. I again advise learning the proper use of these weapons if you choose them. For most people, I think pepper spray is a much better choice.

Personal Alarms

Small, portable handheld alarms are an excellent way to attract attention when you need help, and they're easy enough for small children to use. Several varieties are available. The simplest ones sound a piercing alarm when you push a button or pull a metal pin. Other models combine an audible alarm with a strobe light and flashlight. One model can double as a door or window alarm for travel or at-home use. They can be found at all the usual outlets and on the Internet for less than twenty dollars.

Use What You've Got

Sometimes you may find yourself in a position where you need to defend yourself, but don't have a weapon of any kind. In this case, you may wish to improvise and use whatever's at hand to incapacitate an attacker and/or escape. Here are some suggestions for using things that aren't normally thought of as weapons:

Unusual weapons:

- Grasp your keys in your fist, leaving one key protruding between your fingers. You can drive it into an attacker's face to effect an escape. Remember, you're not fighting—you're escaping.

- Grab a rock and hurl it. Better yet, grab several rocks and pelt the attacker.

- This is one you have to make at home and carry with you. Get a plastic thirty-five-millimeter film canister and fill it with ground cayenne pepper. Yes, the condiment—it's the same stuff pepper spray is made of. If someone is attacking you, open the canister and throw the pepper powder into his face. Even if he gets the pepper on his hands, he's sure to wipe his eyes and feel the effects.

- Here's another make-it-yourself project. Start with a small squeeze spray bottle, like the kind used for nasal spray or eyedrops. You'll need to test a few of these: Some don't propel the liquid well, while others will shoot it out ten feet. To test one, pry off the top and fill it with water. Once you find one that works well, fill it with hot sauce. Make sure it's not the chunky kind. This homemade pepper spray works, though it isn't as effective as a commercial product.

Whatever you do, don't hesitate to scream and run at the first sign of a threat. Don't worry about what you look or sound like. It's better to be embarrassed than mugged.

Do You Need a Firearm?

I was raised on a farm in south Florida, and my father and his brother had been sheriff's deputies. I was used to firearms in the house or in our pickup truck. As a police officer, my pistol was a tool of my trade. I've used firearms in my defense, and I've been threatened with them. I don't recommend firearm ownership for everyone.

Owning a gun is a serious decision, and a very personal one. If you're going to own a gun for protection, you must be aware of the dangers and responsibilities of ownership.

Some problems with guns:

1. Thieves steal guns. If someone knows you have firearms in the house, you can be targeted for burglary. Now you have a thief with a gun.

2. Firearms pose a serious danger to children. My experience has taught me that children are in more danger from the accidental discharge of a firearm than they are from any intruder who may enter your house.

3. Firearms can be used against you by an attacker. Even police officers are sometimes shot with their own guns.

4. Having a firearm readily available can force you to make a life-or-death decision that you'll have to live with for the rest of your life.

A responsible gun owner who has a firearm for personal protection needs to think of that firearm as part of the overall security plan. It's not just a gun you have lying around. It's part of the bigger picture. You need to keep the firearm secured from theft and children, while having it available for use if the need arises.

Gun use and storage tips:

- Have a good secure storage place for guns. When I was a police officer and there were children in my house, I installed a deadbolt on my closet door and alarmed it. As soon as I took my gun off, I locked it in the closet. There were no extra keys to that closet lying around or hidden anywhere.

- Don't keep the gun on the nightstand or under your pillow. Keep it out of sight and hidden in a place only you know about. A suggestion: Attach a holster to the underside of the nightstand near your bed. This will keep an intruder from easily finding it, and you'll have your weapon in a location that allows your to roll off your bed, grab your pistol, and instantly be in a defensive position.

- Learn everything you can about the weapon. Take a class from a firearms instructor and learn proper safety procedures. Police officers and firearms instructors train continually in the use of their weapons. They practice and keep their skills sharp. The more you know, the more comfortable you'll be having the weapon around, and the less chance you'll have of accidents.

- Talk to children about firearms and their dangers, whether you have a gun in the house or not. Encourage them to tell you if another child brings a gun to school or plays with them at all. You must communicate to children the importance of telling you this information so they feel comfortable coming to you. Whether you're for guns or against them, they're prevalent enough in our society that children should know something about gun safety, if it's nothing more than "Don't touch them, and don't play with them."

A Final Thought

I have always believed that personal security is a state of mind, and a state of awareness that comes with practice. Throughout this book, you've learned many simple techniques and tips to help you develop your security state of mind. But remember, it really does take practice to keep that state of mind sharp and alert. Hopefully, you've discovered that it doesn't take a lot of time and effort, that you can develop good security habits without disrupting your lifestyle. And that is what's most important. These techniques have always served me well, and I know they can help you and your family be more safe and secure, even in today's troubled world. Be alert, be aware, have a plan—and be safe.

Resources

National Fraud Information Center
800-876-7060
www.fraud.org

The NFIC was originally established in 1992 by the National Consumers League, the oldest nonprofit consumer organization in the United States, to fight the growing menace of telemarketing fraud by improving prevention and enforcement. It runs the only nationwide hot line for advice about telemarketing fraud.

National Criminal Justice Reference Service
800-851-3420
www.ncjrs.org

The NCJRS is a federally sponsored information clearinghouse for people around the country and the world involved with research, policy, and practice related to criminal and juvenile justice and drug control. Anyone interested in the fields of criminal and juvenile justice and drug policy can use or request NCJRS services and assistance.

National Child Abuse Hotline
800-4-ACHILD (800-422-4453)

The National Child Abuse Hotline offering crisis counseling for children or adult survivors twenty-four hours a day. It also offers referrals for sexual abuse treatment programs, reporting suspected child abuse, shelters, advocacy, mental health, and legal aid. Literature on prevention of child abuse is available upon request.

National Domestic Violence Hotline
800-799-SAFE (800-799-7233)
TDD: 800-787-3224
www.ndvh.org
ndvh@ndvh.org

The National Domestic Violence Hotline is staffed twenty-four hours a day by trained counselors who can provide crisis assistance and information about shelters, legal advocacy, health care centers, and counseling.

National Resource Center on Domestic Violence
800-537-2238 (same as Domestic Violence Hotline)

Federal Trade Commission (FTC)
600 Pennsylvania Avenue, NW
Washington, DC 20580
877-FTC-HELP (877-382-4357)
http://www.ftc.gov/index.html
For consumer information: www.ftc.gov/ftc/consumer.htm

The Federal Trade Commission is the federal clearinghouse for complaints by victims of identity theft. Although the FTC does not have the authority to bring criminal charges, it assists victims of identity theft by providing them with information to help them resolve the financial and other problems that can result from identity theft. The FTC also may refer victim complaints to other appropriate government agencies and private organizations for further action. If you have been a victim of ID theft, you can file a complaint with the FTC by contacting the FTC's Consumer Response Center.

Federal Emergency Management Administration (FEMA)
800-480-2520
http://www.fema.gov

For a free booklet on building a safe room inside your house, call FEMA or visit http://www.fema.gov/mit/tsfs01.htm.

Dr. R. Jerry Adams
Evaluation and Development Institute
4812 Southeast 28th Avenue, No. 506
Portland, OR 97202-4472
503-233-2784
Fax: 503-905-6100
http://www.awesomelibrary.org/road-rage.html
jadams@awesomelibrary.org

Dr. Adams has done research into road rage and is the developer of the SORRY sign for defusing road rage.

National Center for Victims of Crime
2111 Wilson Boulevard, Suite 300
Arlington, VA 22201
800-FYI-CALL (800-394-2255)
www.ncvc.org

The NCVC is recognized as the nation's leading advocate for crime victims, working with grassroots organizations and criminal justice agencies to serve millions of crime victims since 1985. Its goal is to help crime victims rebuild their lives by providing direct services and resources, and advocating for legislation. Write or call to obtain a guide for stalking victims.

Privacy Rights Clearinghouse
www.privacyrights.org
619-298-3396
prc@privacyrights.org

The Privacy Rights Clearinghouse is a nonprofit consumer information and advocacy program. It offers consumers a unique opportunity to learn how to protect their privacy. Its purpose is to raise consumers' awareness of how technology affects privacy, and to empower consumers to take action to control their own personal information by providing practical tips. Contact the group to report privacy abuses and request information on ways to protect your privacy.

KidWISE Institute
888-KID-WISE (888-543-9473)

Index

Acknowledgments

This book became a reality thanks to the efforts of a number of people.

Many thanks to Tom McCarthy, our editor at The Lyons Press, who guided this project with enthusiasm and support, making it both a pleasure and an adventure; to our agents, Marilyn Allen and Bob Diforio of D4EO Literary Agency, who were there every step of the way to brainstorm ideas, handle details, and offer encouragement when it was needed the most.

We also wish to thank our friends who were so generous with their time and talents: Lt. John J. Morrissey, watch commander, Palm Beach County, Florida, Sheriff's Office; Chief James M. Sweat, fire marshal, Palm Beach County Fire Rescue; Bill Pringle, president of Pringle Security; and photographer Thomas L. McCartney.

Personal thanks to Tom Meeteer, Muriel MacFarlane, the Thursday night creativity group (Garrett, Christine, Brenda, Glo and Mike), Danny Callaro, Dori Miningham and Donald McLachlan, and to all our family, friends, and colleagues who inspired and motivated us.